Love the Wild Swan

'Like the wild swan glides, Judith Edwards' writing flows, with great elegance. Her wide-ranging cultural interests combine with her clinical acumen to open new ways of thinking. This book is a really interesting read, both for those in the profession, and beyond.' – **Irma Brenman Pick**, *Distinguished Fellow of the British Psychoanalytical Society and child and adult psychoanalyst.*

'This is a wise and wonderful book of "twisted tales", beautifully calibrated by reference to personal, clinical and cultural life. Coming to know oneself through memoir is the solid and steady background of it all – the intensity of trying to expose and explore the self in the course of psychoanalytically based training and teaching across the life cycle, especially during childhood. Judith Edwards' writing offers a breadth and depth of reference that is both accessible and utterly refreshing. Beneath these lovely pages there lies, fundamentally, a focus on meaning – what does something really mean to someone? How does one gain access to that? Sorting it out, significantly through the quality and capacities for observation, both of self and other, makes genuine growth possible. *Love the Wild Swan* gives us an informed and moving contribution to this process.' – **Margot Waddell**, *Fellow of the Institute of Psychoanalysis, former consultant child and adolescent psychotherapist, and author of* Inside Lives.

Love the Wild Swan is the culmination of thirty years of clinical and teaching experience, undertaken by child and adolescent psychoanalytic psychotherapist Judith Edwards. Along with new material, the book consists of previously published papers spanning Edwards' entire career that have been carefully selected to chart the journey that every clinician and human being makes, from babyhood to adult life.

Edwards offers an example of how the evolution of meanings occur and how lifelong learning about the self and the other takes place. The book is divided into four parts, with sections on observation, clinical work, teaching theory and links between these ideas and ongoing life in the form of the arts, through poetry, film and sculpture.

Love the Wild Swan will be of interest to practitioners and clinicians, as well as appealing to anyone in the field of mental health who wishes to reflect on the nature of human development and growth.

Judith Edwards, PhD, MACP, is a former consultant child and adolescent psychoanalytic psychotherapist who has worked at the Tavistock Clinic since the 1980s. She has been internationally published and is a past editor of the *Journal of Child Psychotherapy*. She edited the collection *Being Alive* (2001), and is the author of the memoir *Pieces of Molly: An Ordinary Life* (Karnac, 2014).

World Library of Mental Health Series

The *World Library of Mental Health* series celebrates the important contributions to mental health made by leading experts in their individual fields. Each author has compiled a career-long collection of what they consider to be their finest pieces: extracts from books, journals, articles, major theoretical and practical contributions and salient research findings.

For the first time ever the work of each contributor is presented in a single volume so readers can follow the themes and progress of their work and identify the contributions made to, and the development of, the fields themselves.

Each book in the series features a specially written introduction by the contributor giving an overview of their career, contextualizing their selection within the development of the field, and showing how their own thinking developed over time.

Titles in this series:

Love the Wild Swan

The selected works of Judith Edwards

Judith Edwards

Routledge
Taylor & Francis Group

LONDON AND NEW YORK

First published 2017 by Routledge

2 Park Square, Milton Park, Abingdon, Oxfordshire OX14 4RN
711 Third Avenue, New York, NY 10017

Routledge is an imprint of the Taylor & Francis Group, an informa business

First issued in paperback 2017

British Library Cataloguing in Publication Data
A catalogue record for this book is available from the British Library

Library of Congress Cataloging in Publication Data
Names: Edwards, Judith, 1944– author.
Title: Love the wild swan : the selected works of Judith Edwards.
Description: Abingdon, Oxon ; New York, NY : Routledge, 2016.
Identifiers: LCCN 2016001738| ISBN 9781138947634 (hardback) |
ISBN 9781138123328 (pbk.) | ISBN 9781315666143 (ebook)
Subjects: LCSH: Child psychotherapy. | Adolescent psychotherapy. |
Developmental psychology.
Classification: LCC RJ504 .E29 2016 | DDC 618.92/8914—dc23
LC record available at http://lccn.loc.gov/2016001738

ISBN: 978-1-138-94763-4 (hbk)
ISBN: 978-1-138-12332-8 (pbk)

Typeset in Sabon
by Florence Production Limited, Stoodleigh, Devon, UK

To Andrew

CONTENTS

FOREWORD

In the introduction to this remarkable book, Judith Edwards tells us that if only books were not forced into a linear form, this collection could be arranged concentrically, starting at the centre with observation, then proceeding in ever widening circles out through clinical work, then onto theory, and then on to even wider links with the arts. She insists throughout, however, that while theory informs, it should not constrain clinical work. Indeed, on the subject of observation she asks, 'Can you fall in love with a method?' She clearly has and she eloquently places close observation at the centre of all her interests. (She is, by the way, a highly skilled photographer judging from her beautiful exhibition of her photographic take on Anthony Gormley's work (Edwards, 2008).) Her love of observation leads to an almost reverential stance in her clinical work, which is characterized by delicacy, tact and attention to nuance. Yet there is always great rigour in her approach. And this is as evident in her teaching as in her clinical work. What I think we can hear in what Yeats called the 'deep heart's core' (Chapter 13) is her feeling for beauty in the arts and in thinking. Yet she honours the sciences too: her discussion of the space–time continuum and of gravitational collapse in black holes is wonderfully clear. Interestingly, although she is speaking metaphorically about black holes in her patient's mind, there are so many correspondences that, given the new findings in the neurosciences, you start to suspect that one day we will realize this may be more than a metaphor, something closer to a microcosm within the brain of a genuine piece of the cosmos (Porges, 2011; Music, 2014). I think she belongs to that group of thinkers characterized by Richard Holmes as belonging to a period when the division between the sciences and the arts was nothing like as extreme as it is now. Coleridge and others were as thrilled and moved by discoveries in the new sciences and the new expeditions as they were by those in literature and painting. Holmes says what brought these together was the sense of wonder and the idea of an often lonely and perilous exploratory voyage (Holmes, 2008). I think there is a deep sense of wonder in Edwards' work and it is extraordinary how she is able to awaken that in her patients, facilitate it in her students, and transmit it to us. The book tackles issues bigger than psychoanalysis although everyone in the psychoanalytic and mental health domain should read it.

In the section on observation, in Chapter 2, she gives a lively example of the way she thinks about the issue of teaching the link between observation and theory. She begins the chapter by stressing the importance of the seminar leader balancing the functions of understanding with those of explication in order to facilitate rather than foreclose on learning. She illustrates this with an observation in which the observer was distressed to have to present an observation where a usually contented and satisfied baby had been very upset, refused the breast and avoided looking at her mother. The observer even apologized for the observation! The mother had shown great patience and persistence in trying to soothe and feed her baby, who began to calm down, then to feed, and eventually to become relaxed and serene. The group discussed this all with considerable feeling but also reflectively, and Edwards began to introduce the concept of splitting and the way in which a previously good object can be felt to turn extremely bad under certain conditions. (They learned that the father was away for a few days, and the mother said that she was feeling quite stressed.) The group was helped by this discussion of a piece of theory. Edwards' point in this chapter is that this kind of experiential teaching involves a fundamental paradox – while theory should not be taught as dogma, the governing principles in psychoanalysis can help to guide the onward paths of both students and teachers.

Chapter 3 concerns the teaching of observation to non-clinical students. She tells us that she often starts with a quotation from an artist such as Matisse, also devoted to the work of observation. She quotes Spurling, (1998: xix):

> No one has described how to paint a portrait more clearly or succinctly than Henri Matisse. He insisted on accuracy, maintaining at the same time that the meticulous production of external detail could never provide more than a starting point. Success or failure at a deeper level was a matter of contemplation, concentration, the force and quality of attention focussed on a subject. Matisse said that nothing should be distorted or suppressed. Anyone attempting a portrait should above all approach the subject without preconception: 'To sum up, I work without a theory. I am aware primarily of the forces involved, and find myself driven forward by an idea that I can really only grasp little by little as it grows with the picture.'

She goes on, 'This idea of painting a portrait without preconceptions is one that the students find curious but interesting, namely, that each observation is in some sense a small art form.' She also cites something written by Grayling (2002), that one needs 'the eager glance of an intelligent eye, unblinkered by conventional education, seeing the value in things without having been told to expect them there, and *therefore seeing them truly*'. The tributes from her students in this chapter confirm their appreciation of her way of teaching the method.

In Chapter 4, 'Towards solid ground', the section on clinical work is another lovely illustration of her method and of her searching and respectful approach. She traces the development of a capacity to think and of a sense of self in a somewhat recovered autistic adolescent who nevertheless continued to suffer from a dread of annihilation and of falling into limitless space. He felt he lived and moved never far from a 'black hole' where he was in danger of gravitational collapse and thus either froze or engaged in repetitive activities to hold himself together. He could not grasp the movement of time, timetables, or time sequences.

I want to select some material from the period when he had become a bit more rooted in solid ground and was able to move forward tentatively into the space–time continuum. In one session he had been exploring the puzzle of time, breaking the session into blocks of minutes, and Edwards tells us:

> I talked about time going on and us going on within it, the links between times and people. He went over to the window and looked out reflectively.

After awhile, he said with the sort of liveliness and curiosity of a young child, 'Where do you think the quietest place in the world is? Where there are no planes and doors and people and cars?' I asked where he thought and he said, 'In the country, I think.' He shut the window and rested his head against the glass, saying, 'so peaceful, so peaceful in here.'

She draws attention to the need in all of us for periods of digestion of and recovery from experience. In a later session he said he could think about timetables in the therapy but not at school because of all the noise. But he did gradually learn to keep out the disturbances and to protect his capacity to think for himself and notice for himself. One day some weeks later, he asked her if she liked Beethoven and Mozart. He said, 'You can hear the silence in between, and then it comes in Da da da DA.' Edwards points out to us that just as the silences could now be perceived as part of the pattern, so he could trust in the continuity of going on being, and that he and she still existed in the silences between the sessions: no one need fall into a hole. He became able to make friends, to get on with his life and to enjoy himself socially. She felt that he seemed, via the thread of time, finally to have entered into the rhythm of the universe. I want to underline the respect she showed for the moment when he could conceive of the quietest place on earth, and the way this allowed him then to find it.

In Chapter 8, 'Before the threshold', the section on theory teaching and learning consists of an important addition to the Kleinian theory of creativity, put forward by Segal, which sees the achievement of the depressive position, where reparative gifts are offered to compensate for past destructive urges, as a necessary prerequisite for creative struggle. Edwards suggests that in fact creativity itself may also develop outside or before this 'position'. She offers the idea that there may be a 'pre-position' related to the impulse to repair the self before reparation of the object. She is drawn to myths in addition to that of Oedipus, those of Ariadne and Orpheus, myths about a 'forward trajectory into relatively unknown territory, via the labyrinth and the underworld'. There is much emphasis in our Kleinian thinking about the importance of weaning and the consequent mourning the loss of the breast (as a precursor to how we process the loss of our loved objects). But Edwards points out that when the baby turns to solid food, new tastes partly contain the representation of the lost object but also the challenge of new experience. I remember the Child Psychotherapist Mirijana Renton once saying that she was sure that architects built 'bigger than their guilt'. This raises the question of identification with potent and creative objects, and perhaps objects potent enough to tolerate, and even welcome, competition. Edwards' point is that the objects need, to some extent, to be able to let the self go and move on. Her patient's poem about the silver surfer, attached to the mother-ship by a line, but nonetheless surfing freely in space, is a beautiful image for this process she is helping us to envisage. Thus, bravery, adventure, playfulness, risk, may all be elements in some types of creativity.

Clearly it is the element of bravery that enabled Theseus and Orpheus, in the first part of their journeys, to enter into the unknown. But neither Theseus nor Orpheus quite made it. Edwards goes on to suggest that both failed in their tasks, not out of unresolved guilt, but because of a conflict between doubt and hope, where the hope/faith is not only in the trustworthiness of the object but in the creativity of the self. A further original point is that the creative act can *lead toward* a more depressive integration rather than arising from it. She emphasizes, on the contrary, the overcoming of fear and the need to move beyond previous parental structures, especially where they may have been genuinely persecutory. She suggests that creative work can evolve where the ' "entry into the depressive position" can be allowed, in a sense, to remain in the background rather than the foreground of the internal world'. Well, it has certainly evolved in this brilliant chapter that involves a major breakthrough in the theory of symbolism.

In Chapter 9, 'Ripples in mental space', still in the theory and teaching section, Edwards once again finds a link between recent hypotheses about the cosmos and her own extension of ideas about the human unconscious mind. She suggests a parallel between the way in which theoretical physicists hypothesize about dark matter by measuring the deformations it causes in surrounding stars and galaxies. She links this with the 'dark matters' existing in the individual's unconscious and 'how things we cannot see may affect the things we can see, and in a sense be measured, as it were not in their own right, but by what they affect'. She discusses the writing of her own previous memoir and reiterates her view on the conflict between the need to find 'safe' answers and the opposing need to eschew closure in order to open up the possibility of fresh understandings. Questions answered then result in further questioning. I want to show once again how this respect for the unknown, even unknowable, infuses her clinical work:

She describes the story of her work with Jim, an adopted boy with a ghastly history of neglect and abuse. For the first period of treatment, he was very suspicious both of her and of his adoptive parents, insisting he didn't believe that his (idealized) birth parents could have done those things to him. But after a year of treatment he began to relax, and come out of his defensive hiding place. He drew some lovely hills and a rooted tree for a cover for a book he planned to write, and then drew a badger waking up and coming out to see a beautiful red sky which he said was the sunset. Notice that Edwards simply commented on the badger emerging into the quiet evening, and the beautiful sky. 'Yes', he said, 'and there's a new moon coming up'. She felt a new cycle of growth and renewal was beginning, but adds that in the meantime he had needed her 'to respect his working under cover of darkness for a long while before he could begin to emerge'. It is this capacity to live through the turmoil and turbulence until the storm has spent itself, or worse, to live through long periods of emptiness and apparent meaninglessness, that is characteristic of the best of psychoanalytic work but it is important to notice also Edwards' readiness to register and then to greet – with not too much excitement – the badger's emergence and then the new moon. I am certain he felt it was as precious to her as to him.

In the section on the arts, the discussions of film, art and literature always observe Edwards' own strictures against foreclosure. The reader will find no neat formulations in them. They are always searching, open-minded, yet filled with illuminating ideas that are never final or presumptuous. Indeed, her writing in all her fields of interest reveals something that I feel goes deeper even than her love of the observation methodology. This is something she calls, in her final words, 'the elusive pursuit of insight', or what Yeats called the pursuit of 'moral radiance'.

Anne Alvarez, London 2016

References

Edwards, J. (2008) Tavistock Art Exhibition.
Grayling, A. C. *Guardian Newspaper*, 13 July 2002.
Holmes, R. (2008) *The Age of Wonder: How the Romantic Generation Discovered the Beauty and Terror of Science*. London: Harper Press.

Music, G. (2014) *The Good Life: Wellbeing and the New Science of Altruism, Selfishness, and Immorality*. London: Routledge.

Porges, S. W. (2011) *The Polyvagal Theory: Neurophysiological Foundations of Emotions, Attachment, Communication, and Self-Regulation*. New York: Norton.

Spurling, H. (1988) *The Unknown Matisse*. London: Penguin Group, p. xix.

ACKNOWLEDGEMENTS

My grateful thanks go to Joanne Forshaw, my editor, and her assistants Kirsten Buchanan and Aiyana Curtis, all of whom have guided me through the process of publishing this book.

Huge thanks to the artist Gino D'Achille who has provided a frontispiece that speaks so eloquently to the spirit of the book, and to Stella Millburn who took the author photograph. I would also like to thank most particularly my dear friend and colleague, Anne Alvarez, with whom I have talked and argued and grown since the day I first met her over thirty years ago. Many other colleagues and friends, including Juliet Hopkins, Anthea Gomez and Maria Rhode, have been an inspiration and a support to me. They are too numerous to mention here, but you know who you are. And finally, to past patients and students over the years, to my analyst and to my family, both external and internal, the greatest thanks of all.

Permission acknowledgements

All of the articles published here were originally published elsewhere in an unmodified form. I am grateful to the editors and publishers who have generously given me their permission to use them here.

'Suffering, weeping and other preoccupations: Darwin's observations and our present-day practice', *Infant Observation* (2003) 6(3), 44–57, copyright © Tavistock Clinic Foundation.

'Early splitting and projective identification', *Infant Observation* (2008) 11(1), 57–65, copyright © Tavistock Clinic Foundation.

'Teaching observation to non-clinical students: Continuing thoughts', *Infant Observation* (2009) 12(2), 207–13, copyright © Tavistock, The Clinic Foundation.

'Towards solid ground: The ongoing psychotherapeutic journey of an adolescent boy with autistic features', *Journal of Child Psychotherapy* (1994) 20(1), 57–83, copyright © Association of Child Psychotherapists. Also published in *Autism and Personality* (1999), edited by A. Alvarez and S. Reid.

'You can't miss what you've never had: can you? The challenges and struggles of single parenthood from a psychoanalytic perspective', *Journal of Child Psychotherapy* (1999) 25(2), 289–307, copyright © Association of Child Psychotherapists.

'On being dropped and picked up: Adopted children and their internal objects', *Journal of Child Psychotherapy* (2000) 26(3), 349–67, copyright © Association of Child Psychotherapists. Also published in *The Emotional Experience of Adoption* (2008), edited by D. Hindle and G. Shulman.

'Before the threshold: Destruction, reparation and creativity in relation to the depressive position', *Journal of Child Psychotherapy* (2005) 31(3), 317–34, copyright © Association of Child Psychotherapists.

'Ripples in mental space caused by dark matters and twisted tales: Some reflections on memory, memoirs and therapeutic work', *Psychodynamic Practice* (2013) 19(4), 390–405, www.tandfonline.com.

'Sifting through the sands of time: A film review'. *International Journal of Psychoanalysis* (2014) 95(4), 791–99. *International Journal of Psychoanalysis* and Wiley. Also published in A. Mauss-Hanke (ed.) (2015) *International Psychoanalyse-Band 10* Psychosozial-Verlag.

'Teaching and learning about psychoanalysis: Film as a teaching tool with reference to a particular film, *Morvern Callar*', *British Journal of Psychotherapy* (2010) 26(1), 80–99, *British Journal of Psychotherapy* and Blackwell Publishing. This paper won the Jan Lee Memorial Prize in 2010 for the best paper in that year linking psychoanalysis with the arts. Also published in *Media and the Inner World* (2014), edited by C. Bainbridge and C. Yates, London and New York, Palgrave Macmillan.

'Teaching, learning and Bion's model of digestion', *The British Journal of Psychotherapy* (2015) 31(3), 376–89.

'The elusive pursuit of insight', originally published in *Acquainted with the Night: Psychoanalysis and the Poetic Imagination*, edited by H. Canham and C. Satyamurti, Karnac Books (2003) and reprinted with kind permission of Karnac Books.

'Seeing and being seen: The dialectics of intimate space and Anthony Gormley's *Event Horizon*', originally published in *Free Associations: Psychoanalysis and Culture, Media, Groups, Politics* 68 (December 2015).

Note on confidentiality

Names and some circumstances of those whose clinical material has been used in this book have been changed in order to disguise identity in a way that does not change the meaning of the clinical material used.

INTRODUCTION

The title of this book derives from a poem by American poet Robinson Jeffers (1887–1962) (Jeffers, 1959) where the poet is regretting that he can never fully describe what he wishes to portray. He mitigates his frustration by exhorting himself to observe closely, and to translate the thunder of the swan's wings into the music of words. The poet himself elsewhere called this 'the exciting truth'.

This book is a collection of papers that have been written over the years in this spirit, deriving first from observation, both of other and of self, which is the foundation of all psychoanalytic clinical endeavours, as well as of the thinking that proceeds from these.

The artist Matisse is in the same territory when he says 'To sum up, I work without a theory. I am aware primarily of the forces involved, and find myself driven forward by an idea which I can really only grasp little by little as it grows with the picture' (Spurling, 1988, p. xix). This seems to mirror the idea of authentic growth in us all.

Psychoanalytic thinking is, I believe, of central relevance in understanding personal relationships, and this relevance is enhanced by its relationship to other fields of enquiry. Lateral thinking offers a gain in disentangling and explaining complex ideas. Alexander Luria, the great Russian neurologist, maintained that the main goal of scientific observation is not mere fact-gathering; it aims to view an event from as many perspectives as possible (Luria, 1987).

The child psychotherapy consulting room is a scientific site of enquiry in an increasing body of qualitative research. The setting is a regularly offered space furnished with toys, both communal (the dolls' house) and personal to the child in a separate box, and drawing materials. Here play (and sometimes the absence of play), drawings and dreams offer over time material that elaborates the meaning of a symptom and the unconscious phantasies connected to it. There is in this setting both the opportunity to observe the unfolding of the transference (what the child brings from past relationships into the present one with the therapist) and the counter-transference (what is experienced by the therapist that may have central importance in terms of what the child splits off from consciousness, or is unable to experience consciously at that point). While there is still a concern with lifting repressive barriers where appropriate, there has been over the years an increasing aim to extend the boundaries of the self and to regain 'lost' split-off parts of the personality. Kvale (1999) described the therapeutic encounter as a 'construction site of knowledge' where layers of self-understanding not made accessible in briefer encounters can be gradually made available both to the therapist and the patient.

We need to be open however to questioning ourselves, and questioning what we think we 'know'. Bion (1990) advised 'Keep your questions in good repair'. There will inevitably, and valuably, be multifaceted aspects of our understanding as clinicians raised in differing traditions under the umbrella of psychoanalysis. We need to acknowledge the limits of our own subjectivity, feel supported by 'usable theory' without allowing it to cloud the clinical encounter, and honour the legacy of our training while allowing space in our minds for new thoughts. In essence, this is a kind of 'play' that allows for creativity to make new connections, rather in the way a child rummaging through a bowl of Lego pieces builds something new. It will be noticed in this book that I return several times to some pieces of clinical work over the years, making new connections linked to my own ongoing 'play' of thinking.

The Nobel prize-winning scientist Stephen Weinberg thinks that it may never be possible fully to explain the world. The universe simply may not fit any framework human beings can devise. Science [and psychoanalysis – JE] may offer pleasure, but not certainty. 'Like me', he writes, 'most physicists today are resigned to the fact that we will always have to wonder why our deepest theories are not something different' (Weinberg, 2015). And as Money-Kyrle (1988, p. xix) said in his Introduction to Melanie Klein's work, 'as in physics, so in psychology, ultimate truth is perhaps of infinite complexity, to be approached only by an infinite series of approximations'.

There is no marked road forward, and new paths may open up in both our understanding and our practice. But it is part of the pleasure of the journey, as I understand it, to create a path that while it may intersect with those of others, and be influenced by them, will be unique, just as each clinical encounter will be unique. The very nature of psychoanalytic enquiry is such that its discoveries need to be regarded as provisional, to be discarded perhaps later as new insights and knowledge become apparent. As Eric Rhode says (Rhode, 2014, p. 48) 'even the concept of observation becomes a burden if it is too securely defined'.

Given what I have outlined above, if books were not forced into a linear development by virtue of their construction, this collection would be arranged concentrically. It would start at the centre from observation, and what observation then brings both to the clinical encounter and to the evolution of the mind itself. It would then proceed in ever widening circles. Clinical work then forms the next circle, followed by theory, which contains and informs the clinical work but does not hopefully constrain it. Other circles then expand outwards to include links and associations that can be made, as psychoanalysis takes its place alongside other creative and scientific vertices. And as Bion observed in his *Memoir of the Future* (1991) 'psychoanalysis is just one stripe on the side of the tiger'.

Since we are faced here with the constraints of the medium of a book, the chapters will follow this concentric path but perforce in a linear way. I hope that readers will bear this model in mind as they too proceed along the learning curve that is the trajectory of our clinical as well as our human development.

There is a danger always in striving for what you might call 'cognitive neatness' – avoiding what one observation student ruefully admitted were 'the messy bits' when she did not want to observe a nappy change. The linear narrative can beguile us: any written case history is already a 'fiction' – but a fiction that is hopefully constructed in order to help both the patient, the therapist and the reader.

Symbolic correspondence or consonance, i.e. when something outside connects with something already existing inside the mind, may occur at any time, and is a generative mode of being, producing what might be called 'an ah-hah moment' if its meaning is fully attended to. But that is never the end of it. The poet Rimbaud observed that 'the word is a forest of symbols' and they may come to mean different things to us at different times. There are three categories into which symbols can be roughly broken: those mass symbols on which we may all agree, those that are personal to us, and those that are personal to our patients. It is of technical importance to be able to discriminate between these within any analytic session, be it with child or adult, in order not to trespass inappropriately into the interior drama of another in an intrusive way. It is in this way that the skill of the analyst or therapist develops over time, and it cannot be rushed. So in a sense it can be suggested that internal as well as external conversations take place. While the analyst or therapist is in some ways in a 'parental' role, these conversations also have a co-equal existence within two minds, and necessarily so, taking place in what Adrian Stokes, poet and art critic, called 'the spirit of brotherliness' (Harris Williams, 2014, p. xxi). So, one of the family, not the head of it. The power to communicate and to receive communications is one of the central hallmarks of sanity, and the word 'hermeneutics' is derived from the ancient Greek word meaning the art of midwifery. By reading and listening to the words of others we release, give birth and foster our own intuitional abilities. We are each in the process of a continual becoming, and for my understanding no observation, no theory and no 'clinical fact' is ever a finished thing.

Nietzsche said in 1878 'Convictions are more dangerous enemies of truth than lies'. Each of us will be in the continual process of creating a sense of what is 'true' for us at any point. This is a fluid history, and this process is reflected in this collection, and in the evolution of its author. The 'wild swans' appear too in the last chapter of the book, in W.B. Yeats' poem 'The Wild Swans at Coole'. Yeats could at that point in his life accept that they would 'fly away' after he had observed them, but that they and he would have had this important intersection that joined them, and that spoke to him in a way that had both personal and more general significance. This collection, which has grown over years of practice as well as years of reading theory and relating it to fields beyond that of psychoanalysis, aims to show by example how one person's development may reflect simultaneously both something particular and something universal in our development as clinicians and as human beings.

References

Bion, W. R. (1990) *Brazilian Lectures*. London: Karnac.

Bion, W. R. (1991) A *Memoir of the Future* (3 vols, 1975, 1977, 1979). London: Karnac.

Harris Williams, M. (ed.) (2014) *Art and Analysis: An Adrian Stokes Reader*. London: Karnac.

Jeffers, R. (1959) *Penguin Book of Modern American Verse*. Harmondsworth: Penguin, p. 126.

Kvale, S. (1999) 'The psychoanalytic interview as qualitative research'. *Qualitative Enquiry*, 5(1), 87–113.

Luria, A. R. (1987) *The Mind of a Mnemonist*. Cambridge, MA: Harvard University Press.

Money-Kyrle, R. (1988) 'Introduction' in M. Klein (ed.), *Love, Guilt and Reparation*. London: Virago Press, pp. xv–xvi.

Nietzsche, F. W. (1878) *Human, All Too Human*.

Rhode, E. (2014) *On Revelation*, London: Apex One, p. 48.

Spurling, H. (1988) *The Unknown Matisse*. London: Penguin Group, p. xix.

Weinberg, S. (2015) *To Explain the World*. London and New York: Harper Collins.

PART 1

ON OBSERVATION

Mother, you and he began together
You learned together
You protected his newly opened eyes from fear,
Cradling him in your friendly arms
                    (Rilke, Duino Elegies No. 3, translated by Judith Edwards)

Can you fall in love with a method? Observation is not a skill confined to training as a psychoanalytic clinician: it is one that is also practised across the spectrum of the creative arts as well as the sciences. Indeed the title of this book derives from this very impulse which lies at the heart of so many areas of life. 'Being there' is a vital component of witnessing what goes on in any observational transaction, be it between hand, mind and external object, or in our own discipline between the observer and the observed environment, with the infant placed centre stage. It has of necessity a great deal of heart as well as mind in it; empathic observation cannot be practised by a disinterested or dissociated observer. The three chapters in this section have been written over the years while having the privilege to participate as a seminar leader in many groups of students, observing many babies. This is how future clinicians fine-tune their responses: learning much about how to unlock what might be called the existential codes of all beings, while observing the development of just one. The 'personal style' of babies can be seen to emerge in observations over time, as they use these universal 'codes', seen from a psychoanalytic point of view to be locked in unconscious processes such as splitting, integration, anxiety, guilt, denial and reparation (to mention just a few). So observing a baby is essentially also a kind of self-education. As A. C. Grayling (2002) said about educating the self, 'one imagines the eager glance of the intelligent eye, unblinkered by conventional education, seeing the value of things without having been told to expect them there, and *therefore seeing them truly*' (emphasis added). There are of course many factors to consider here: do observations change what is being observed? What can you see in a short observation of an hour, one of twenty-four in the day and seven times that in a week? What do you need to be aware of? And what wary of? Truly 'being there' involves looking, taking in, digesting, feeling and reflecting, making hypotheses and then testing these over time. The role includes that of self-reflection and self-enquiry, as well as the strength to resist a position of 'certainty'. We're thinking about structure rather than rigidity here. These necessary skills of the psychoanalytic observer are also learned by the human baby as she observes and experiences the world and builds up an internal picture based partly on the external world and the care-taking environment, partly on how she is able to receive it. Thinking about Darwin and his observations of his infant son Doddy, to the present day student who might not necessarily want to do a clinical training, these chapters represent some of the dilemmas that are common to us all, while these are being observed in detailed word pictures of specific infants.

References

Grayling, A. C. (2002) *Guardian*, 13 July.
Rilke, R. M. (1923) *Duineser Elegien*. Frankfurt: Insel Verlag.

CHAPTER 1

SUFFERING, WEEPING AND OTHER PREOCCUPATIONS

Darwin's observations and our present-day practice

This chapter aims to look at Darwin's observations, locating them within a pre-psychoanalytic history and culture, and within Darwin's project of establishing man's connection with the earthly animal kingdom and the notion of evolution. Can we find evidence in Darwin's observations of the sorts of issues we would think about, even though Darwin himself was looking with another purpose? This chapter charts Darwin's observations of his son, published thirty years after he made them originally, and ends by contrasting Darwin's short description of a 'peep-bo' game with a modern piece of observation showing how such a game emerges in a situation related to frustration by mother and the presence of the observer:

> Plans were announced in 2002 for an international day to celebrate Darwin's achievements (his birthday, February 12th), and Richard Dawkins, President of the Darwin Day Organisation, declared that along with Shakespeare and Newton, Darwin is 'our greatest gift to the world'. The philosopher David Dunnett has talked of evolutionary theory as 'the single best idea anyone has ever had'.
>
> (*Observer*, 13 January 2002)

Although it was Esther Bick, with the encouragement of John Bowlby, who set up the practice of infant observation as a pre-clinical prerequisite for training as a child psychotherapist in 1948, she had weighty and honourable forebears in the field. As is well known, Freud's one extant observation, that of his grandson playing the *fort-da* reel game, was published in 1920. This revealed for Freud the extent to which his grandson was trying to master his anxieties over separation from his mother, and it was a cornerstone in the building of his ideas about what happens 'Beyond the Pleasure Principle' as a child struggles with the realities of life as it develops over time outside the womb. His observation is still on our reading lists today, and Alvarez (1992) has further elaborated his original text, already commented on by Isaacs (1952) in terms of object-relations theory, by pointing out the different states of mind in which this game could be played, then and now.

Freud was for all his life a staunch admirer of the man he called 'the great Darwin' (Gay, 1988, p. 36), wanting to emulate him in establishing a scientific base for psychology. It was seventeen years before Freud's birth that Charles Darwin embarked on the project of observing his own first son, William Erasmus Darwin (nicknamed 'Doddy'), born in 1839. Darwin had decided on marriage because he thought that to have a wife was 'better than a dog anyway', and he complained about the parental impact of having a baby: 'what an awful affair confinement is: it knocked me up, almost as much as it did Emma herself' (Desmond and Moore, 1991, p. 287). So we can speculate whether his scrupulous observation of his son from his first day of life could be called 'primary paternal preoccupation' or was something he embarked on partly in the service of his recovery from this 'awful affair'. Emanuel (2002) talks of the traumatic impact on fathers who witness the birth of their baby, but we must assume that in the tradition of the nineteenth century Darwin was not present at Doddy's birth. We can also wonder about the impact on Doddy as his father observed his upsets and took detailed notes on them rather than intervening in a more usual parental way:

> In addition, it was also very much part of Darwin's project to demonstrate that man is descended from apes rather than God, and it was Freud who allied himself with Darwin and Copernicus in considering that the three men had delivered three narcissistic blows to mankind: that the earth moves round the sun rather than vice versa, that we are indeed descended from apes rather than gods, and that a good part of our nature may remain largely unknown or unconscious even if we work at it.
>
> (Gay, op. cit., p. 449)

Darwin's observations

It was over thirty years later that Darwin made extensive use of his notes on Doddy, in *The Expression of Emotions in Man and Animals* (1872) and later still in 'A Biographical Sketch of an Infant' (1877) in response to an article about the mental development of an infant published in the previous edition of *Mind*. In Chapter Six of his book, called 'Special Expressions of Man: Suffering and Weeping', his chapter subheads listed at the beginning indicate that he was in territory familiar to observers today, looking for causes but seeing them physiologically rather than psychologically or psychoanalytically:

> The screaming and weeping of infants – forms of features – age at which weeping commences – the effects of habitual restraint on weeping – sobbing – cause of the contraction of the muscles round the eyes during screaming – cause of the secretion of tears.
>
> (Darwin, 1872)

So, we would consider this to be a picture of infancy where labile emotions are affected by fluctuating states of mind, of extreme happiness and unhappiness (with Darwin for his own purposes concentrating on the latter at this point), mitigated and helped in most cases by the ministrations of the caretaker. Darwin, however, did not put great stress on the interpersonal nature of a baby's world from the beginning, although he later made reference to social interactions between Doddy, his mother and his nurse. How the mind grew was, he thought, beyond his range. He said modestly that he thought his gifts were unsuited to 'the study of higher mental processes'. Largely, however, his nineteenth century mindset saw a rather mechanistic view of the subject or 'organism' in its reaction to pleasure and pain. Darwin lived in an age where the internal world and indeed even young babies' emotions were not accorded the same significance as we give them now. He says:

No suffering is greater than that from extreme fear or horror, but here a distinct emotion comes into play, and will be elsewhere considered. Prolonged suffering, especially of the mind, passes into low spirits, dejection and despair, and these states will be the subject of the following chapter. *Here I shall confine myself to weeping or crying, more especially in children.*

(Darwin, 1877, emphasis added)

What is being noticed is the physiological form of suffering but not its impact. We encourage observers to be sensitive and open to this in their counter-transference, to note their shifting identifications with mother and baby, and to make sense of these in terms of what is being projected, what is being denied or repressed, and how the baby's fluctuations between persecution and bliss (and states in between) become gradually modified so that self-containment will be the ultimate goal of being initially contained by the other. However, Darwin declares 'it is easy to observe infants while they are screaming' and he wrote down his scrupulously detailed observation of Doddy:

I often observed that the first sign of a screaming fit, when it could be observed coming on gradually, was a little frown, owing to the contraction of the corrugators of the brows; the capillaries of the naked head and face becoming at the same time reddened with blood. As soon as the screaming fit actually began, all the muscles round the eyes were strongly contracted, and the mouth widely opened in the manner above described, so that at this early period the features assumed the same form as at a more advanced age.

(Darwin, 1877)

One of the difficulties new observers often report is that of watching and containing an infant's distress rather than intervening in an active way. This capacity to watch and think about painful states that can stir up a painful affect in the observer is the prerequisite for being effective later in clinical work. And there is frequently some initial surprise on the part of observers at the way that many babies can indeed use the observer's thoughtfulness and feel contained and helped by it. Darwin's description quoted above does seem to have some unconscious resonances with his son's distress – in the use of the description 'naked head' for instance indicating his awareness of something helpless and vulnerable, unprotected from its own excesses of feeling – and yet it also seems that Darwin armed himself against his baby's distress too by the assumption that these 'screaming fits' were unallied to real and deep suffering, at that moment when these physical enactments took place. The last sentence, where he mentions the physical features of distress in a baby resembling those of people 'of more advanced age', might seem to be the beginning of an idea of equivalent feelings, but he does not develop this. His task was a different one, and it might also be seen to have been a protective one for Darwin himself.

Later in the chapter Darwin notes that photographs of adults crying show facial expressions similar to those of children, and also 'while very characteristic of the expression of a crying child, a nearly similar fold is produced in the act of laughing'. Could we infer from this some protorealisation of the rapid oscillation of moods that characterises the life of babies?

Darwin admired people who possessed exceptional observational powers, and he notes with satisfaction the work of 'that excellent observer' Mrs Gaskell (in her novel *Mary Barton*) who described a baby crying while it was being fed: 'it made its mouth like a square, and let the porridge run out at all four corners'. We might think of a baby being completely possessed by a state of mind antithetical to taking in anything, and especially perhaps porridge which might be felt to be full of the baby's angry projections, possibly around weaning. Darwin however notes the strong action of the depressor muscles that keep the mouth open thus ensuring that the baby's cries 'emerge at full volume'. He observes that older children often use only the upper set of these muscles 'but this may perhaps be due to older children not having so strong a tendency to scream loudly'.

Infants, Darwin observed, do not weep tears, and the first time he saw Doddy cry 'real tears' was when he was 139 days old (although he had been 'positively assured' – either by the child's mother or his nurse) that tears ran down the cheeks of another of his ten children 'at the unusually early age of 42 days'. This seems to be very much linked in Darwin's mind to the reality or not of children's suffering, because he feels that with the onset of the production of tears 'this expresses in the clearest manner suffering of both kinds, both bodily pain and mental distress'. He is also very interested in sobbing which he feels is connected with actual crying being repressed; here Darwin seems to allow in the notion of feeling although it is allied to physical manifestations, and Doddy of course had to grow up to be an Englishman. 'Englishmen rarely cry, except under the pressure of the acutest grief; whereas in some parts of the Continent men shed tears much more readily and easily.'

As the chapter proceeds Darwin becomes more and more technical and 'scientific', leaving behind the idea of the infant screaming, the rejected food, and passing on to the observations of others, for instance a certain Sir C. Bell, who is quoted as having separated the eyelids of a child while it was crying and struggling with passion. He quotes the tears noticed of an Indian elephant, and then ends the chapter with an assertion that Bowlby was to take up much later in terms of attachment theory and the 'environment of evolutionary adaptedness' (1982):

> Children, when wanting food or suffering in any way, cry out loudly, like the young of most other animals, partly as a call to their parents for aid, and partly for any great exertion serving relief . . . as much as the weeping is more violent or hysterical, by so much will the relief be greater.

In the 'Biographical Sketch' Darwin gives us a more rounded picture of the whole infant: he describes with pride how 'well performed' were Doddy's first actions of sneezing, hiccuping, yawning and stretching. He talks of the reflex to suck that occurs when he brushes the baby's cheek with his warm hand. He felt this had to be described simply as a reflex because 'it is impossible to believe that experience and association with the touch of his mothers breast could so soon have come into play'. This was when Doddy was a week old, and now we would think not only of a preconception of a breast having met reliably with a realisation (Bion) to form a concept, but of the beginnings of introjection of the satisfying breast that results from repeated experiences – a kind of psychophysiological associationism, where the meeting of the instinctual needs by the external object, the caretaker, results both in physical and psychological satisfaction and the beginning of the infant's own mental development (Shuttleworth, 1989). This way of thinking does not of course replace the idea that some actions are indeed reflex in origin, but suggests that the building up of experience from both physiological and psychological motivation is interdependent and complicated too by the baby's own capacities to make something from what he (in this case) receives. In the same paragraph Darwin describes an adverse reaction to father's sneezing which persisted for at least an hour when Doddy was nine months old, 'afterwards he was in a state which could be called nervous in an older person, for every slight noise made him start'. One could speculate on a hostile projection of Doddy's own being visited on Darwin, who was by all accounts rather a mild man, so that this sneeze could have seemed to enact Doddy's fears of retaliation, perhaps for his own wish to exclude his father and have sole possession of his mother. (By this time Mrs Darwin was pregnant again, and Anne, who was to be both her parents' darling, died of fever when she was eleven, an event that Doddy reacted to with particular grief (Desmond and Moore, op. cit.).) Again we might think about the omnipotent fears around his own hostility at being supplanted so early in his infancy, where at an unconscious level he might have linked his murderousness with Anne's actual death. The book *Annie's Box* (Keynes, 2001, reviewed by Urwin, 2002b) shows how much her parents were affected by her death, but there must have been a huge impact on Doddy in particular because of the closeness in their ages. There was also an intergenerational link: Charles Darwin himself had been supplanted by a sister when he was only fifteen months old.

But there is also evidence that Darwin could appreciate the interpersonal nature of development, and that the infant's capacity to relate empathically to his nurse by crying when she pretended to cry, and introject qualities from his objects, was something he noticed: 'an infant understands to a certain extent and as I believe at a very early period, the meaning of the feelings of those who tend him, by the expression of their features.'

Further observations of Doddy

Darwin noticed a tendency in Doddy to 'fix' on an object, a behaviour that would be observed and identified by Esther Bick (1964) as 'adhesive identification': a normally evolving behaviour that can be used as a primitive defence to hold the self together in times of stress:

> With respect of vision, his eyes were fixed on a candle as early as the 9th day, and up to the 45th day nothing else seemed thus to fix them; but on the 39th day his attention was attracted by a bright-coloured tassel, as was shown by his eyes becoming fixed and the movements of his arms ceasing.

The importance of orality in exploration and early tendencies towards some kind of primitive splitting mechanisms was observed by Darwin (although of course he did not have these formulations in mind) and collated by him into a paragraph pondering on the development of rational intention:

> The movements of his limbs and body were for a long time vague and purposeless, and usually performed in a jerking manner; but there was one exception to this rule, namely that from a very early period, certainly long before he was 40 days old, he could move his hands to his own mouth. When 77 days old, he took the sucking bottle (with which he was partly fed) in his right hand, whether he was held on the left or right arm of his nurse, and he would not take it in his left hand until a week later although I tried to make him do so; so that the right hand was a week in advance of the left ... when between 80 and 90 days old, he drew all sorts of objects into his mouth, and in two or three weeks time could do with some skill; but he often first touched

his nose with the object and then dragged it down into his mouth. After grasping my finger and drawing it down into his mouth, his own hand prevented him from sucking it; but on the 114th day, after acting in this manner, he slipped his own hand down so that he could get the end of my finger into his mouth. The action was repeated several times and was evidently not a chance but a rational one ... when four months old he often looked intently at his own hands and other objects close to him, and in doing so the eyes were turned much inwards, so that he often squinted frightfully.

After short paragraphs about fear (of his father's unpredictable 'strange and loud noises') and anger: 'a small cause sufficed; thus when a little over seven months old he screamed with rage because a lemon slipped away and he could not seize it with his hands' (which we might be tempted to connect at least hypothetically with weaning and anger at loss of the breast), Darwin talks of 'Pleasurable Sensations'. In this paragraph he mentions the development of the 'peek-a-boo' game. I would like to contrast Darwin's description, which is largely behavioural rather than one that sees the game in terms of an intersubjective and intrasubjective agenda (although 'peek-a-boo' has of necessity to occur within a two-person exchange), with a description taken from a modern-day infant observation. As we know, Melanie Klein's view was that the infant was object-related from birth and that the development of mental life began at that point (this is now postulated as even earlier because of the foetus's capacities to hear sound within the womb (Maiello, 1995)) – confirming the way in which psychoanalytic formulations help us towards understanding the processes that underlie external behavioural developments.

Pleasurable sensations

It may be presumed that infants feel pleasure whilst sucking and the expression of their swimming eyes seem to show that this is the case. This infant smiled when 45 days, a second infant when 46 days old, and these were smiles indicative of pleasure, for their eyes brightened and eyelids slightly closed. The smiles arose chiefly when looking at their mother, and therefore were probably of mental origin, but this infant often smiled then, and for some time afterwards, from some inward pleasurable feeling, for nothing was happening which could have in any way excited or amused him. When 110 days old he was exceedingly amused by a pinafore being thrown over his face and suddenly withdrawn; and so he was when I suddenly uncovered my own face and approached his. He then uttered a little noise which was an incipient laugh. Here surprise was the chief cause of the amusement, as is the case to a large extent with grown-up persons. I believe that for three or four weeks before the time when he was amused by a face suddenly being uncovered, he received a little pinch on his nose and cheeks as a good joke. I was at first surprised at humour being appreciated by an infant only a little above three months old, but we should remember how very early puppies and kittens begin to play.

(Darwin, 1877)

'Stumbling into peek-a-boo'

I want to end by quoting from an observation brought to a Child Development seminar some years ago in order to connect up the student's experience in her observations with the texts of child development research on the subject of object constancy, and Freud's ideas about the evolution of play in order to work through understanding of separation (Freud, op. cit.). In my experience it is in such moments in a seminar group where different paradigms may be examined and seen to be mutually illuminating rather than mutually exclusive that valuable learning and the capacity to make one's own links is promoted for group members. This has, I think, great relevance to the evolution of the creative process within the self, and the capacity to tolerate the unfamiliarity, even confusion, out of which new ideas will evolve. I explore this elsewhere, in terms of the dialectic between defensiveness and openness that can be seen to be at work throughout the life process (Edwards, 2002 and Chapter 13, this volume).

This observation, of a six-month-old baby, was the second visit following the Easter break. The previous week, the baby had avoided the observer's eyes. Maternal grandmother was also visiting; mother herself had been in conflict with her own mother on the subject of mess, and there were also issues around weaning; the baby was eating *fromage frais* as well as being both breast and bottle fed.

Mary (mother) removed the arch of the baby gym from the mat and helped Tina (the baby) to sit upright. She placed two cushions on either side of Tina and explained to me that she was scared of Tina falling backwards and injuring her head. This was the first time I had seen Tina sit independently of Mary's support.

As I watched, Tina appeared to straighten her spine and use her arms to balance and steady herself. She watched intently as Mary placed toys just within her reach on the mat. She seemed to be particularly attracted to a plastic cube that had a different basic musical instrument on each surface. She lunged forward, wobbled momentarily but succeeded in grabbing a plastic ring attached to the cube. As she pulled it nearer to her, the cube made a sudden 'miaow' like a cat.

Tina's eyes opened wide and her mouth opened and closed in quick succession. This was swiftly followed by a very 'blank' or 'flattened' expression when her face became very still. She held the ring in both hands and drew it to her mouth. The exertion of this movement caused her to rock forward with her head bobbing downward towards her toes. Tina's left arm shot out to balance herself and she straightened up, looking at us both and smiling. She gave a short 'ehh-ehh' sound and settled herself back on the mat.

Mary asked me whether I remembered when Tina often used to make that sound as a way of checking that everything was all right. Nowadays Tina's sounds are less sharp and defined and have been replaced with a more continuous babble.

Mary moved and sat on the floor next to Tina and smiled directly at her. She smiled again while saying that the next thing to do was to talk. Mary repeated 'Da, da, da' in a high-pitched voice to Tina. As Mary's pitch rose she began to move her face to within a few inches of Tina's. Simultaneously Tina turned her attention to the ear of a sensory toy elephant and as Mary moved closer, Tina began to hit the crackling material with her fist, until they were both making competing sounds.

The observer watches this 'competition', which culminates in mother finally managing to draw her child's attention to herself and the butterfly rattle she is waving at her:

> Mary smiled at Tina and began to move the butterfly in and out between them both. They both smiled and became visibly excited.
>   The game continued for about two minutes. Mary was making 'ahh' and 'ooh' noises and as the intensity of the game increased so did the speed with

which Mary pushed the butterfly towards Tina. At its peak Tina wobbled backwards and the game ended abruptly.

When she had regained her balance Tina slowly turned her face to me. She lifted up her bib and tried to put it in her mouth. The bib obscured her eyes, so she pulled it back down slightly, smiled at me and then pulled it up again over her eyes. Slowly she repeated it, and at the point that she drew it away from her eyes for the second time we both laughed aloud. It felt like an accidental stumble into a game of peek-a-boo. Tina let go of the bib and laughed again. She turned to look at Mary, who smiled back warmly.

Mary then reintroduced the cube and began to play with Tina in a calm and gentle way. Tina was interested in what she was doing and began to mimic her wider movements. Mary copied Tina as she banged the xylophone, waved the cube and pulled the plastic ring. This five-minute period was like a dance between the two with fluid and synchronous movements and complementary facial expressions. It reached its peak naturally and then slowed to a thoughtful pace where they were both looking at the pictures on the cube. Their bodies were close to each other and their heads were both bent in concentration.

Suddenly Mary heard her mother move upstairs and, in a quick movement, went from Tina to the window and began to speak in a worried voice about the weather.

(Burhouse, 1999)

Discussion

What this observation shows, I think, is the rich description that can be achieved, where no particular agenda is paramount beyond that of building up over the period of two years a detailed, thoughtful 'biography in depth' of an infant, and where gradually detailed observations can be linked to theoretical explanations. There are many comments that could be made about the observation above, in terms of the introjection of a particular object relationship and the building up of this little girl's particular internal world – what one might call the evolution of mental space, in relationship both to external events and the internal object relationships brought to the situation by her mother. As I have previously said, it also interests me a great deal in terms of the creative process, and what may emerge out of a period of 'chaos'. I use it here to illustrate something about the peekaboo game. While Doddy's experience of peekaboo was literally thrust upon him to begin with, Tina's game evolved out of her own discoveries, related to presence, absence and the thoughtful containment offered by the observer. She might also have been indicating something about her own ability to screen what she takes in with her eyes, and her enjoyment of this potency (Anne Alvarez, personal communication). The observer brought it because of the evolution, before her eyes, of the game, which could be related to the observer's absence and presence around the Easter break. The observation also illuminated the link between the inevitable vicissitudes in the external mother–baby relationship and what this particular baby makes of it inside her mind. What is particularly noteworthy is the way in which both mother and baby appear to be able to use the containing mind of the observer and achieve a less frantic and more harmonious interaction (which is then interrupted by mother's other preoccupations to do with the relationship she has with her own mother, both externally and internally).

The game of peekaboo that then develops into hide-and-seek has important ramifications too in later clinical work with deprived children in treatment. 'You be the seeker!' a small, deprived boy would instruct me eagerly, once he had been able to build up in his previously highly persecuted mind the idea of an object who was glad to see him, and to seek him out. As Alvarez (op. cit., p. 173) notes, the complicated mixture of emotions present in the playing of the game includes genuine delight in being discovered that is not manic or triumphant, and this can evolve to produce real change in the internal world. The elaboration of these implications lies outside the parameters of this paper; however I simply want to make the internal and external developmental link, and link it too back to Darwin's and Doddy's 'discovery' of the game.

In a paper on a psychoanalytic approach to language delay, Urwin (2002a) suggests that peekaboo is 'the hallmark of the emergence of the non-autistic personality . . . it is to support such a process (of separation and individuation and self/other distinction) that the I-me-you games of infancy are so important.' Indeed the observer herself went on to write a dissertation on this subject, bringing together thoughts from cognitive psychology, child development research and psychoanalysis (Burhouse, 1999, 2001).

Darwin's discussion based on his observations of Doddy and his other children aimed to show that much human behaviour is instinctive and derived from animals. He did not explain how mental development comes about in infancy, and *indeed* saw no gulf between the mental lives of human beings and animals. How the mind grew was, he thought, as I have said previously, beyond his range. We can look at the detail and cumulative power of his observations of Doddy and put onto them our own retrospective gloss, and it makes for fascinating conjecture. I hope this chapter may stimulate readers to go back and look at Darwin's observations and make their own connections. Darwin's observations were driven by his theory of evolution, ours by the theory of an internal world and internal object relations.

We are now so accustomed to the theory of evolution that it is impossible to stand outside it and take on our ancestors' view of men as upright beings descended from gods, as far back as when Odin and his brothers carved the elm and the ash into the first couple. Our outrage cannot be stirred as was that of Darwin's contemporaries, in thinking about a far more earthly 'ascendancy' from ape to man, just as ontogeny may be seen to reflect the wider picture as the infant crawls on all fours before becoming upright. Observation too has evolved from Darwin's rigorous efforts to observe with his agenda related to animal behaviour, to the work of observation students today who stand in an honourable line both to confirm psychoanalytic findings in which individual accounts act cumulatively as a research tool (Rustin, 1989, 1997) and carry the thinking forward. In Darwin's observations of Doddy we can see the seeds of future growth, as we notice the same phenomena but attribute possible internal and unconscious meanings to the observed behaviour of infants with their caretakers.

While Darwin himself rejected the notion of evolution being necessarily allied to progressive development (Gould, 1995) we can I think see at least a development in the interpretive art and science of infant observation from the nineteenth to the twenty-first century. As Gould (1995, p. 19) said, 'science is an integral part of culture: it is one of the glories of human intellectual tradition.'

Just as evolution, Darwin thought, was a question of struggling for existence at both macro and micro level, so ideas have become more complex in terms of the complexities and contingencies of human behaviour using the paradigm of psychoanalytic infant observation, in which we too as clinicians and thinkers are now historically and culturally embedded. Increasingly we are becoming interested in the way paradigms can be accepted as different and yet often producing complementary understandings that enhance rather than undermine our own work, as Rustin (2002) indicates, bringing together the ideas from chaos theory first posited as being psychoanalytically relevant by Moran (1991) and further elucidated by Scharff and Scharff (2000). We live in exciting times.

Acknowledgement

I am indebted to Anna Burhouse for permission to use an excerpt from her infant observation.

References

Alvarez, A. (1992) *Live Company*. London: Routledge.

Bick, E. (1964) 'Notes on infant observation in psychoanalytic training'. *International Journal of Psychoanalysis*, 45, 558–66.

Bowlby, J. (1982) 'Man's environment of evolutionary adaptedness'. In *Attachment and Loss, Vol. 1: Attachment*. London: Hogarth Press.

Burhouse, A. (1999) Me, You and It: Conversations about the significance of Joint Attention Skills from cognitive psychology, child development research and psychoanalysis, MA Dissertation, London, Tavistock Clinic, published *International Journal of Infant Observation*.

Burhouse, A. (2001) 'Now we are two, going on three: triadic development and its link with development in the context of young child observation'. *International Journal of Infant Observation*, 4(2), 51–67.

Darwin, C. R. (1872) *The Expression of the Emotions in Man and Animals*. London: Murray.

Darwin, C. R. (1877) 'A biographical sketch of an infant'. *Mind*, 2, 285–94.

Desmond, A. and Moore, J. (1991) *Darwin*. London: Joseph.

Edwards, J. (2002) 'The elusive pursuit of insight: 3 poems by W. B. Yeats and the human task'. In H. Canham and C. Satyamurti (eds), *Poetry and Psychoanalysis*. London: Karnac, pp. 167–87.

Emanuel, R. (2002) 'On becoming a father: Reflections from infant observation'. In J. Trowell and A. Etchegoyan (eds), *The Importance of Fathers*. London: Brunner-Routledge, pp. 63–79.

Freud, S. (1920) *Beyond the Pleasure Principle*, S.E. 18.

Gay, P. (1988) *Freud: A Life for Our Time*. London and Melbourne: Dent.

Gould, S. J. (1995) *The Individual in Darwin's World*. The Second Edinburgh Medal Address. London: Weidenfeld & Nicolson.

Isaacs, S. (1952) 'The nature and function of phantasy'. In M. Klein, P. Heimann, S. Isaacs, M. Klein and J. Riviere (eds), *Developments in Psychoanalysis*. London: Hogarth, pp. 67–105.

Maiello, S. (1995) 'The sound-object', *Journal of Child Psychotherapy*, 21(1), 23–41.

Moran, M. H. (1991) 'Chaos theory and psychoanalysis: The fluidistic nature of the mind'. *International Journal of Psychoanalysis*, 18(2), 211–21.

Rustin, M. (1989) 'Observing infants: Reflections on methods'. In L. Miller, M. Rustin, M. Rustin and J. Shuttleworth (eds), *Closely Observed Infants*. London: Duckworth, 52–75.

Rustin, M. (1997) 'What do we see in the Nursery? Infant observation as "laboratory work"'. *Journal of Infant Observation*, 1(1), 93–109.

Rustin, M. (2002) 'Looking in the right place'. *Journal of Infant Observation*, 5(1), 122–44.

Scharff, J. S. and Scharff, D. E. (2000) *Tuning the Therapeutic Instrument*. London and Northvale, NJ: Aronson.

Shuttleworth, J. (1989) 'Psychoanalytic theory and infant development'. In L. Miller, M. Rustin, M. Rustin and J. Shuttleworth (eds), *Closely Observed Infants*. London: Duckworth, pp. 22–51.

Urwin, C. (2002a) 'When autistic is not necessarily autism'. *Journal of Child Psychotherapy*, 28(1), 73–93.

Urwin, C. (2002b) 'Review of *Annie's Box*'. *Journal of Infant Observation*, 5(1), 145–56.

CHAPTER 2

EARLY SPLITTING AND PROJECTIVE IDENTIFICATION

In this chapter, starting from the idea of the relationship between maternal and paternal functions in the processing of experience, I take as the object of my thinking an account of a particular observation and its discussion in an observation seminar group. Using the example of early splitting and projective identification, first delineated in terms of Klein's (1946) seminal paper, 'Notes on some schizoid mechanisms', I reflect on this process in the observation, the group and in the mind of the teacher. The seminar leader is also involved, I suggest, in an ongoing process. She needs to exercise caution in the fine balancing of her own maternal containing and paternal explicating processes, in order to facilitate rather than foreclose on the learning that can take place in the experiential group setting. I go on to exemplify this in a particular narrative of teaching and learning that occurred within a single seminar, halfway through the first year of the students' experience.

Observation and theory – the inseparable couple

Having taught both Observation and Kleinian Theory at the Tavistock for many years, I was pleased to be asked to contribute the first of a series of articles in *The Journal of Infant Observation* on the topic of elucidating the theoretical concepts that surround and infuse the observational task, particularly since the issue had been at the forefront of my mind. This was for two reasons: the first was that I had read Maiello's paper (2007) in *The Journal of Infant Observation* on 'Containment and differentiation: Notes on the observer's maternal and paternal function'. In this the author was focussing on emotional aspects of the observer's learning experience, in terms of the capacity both to contain complicated projections of primitive mental states in a maternal way, and then to disentangle them in order to differentiate their origin, function and meaning (the paternal function). This work enables the observer over time to develop the vital skill of being able to be both receptive and interpretive, which is the core need in therapeutic work with children (and also with adults), as Sternberg (2005) explicates so tellingly. As Maiello suggests, this 'remaining in the third position' enhances the maturational process of the observer, as she comes into contact and communicates with her own infantile self as well as that of the baby she is observing (2007, p. 46). I will return to this later in terms of the observational material presented here.

I was struck by this thought too in relation to the seminar leader's function in the group. I had previously written a paper with some colleagues (Edwards *et al.*, 2006) about the different layers that are at work in what I called circles of 'concentric containment': held at the periphery by the seminar leader, and focussing inwards on the different containing circles that originate in the mother's arms held around her baby. In other words, the holding function (Winnicott, 1956) that gradually enables a baby who feels physically and psychologically contained to achieve a growing measure of self containment over time. We generally tend to feel strongly, and I think rightly, that the experiential group and each observer should not be too burdened by theory at the outset, (i.e. that the leader performs her maternal function, but contained by her own knowledge of theory and the experience of its use) in the very disentanglement described above. But when should she call on what might be called her more paternal function, and refer directly to these same governing principles of theory? This of course has an interface with the academic demands that are placed on the student, but with infant observation, in the Tavistock/University of East London model; the essay on the whole process is not written until the end of the second academic year. However, many of these essays tend to focus on developments during the first year of life.

As is frequently the case in my experience, once one starts thinking of a problem and how to understand it, the opportunity emerges to exemplify it and think about it further, in this case in a teaching experience within a group. Thus the learning experience extends to the teacher, who must think carefully about how to find the right timing and approach in order to enhance learning rather than foreclose on thinking by the premature introduction of theoretical concepts. There needs, in sum, to be an awareness of the fine balance necessary in the teacher, in terms of the exercise of the maternal containing and paternal explicating processes.

The theoretical/paternal side: early splitting and projective identification

The concept at issue here is one that begins to operate at the very start of life. Melanie Klein (1946) wrote her seminal paper, 'Notes on some schizoid mechanisms', based on the 'Controversial discussions' that took place between the British and Viennese schools of psychoanalysis (1943–44) in order to clarify her views on splitting and projective identification in 'the paranoid-schizoid position'. This was the first time that she pulled together her description of what she had previously called 'paranoid' anxieties during the first three months of life into a more organised account. As anyone who observes small babies will soon become aware, their lives tend at times to be either threatened or completely overwhelmed at the beginning by feelings of terrifying chaos and abandonment. The early fragile ego is beset with strong anxieties, and the baby needs the care and devoted understanding of his carers in order to avoid falling apart. He is, as Bick (1968) so memorably put it, like an astronaut shot into space without a space suit.

In this 1946 paper, Klein introduced the crucial concept of 'projective identification', a type of omnipotent impulse at the level of unconscious phantasy that is vital for the first weeks of existence, but that if it is reverted to in adult life is linked in its pathological intensity with schizoid states. This projective identification, she said, was a combination of splitting, projecting or expelling feelings, and identifying these same unwanted feelings elsewhere, in an object. The contents of the ego are not split off completely but are rediscovered in the object, so that there is in effect, for a time, a confusion. However, this is a necessary defence in the early weeks, when it is vital for the baby to recognise quite plainly the difference in objects and experiences between 'good' and 'bad', towards the building of a coherent internal world. It is the mother (or other carer) who by her reverie (Bion,

1962) digests the projections without prematurely returning them. Then after she has mulled over them, she returns them in a more manageable form.

Sorensen (2000) describes what she calls 'transition-facilitating behaviour', intimately connected with what I have just described, which a mother uses in order to help her baby manage change and the extreme states that may be stirred up in the tiny baby's mind. This primary splitting is fundamental to the unfolding of normal development as the baby experiences states such as being full and then feeling hungry and empty, mother 'here' and mother 'gone'. For a tiny baby, these may be felt at the time to be life and death issues. It is mother's understanding and containing mind, performing her maternal containing function over and over again as part of her repertoire of tasks, that helps the infant gradually to become less terrified, in other words, to feel emotionally contained and understood in all his most extreme raw states, in what Sorensen (2000, p. 52) calls 'the gradual accumulation of the smallest moments that make a life'. The mother develops her ability to see life from the baby's point of view, and act in order to mediate extreme states. Stern (1985) described these maternal capacities as contributing to the building up of what he called RIGS – representations of interactions that become generalised. This containment will enable the baby gradually to move towards self-containment and a more realistic picture of the world. These skills will also be core for the work of child psychotherapists working with their most deprived and borderline patients, and it was Schore (2001) who discussed how these fragments expelled in terror and projectively identified with the object will become experienced in the counter-transference of the therapist, as emotional states of primitive intensity, experienced by both partners in the right brain, which has been gradually developing in the early preverbal time of an infant's life.

The trauma of birth, the first terrifying feelings of separation, the frustration of bodily needs and the hatred arising from these states, all felt to be caused by objects, usher in this necessary unconscious defence from the beginning of life. Klein saw these omnipotent phantasies as defences against the dread of separation, dependency, and primary envy of the object, which becomes more frightening when the infant may fear that it is now filled with his own hostile and destructive urges. In observation groups, those who have the opportunity of observing a baby from the first days or even hours, frequently have the chance to see how labile is the mind of the infant, veering between extreme states of terror, the phantastically bad (perhaps feeling terrifyingly exposed for a nappy change) and ecstasy, the phantastically good (feeling full after a feed, and held in mother's arms). Thus the vulnerable infant maintains the possibility of preserving the good object by splitting, an impulse seen by Melanie Klein to be at the core of healthy development. Students may then understand why we ask them to observe from as near the beginning of life as possible, because gradually things settle down, the extremes are less intense, and something else begins to happen, in the context both of the developing brain, and developing relationships. This 'move' will be described in later chapters, and for my purposes here I want to concentrate on these first impulses (though of course it is also important to acknowledge that these defences are never fully outgrown; we can all resort to splitting even as 'mature' adults). So from Freud's ideas about somatic tension and subsequent discharge for relief, Melanie Klein introduced the notion of something being done by someone to somebody – object relations from the beginning. The infant ego may either fall to pieces, or split itself actively, employing the good offices of the caretaker to survive in this new and terrifying world. As Klein said 'the early ego lacks cohesion, and a tendency towards integration alternates with a tendency towards disintegration, a falling into bits' (1946, p. 4).

The theory group

A few weeks after having read Maiello's paper, I had been reading this 1946 paper one morning with a student group. These pre-clinical second-year students had struggled with doubts and anxieties about the complexities of Kleinian thought, and tended to approach reading assignments such as this dense paper with trepidation. They were halfway through the year at this stage, and we were able to think about the early stages of their observations, which had been done a year previously, and link those experiences with what Klein was describing. Individuals within the group offered some instances from their observations that might be seen to be relevant to this notion of primary splitting. One student voiced the thought that she wished she had known about this paper then, and others agreed. I responded that maybe it was also important to think about the chance to have the experience first without wanting to put a label on it, a defence perhaps deployed in order to avoid the anxiety aroused by witnessing such extreme states.

The observation group

That same day in the afternoon I was meeting with first-year students for an observation group, and we had similarly been meeting since the previous October. There were four students in the group since the fifth student had to withdraw after a family accident. All had been observing since some time during the first term.

A baby whom I will call Lily was being presented. Lily was nearly four months old, and until that time we had indeed not witnessed any extreme and difficult states in the observations. The observer felt that the mother was a patient, thoughtful carer of her infant daughter, well supported by her husband. I had wondered about a certain amount of idealisation, and there had been an issue previously around when the observer described how she had felt reluctant to follow the mother with her baby into another room for a nappy change. The group thought with her about this, and she had been able to reflect about her own wish to avoid 'messiness'. As she handed round her observation notes on this particular week, the observer said she was worried, this had been such a difficult observation – she had never seen Lily like this before. This seemed at first hearing to be a comment that contained some embarrassment, as if the observer felt Lily or indeed the observer herself had 'failed' in some way, by Lily behaving as it were so out of some character previously hypothesised by the observer to be the total picture. She said she had felt like 'an intruder' for almost the whole hour, and had come away feeling rather shattered by an experience of extreme emotional intensity.

The observation

The observer described knocking at the door, hearing a baby crying, and being hastily let in by the mother (Mary). Mary was holding a frowning Lily diagonally across her body, with Lily's face turned outwards. Lily looked as though she had been crying, but had momentarily stopped. Mother went ahead into the living room, and the observer joined them, sitting on a sofa opposite:

> Lily's face was expressionless, and as Mary tried to settle her in a position comfortable for both of them, Lily appeared to resist her, arching her back

and straightening her legs. Mary said 'OK, you don't like this' and lifted Lily so that they were facing one another. 'What are we going to do?' Mary asked, looking closely at Lily. Lily let out a loud cry. 'Oh no, maybe some milk will help', Mary said, and she put Lily in her lap so that she could feed from the left breast. She held Lily with her left arm and started to expose her breast, but did not get very far with this as Lily started to kick her legs in small movements, pulled her face into a grimace, closed her eyes and opened her mouth wide to let out another loud cry. Mary brought Lily close into her body, rubbed her back, and spoke softly to her. Lily continued to cry with her eyes tightly closed. Mary took out her left breast, and offered it to Lily by slowly lowering her upper body, so that Lily could feel the nipple on her lips. This did not soothe Lily; she arched her back and threw her head backwards, making it hard for Mary to hold her. She seemed very angry, not about to be pacified easily, as if maybe Mary had responded to her needs too slowly and she would not be easily forgiven.

Once again Mary tried to offer her breast, but Lily was not having any of it. She continued to fight her mother's efforts, and cried with her eyes closed, making no eye contact with her mother. Mary continued in her efforts to offer the breast, but because of Lily's jerky movements of refusal as she arched her back and kicked her legs, Mary's movements too became lacking in fluidity, and there was not the coordination and harmony I had observed previously during breastfeeding. The struggle continued: Mary holding Lily close to her, trying over and over again to offer the breast, and Lily persistently arching, kicking and crying loudly.

This went on maybe for around 5–7 minutes, but to me it felt like fifteen minutes or more. I felt guilty and anxious that I had arrived at a bad time. I recalled hearing Lily crying when I knocked at the door, and thought that I must have disturbed the beginning of a feed.

Then slowly something seemed to change. Lily calmed a little, as if she was exhausted by her crying. A sleepy look came over her face. She settled more in her mother's lap, stopped wriggling so much, and Mary once again offered the breast. Lily then opened her eyes, for the first time since the crying episode had begun, and looked at her mother through her tears. After a couple more attempts on Mary's part, Lily took the breast. Now she appeared to relax, seeming almost to burrow into her mother's body. As they both settled, Mary stroked her baby's face, speaking softly to her, then repositioning her so that they both looked comfortable. Lily closed her eyes again, but now she was holding on to Mary's forefinger as she fed.

At first she sucked greedily, making loud smacking and rather desperate noises, then after a short while she slowed down, and the noises became calmer, seeming more to be those of satisfaction and enjoyment. Mary looked rather frazzled, and also relieved.

Once Lily had settled, it was almost as if Mary noticed I had been there all along, and she said 'I can only remember her doing that on one other occasion, and that was when she had her first immunisations. I don't know what upset her so much this time.' It felt like an apology, and I felt embarrassed, as I felt like an intruder. Mary spoke to Lily again: 'What was it baby, it's all right now, it's all right.' They both looked peaceful. Lily's body and face were turned into her mother's body, her left arm was not visible, and with her right hand she continued to hold on to Mary's forefinger. They stayed like this for about twenty minutes, and Lily appeared to have fallen asleep.

Her face looked serene, and Mary too looked relaxed. Lily's breathing was deep and even, and intermittently she sucked for a few minutes, in this half asleep, drowsy state.

While Lily slept, Mary told the observer that her husband was away for a few days, working. She talked of the huge adjustment to being 'a single parent' with no time for herself, and she realised how much both she and Lily relied on her husband. How did single parents manage? The rest of the observation was done in silence, with the observer watching Lily, cocooned and content in her mother's arms.

Discussion with the group

After she had finished reading out her observation, the observer too looked somewhat 'frazzled' and concerned. As we as teachers are aware, reading out a previously written-up observation creates something that happens again, and is not simply a re-presentation of what went before. It possesses a new and added dimension in being recalled, digested and discussed in the seminar group. In a sense, the presenting observer has three opportunities to experience her observation: in the lived experience, in the subsequent writing up of the material, and then in the seminar group.

We thought about the observer's guilt at being the intruder (and mother had talked about the upset over the intrusion felt by Lily at the time of the immunisations) as also perhaps a projection of mother's own guilt at not 'managing'. This persecuted feeling of having her space taken over without father's usual protection may also have been projected into the baby, and, as Bick (1986) noted, the baby's loud sense of grievance, with its potential attack on mother's sense of 'goodness', might well have stirred up guilt that had roots in her own infantile complaints about the inadequacy of her own mother. The observer then became the unwelcome rather than the desired third, and mother and baby were locked into a dyad of intensity and despair. The baby, with her eyes tightly closed, was in a persecuted state, and would not look at her mother, who also did not appear to 'see' the observer until the storm had passed. We thought about the observer's sense of guilt in relation to a baby self that had tried to adapt and become overwhelmed by failure, terror and an identification with mother's own sense of loss with relation to her husband, almost as if his physical absence had given rise to a persecuted feel of an almost concrete presence, in both mother's and baby's minds. Again, as with the previous issue around 'mess', the observer became reflective about what she, too, brought in terms of transference (and of course there is also the inevitable transference to the seminar leader to think about here).

One student recalled how another person in the group had previously observed that there was a sense in which 'mother always offered milk'. The other student could not remember this at first, but then agreed, saying she felt mother was offering 'the wrong thing' – the baby quite clearly didn't want it. The observer then talked more about how confused she too had felt: 'I just didn't know, Lily didn't know what she wanted, Mary didn't know what Lily wanted.' At this point I felt as seminar leader that I was not quite sure what was needed here. I too was assailed by some contradictory impulses about what and how to offer some additional thinking, and the timing of this. I was acutely aware of the danger of offering too much, too soon. I hesitated, and then asked the group for any further thoughts. The student who had just projected her own sense of mother's failure onto a comment by another student in a previous seminar, now offered that she felt mother had actually been helpful, trying gently to put the nipple in the baby's mouth – and yet, it hadn't worked – why was that? Because later it *was* what Lily wanted, and she had become settled in a feed, which ended in a sleep and a feeling of calm and closeness between mother and baby. We discussed Lily's holding fast onto her mother's finger, which might be thought of as the restoration of a 'third area', and also perhaps a reference to the absence of father, felt keenly by both mother and child.

We returned to the beginning of the observation, where the observer had wondered (probably rightly) whether she had disturbed a feed. We thought about the differing views in the group, with one representing the view of something done 'wrong', another that here is a mother trying in vain to do something ultimately 'right'. The observer herself represented the position of no one knowing anything, but there was no blame attached to this confused state. The group had grown accustomed to expressing differential viewpoints and considering them, and were somewhat open to this state of 'not knowing' by this time in the year. Apparent vulnerabilities and possible 'blind spots' had been discussed where relevant, and a trust in the value of this process, hopefully relatively non-persecutory over time, had been built up in the group. A 'third area' for reflection in the group had emerged that could then enable us to think about apparent contradictions and their possible implications.

I suggested that Lily did know what she did *not* want and was making that abundantly clear through her loud crying. I then talked briefly and as simply as possible about Melanie Klein's notion of primary splitting: that Lily had transformed her mother's previously 'good' breast into something bad and unacceptable, changed by her own anger into something quite impossible to accept. She closed her eyes, because it was too terrifying to 'see' this bad mother. Then she had gradually been able to calm down, aided by mother's steadfast efforts to endure her daughter's rejection as she lay stiff-legged and rigid, a great contrast to the way in which she had finally been able to mould, even 'burrow' as the observer noted, into her mother's body, exhausted by her previous terror. Then when she was able to open her eyes, through her tears she rediscovered her 'good' mother, reinstated in her mind as a good object after the terror she had felt at being possessed of something monstrously bad. It was then that Mary 'discovered' the observer, and talked of the absent father, while Lily held on to her forefinger as she slept and sucked in her sleep. In a sense, there was a concentric process of 'making room' for something new; within the mother/baby dyad, within the observer, and within the group – what Ogden (1994) called 'the analytic third'.

Although Klein's detractors tend to insist that she ignored the impact of the external world, she was clear that it was indeed mother's repeated external proofs of her understanding and her return that helped the baby understand that she was not destroyed by his or her attacks. This then makes the vital contribution in the building-up of a secure internal world of good objects – although Klein also stressed in many of her works that this capacity for understanding and relief would vary with each individual. This process had been at work, I submit, in the observation quoted above.

I referred directly to Klein's seminal 1946 paper, addressing the importance of the capacity to split in order to preserve the good object, and how vital this was in the early months in order later for true integration to begin to take place – in other words, the emergence of the idea of a whole object, loved but also hated, based more on the reality principle, and with a measure of concern becoming more evident. The students were extremely interested, and the observer felt it was the first time she had really been able to fully understand something of how theory could help disentangle what goes on in the observational setting. I think what she was perhaps experiencing was a sense of emotional and intellectual understanding coming together in a meaningful way. She talked about how privileged she felt to be able to see how what she called 'a storm in a teacup' could become such a stark drama for them all, threatening to overwhelm baby, mother and observer. I found myself nevertheless apologising for holding a more didactic seminar than usual (I had also mentioned their essays at the end of the second year). I recalled to myself Bick's (1968) caveat about 'premature theorising'.

Conclusion

In conclusion, what took place in this seminar that represented an episode in the ongoing narrative of both learning and teaching, led me to consider both pace and timing in terms of a link, rather than a split, between academic and experiential learning. I wondered whether we may fear too much that theory will overwhelm experience: that our paternal function will hold sway and prevent students from truly experiencing in depth the powerful emotions that assail babies and their carers, and by extension sensitive observers who are able to process what they will later learn to call their counter-transference, for digestion and reverie, the maternal function. This is obviously something that one needs to debate within oneself in terms of the capacities of the particular experiential group. It is also valuable, I suggest, sometimes to revisit these thoughts in terms of where we are now in relation to academic requirements, and our ability to equip our students with the necessary tools both to experience the lived moment, and to be able to call on theory subsequently to elucidate it. This refers directly back to Maiello's paper, and I think applies to seminar leaders as well as students. We need to be alert to the danger that psychoanalytic theory may be used to corroborate observation, or vice versa: the issue of remaining 'experience near' as opposed to 'experience far' (Sandler and Sandler, 1994).

What was interesting for me was the juxtaposition of the two seminars, what took place within each, and how they were linked in terms of learning, my own included. In terms specifically of the Tavistock/University of East London courses, perhaps it is wise not to teach Kleinian theory until the second year, in order not to foreclose on the aforementioned need to be able to live with not knowing. However, in order not to maintain a rigid split, as baby Lily demonstrated with her stiff legs, perhaps we also need to think how to mould the two tasks together without feeling that the paternal function may compromise the maternal. The ultimate essay on the observation is both an internal emotional task and also an academic one – the core issue seems to be for seminar leaders to enable students to maintain some kind of dynamic tension between the two, and I suggest this is an ongoing process.

A social research student who undertook an infant observation then wrote about the process in terms of her experience and the social science concepts of reflexivity and reflection (Brown, 2006). She quotes Finlay (2003, p. 108) who says:

> These concepts are perhaps best viewed on a continuum. Reflection can be understood as thinking about something. The process is a more distanced one and takes place after the event [as in writing up an observation]. Reflexivity,

by contrast, involves a more immediate, continuing, dynamic and subjective self-awareness.

These linked functions come into triangular relationship I suggest with one's own epistemological frame, that of psychoanalysis, to give us the third area in which to carry on thinking.

I want to end by briefly quoting from Ogden's (2006) paper on psychoanalytic teaching, which I think sums up what I have been trying to articulate:

> Psychoanalytic teaching at its best opens up a space for thinking and dreaming in situations where the (understandable) impulse is to close that space. To fill that space as a teacher is to preach, proselytise, to perpetuate dogma; not to fill it is to create conditions where one may become open to previously inconceivable possibilities. The central goal of analytic teaching [and I would include teaching of observation here – JE] is the enhancement of the analyst's [observer's – JE] capacity to dream those aspects of experience in the clinical [observational – JE] experience s/he has not previously been able to dream.
>
> (Ogden, 2006, p. 1083)

I think we might all agree that these eloquent words sum up a process that is not at all easy to maintain at times, when we too may wish to fill a space with what Ogden called 'dogma'. And yet our governing principles exist to guide our onward paths, as students and as teachers. Perhaps this is a paradox that we need to tolerate, respect and live with.

Acknowledgements

I would like to thank the members of my observation group for their permission to discuss this seminar: Tendai Chikohora, Laurence Kalbreier, Liberty Mosse and Traute Paulin.

References

Bick, E. (1968) 'The skin in early object relations'. *International Journal of Psychoanalysis*, 49, 484–6.

Bick, E. (1986) 'Further conclusions on the function of skin in early object relations'. *British Journal of Psychotherapy*, 2(4), reprinted in A. Briggs (ed.) (2002) *Surviving Space: Papers on Infant Observation*. London and New York: Karnac, pp. 240–56.

Bion, W. R. (1962) *Learning from experience*. New York: Heinemann.

Brown, J. (2006) 'Reflexivity in the research process: Psychoanalytic observation'. *International Journal of Social Work Methodology*, 9(3), 181–97.

Edwards, J., Arnold, K., Hanson, C., Ngah, Z., Oclander-Goldie, S. and Segal, B. (2006) 'Making connections: Teaching observational skills to non-clinical students on an MA course in psychoanalytical studies'. *Journal of Infant Observation*, 9(3), 221–32.

Finlay, L. (2003) 'The reflexive journey: Mapping multiple routes'. In O. Finlay and B. Gough (eds), *Reflexivity: A Practical Guide for Researchers in Health and Social Sciences*. London: Blackwell, pp. 104–24.

Klein, M. (1946) 'Notes on some schizoid mechanisms'. In M. Klein (ed.) (1975) *Envy and Gratitude and Other Works 1946–63*. London: Hogarth Press, pp. 1–24.

Maiello, S. (2007) 'Containment and differentiation: Notes on the observer's maternal and paternal function'. *International Journal of Infant Observation*, 10(1), 41–9.

Ogden, T. H. (1994) 'The analytic third: Working with intersubjective clinical facts'. *International Journal of Psychoanalysis*, 75(5/6), 3–19.

Ogden, T. H. (2006) 'On teaching psychoanalysis'. *International Journal of Psychoanalysis*, 87, 1069–85.

Sandler, J. and Sandler, A-M. (1994) 'Comments on the conceptualisation of clinical facts'. *International Journal of Psychoanalysis*, 75(5/6), 995–1011.

Schore, A. (2001) 'Neurobiology, developmental psychology and psychoanalysis: Convergent findings on the subject of projective identification'. In J. Edwards (ed.), *Being Alive: Building on the Work of Anne Alvarez*. London and New York: Routledge, pp. 57–74.

Sorensen, P. (2000) 'Observation of transition-facilitating behaviour: Developmental and theoretical implications'. *Journal of Infant Observation*, 3(2), 46–54.

Stern, D. (1985) *The Interpersonal World of the Infant*. New York: Basic Books.

Sternberg, J. (2005) *Infant Observation at the Heart of Training*. London: Karnac.

Winnicott, D. W. (1956) *Through Paediatrics to Psychoanalysis*. London: Hogarth Press.

CHAPTER 3

TEACHING OBSERVATION TO NON-CLINICAL STUDENTS

In this chapter I explore thinking around the teaching of observation to students who are not planning to become clinicians. Is it relevant? What is its impact? Using experiences from two groups and comments from students themselves, I suggest that infant and young child observation is not only the province of pre-clinicians – there is a profound learning experience inherent in the task, having, as I suggest, its roots in the primal relationship between infant and caretaker, and the vital role of this in the unfolding of psychic life.

Introduction

Observation, as I think all clinicians would agree, is a vital tool in preparing pre-clinical students for attention to the minutiae, both of body language and of feeling, in patient and practitioner, that will lie at the core of clinical work; as Sternberg (2005) so eloquently expressed it, 'feeling the music' (p. 84). Many, although not all, clinicians working with children retain that sense of devotion (and maybe that is not too strong a word) they recall from their own observations, and have a commitment that lies at the heart of their wish to pass on these vital skills to future practitioners. These future practitioners are usually in analysis or therapy, where the turmoil concerning their own infantile selves stirred up by the experience of observing a baby can be held and thought about over time.

But why should there be any need to extend this experience further, to those who are not going on to train in this work? I have been continuing to reflect on this, since I am involved in two courses with different cohorts of students where observation, either directly or indirectly, is part of the curriculum. One of these (which I will call Course A) comprises a body of people very probably not going on to train as psychotherapists, and largely not in therapy or analysis themselves, but already employed in what one can loosely call 'the helping professions'. The case has been most convincingly made (see for example several papers on this topic in *Journal of Infant Observation* (1999) and Rustin and Bradley (2008) for the value of observation, for instance for hard-pressed social workers). Thoughtful observations of children in problematic family situations may go a long way in helping sort out the knotty and painful questions to do with adequate care, strengths of relationships, and defences that can also plague the network charged with supervising and regulating the lives of the most vulnerable members of society.

The other cohort with whom I have contact is a body of students (on what I will call Course B), many of whom are not in the caring professions, but have been drawn by their own personal experiences to the idea that thinking about the internal world and the dynamics of the unconscious would be a worthwhile and rewarding experience. Some of them are fascinated by the idea of observation, some are in awe of the task, some are frankly extremely concerned and worried about their capacity to do something so new and so challenging. I wrote with my colleagues on this course in a previous paper (Edwards *et al.*, 2006) about the particular issues inherent in this task, both for students and teachers.

Work with the two groups

Course A

With Course A, I meet them as a course group in the first term to think about the benefits and challenges of observation (sadly they do not have the space in this one-year course for an observation module per se). I have asked them previously to do a small piece of observation, be it at a bus stop, at a café, in the park, to have some idea of what might be involved. While I don't then ask them for details of what they observed, I do ask them for a free association of words to sum up that experience, before we begin to think about observation in general. Over the years these words have included 'intrusive' (nearly every cohort produces this word), 'surprising', 'uncomfortable', 'anxious', 'embarrassing', 'unclear purpose', 'curious', 'self-conscious'. Teachers of Infant Observation may recognise how often these same words come up in their seminars, at the beginning, and clearly the task, either undertaken for ten minutes or two years, engenders a range of feelings, many of which can seem overwhelming. Ambiguity, complexity, uncertainty – there is a process going on from the start.

After we have begun the seminar in this way, I then introduce a quotation about an artist, also devoted to the work of observation:

> No one has described how to paint a portrait more clearly or succinctly than Henri Matisse. He insisted on accuracy, maintaining at the same time that the meticulous production of external detail could never provide more than a starting point. Success or failure at a deeper level was a matter of contemplation, concentration, the force and quality of attention focussed on a subject. Matisse said that nothing should be distorted or suppressed. Anyone attempting a portrait should above all approach the subject without preconception: 'To sum up, I work *without a theory* [my italics: I have written previously about the balance needed here between observation and theory in observation seminars, Edwards (2008 and Chapter 2, this volume)]. I am aware primarily of the forces involved, and find myself driven forward by an idea that I can really only grasp little by little as it grows with the picture.
>
> (Spurling, 1998, p. xix)

This idea of painting a portrait without preconceptions is one that the students find curious but interesting: that each observation is in some sense a small art form. Then as the seminar continues they talk about their own observations at work, and begin to have some appreciation of how detailed observation, of what you might call almost the nerdy kind (no accident I think that the first book about Infant Observation was called *Closely Observed Infants* (Miller, Rustin, Rustin and Shuttleworth (eds), 1989) after a film about an obsessive and enthusiastic train spotter, *Closely Observed Trains* (Menzel, 1966), is helpful in order to aid meaning, and that this will include one's own feelings as part of the venture. It is a unique kind of self-education, being in the room with the baby and the caretaker; before the observation is then discussed in the experiential group. As Grayling (2002) so succinctly put it in a piece on self-education, one needs 'the eager glance of an intelligent eye, unblinkered by conventional education, seeing the value in things without having been told to expect them there, and *therefore seeing them truly*'.

I have no idea whether the students in this cohort do indeed subsequently go on after this course has finished to observe a baby or young child within the frame of an experiential group (I think most do not), but they do seem to be fired by the idea that observation is a worthwhile venture, both professionally and personally.

Course B

In Course B, the student cohort is of a much more varied makeup: there are indeed clinical psychologists, teachers, sometimes therapists, but also lawyers, actors, novelists, managers of companies, and other interested participants from various professions, from around the world. Some may indeed become so interested in what they receive and learn that they go on to train in working either with adults or with children, but many do not. However they take what they have learned back into their own professional tasks, and into their personal lives. (Again, see Edwards (2006) for examples of how a mediator and a manager in the civil service found what they learned to be of value in their own work.)

A recent prospective applicant from overseas (she is a manager in a large airport) talked of how she felt that the observation would be a 'unique and thrilling opportunity' to integrate theory with knowledge from real-life situations: what she called 'a healthy way of theory production'. Looking back over the feedback forms specifically about observation on this course over the last few years, and also from face-to-face feedback in course committees, it has become increasingly evident that this experiential part of the course has enormous core value, even for non-clinicians. There is appreciation of the open discussions, where 'things are held tentatively' – what a descriptive phrase – rather than being part of a rush towards explication. 'Exploring new ideas with others, and enjoying the process – I did not expect that!' as one student wrote. 'I have been surprised by the amount I have learned' wrote another. A third wrote:

> I must thank you so much for this opportunity to observe a baby. Even if I do not do well on this course, it has been one of the most significant and enriching experiences in my life on many levels. I would describe it as truly enabling. There is no better compliment that I could give.

To conclude, I asked three students (two of whom had already completed the course), a GP, a journalist and a strategic consultant respectively, if they were able to put down some thoughts about the observation task and its impact. What had they been looking for? Did they find it? How has it affected them?

First, the GP view:

> I had not expected to enjoy the Infant Observation module as much as I have. As a GP I have carried out innumerable examinations on children as well as hundreds of newborn and six week old infant checks. While doing these I am used to noting the colour and condition of their skin, the presence or absence of facial expression or eye movements, any limb activity and so on. Some

infants glow and some are pale and wan, some seem happy and others grizzle. As one examines and handles them they all feel so very different and individual. I may be aware of restlessness, passivity, being accommodated and wilfully resisted. But without fail I come away from an infant examination feeling that I have briefly met an individual.

Infant Observation is quite different. First of all there is no gain of intimacy from touch, movement or direct interaction. The infant is observed from a distance and the family style must be respected. One must obtrude as little as possible between the baby and the family. At first I found this strange but soon realised that I had to rely on my wits and senses in a different way to assess what was going on. In being aware of how he is held and treated, of his tiny movements and gestures I have found that I conceptualise 'my' infant's immediate life in a way that I had not, either as a father or a GP. I am aware that I am not scoring his health or development but simply watching and sharing in it. I now feel his helplessness, his pleasures and disappointments and occasionally feel what his skin and muscles must feel when he is held in certain ways. I guess a little at how wonderful feeding, his mother's voice or some music must seem to him, and I wonder about the times when he seems to communicate but is not heard or noticed.

A poignant moment occurred in one of my early observations when the baby was being held awkwardly and horizontally in his father's arms. He looked with great concentration up at his father's face while his father talked about him to visitors. His gaze remained fixed and imploring for a long time and eventually his proud father glanced at him briefly before carrying on with his conversation – and still the baby looked up at his father's face with hope and expectation. After a time his gaze and expression changed and quietened so that I felt a moment had been lost forever. I know that I felt so much on his behalf and wished his need had been recognised and held. It made me think about being a 'good enough' parent and what it means to be a 'good enough' child.

I realise that I am getting to know this baby from how his life is, and I enjoy the struggle of making sense of this experience, and writing it up each week. All very different from the insights of a busy GP. Finally I can quietly reflect upon this intense and personal experience, on how my own infancy might have been and on how all this can be related over time to Freud, Klein, Bion and Winnicott. A new, different and rich experience which I wish that I had had before.

Next, the account of a journalist and novelist:

I was particularly nervous about the observation strand of the course. I am very talkative and opinionated in general, and am the mother of two children, so I couldn't imagine being able to sit quietly and observe without judgement. I also felt guilt both before and during observations at many times . . .

One of the observation groups was wonderful, inspirational. [This student did the course in one year, and conducted two observations simultaneously, of a baby and a young child, no easy task.] I often felt that my observations were boring, yet my seminar leader's thinking and group discussion about this always transformed the most ordinary aspect of a baby's life into something revelatory. The whole experience was very emotional for me as a mother. I wished I had done the observation before having children! My first ever observation, of a new baby, left me feeling devastated. Every time the baby lost sight of her mother's face she seemed literally to crumple. Had I known what effect my absences may have been having on my own babies I am sure I would have tried to do things differently. The seminar leader's interpretations were always fascinating, and the way she thought about toddlers too very much made the link for me between Infant Observation and the role of the analyst.

The Infant Observation was rather disturbing. I was observing in a family where mother bottle fed her baby at an enormous distance, seeming barely to interact with the baby, and often propping the bottle up and leaving the baby to feed when she was a week or two old. Cultural similarities between myself and this mother led me not to notice this as unusual, even though I had fed two babies myself. It took the astonishment of the group to show me the things towards which I was turning a blind eye.

Finally, the views of a strategic consultant:

Let me start at the end: child observation reconnected me to the child I was, and in many ways to the child I remain. It has had a profound effect on me and continues to inform my view and apprehension of the world around me.

I assumed that observation was going to be a task like any other I would undertake in my daily work life. I would observe this child as I would analyse a market or a business opportunity. This would be an objective study that I would rationalise using my newly developing psychoanalytic knowledge. This could not be further from the beautiful reality of my experience.

I began my observations nervously, as I could not escape the almost predatory quality I experienced while observing. It was odd, given that I had listened to the notion of being held, in mind or in gaze, but my experience seemed contrary to this. This was a reflection of some of my own less pleasant childhood experiences – no surprise to me once I had realised this. But what did surprise me was just how much I blamed myself as a child for ever having been vulnerable. I recognised in this dear little human being that I was observing the same vulnerability, which I found intolerable at first and then began to understand as empathy and intuition born of many factors that drive us to survive. This little girl negotiated territory I sometimes barely can as an adult; notably desire, and rage – but most of all plain old unfairness. As in getting bellowed an instruction from a nursery nurse, following it but getting told off anyway. I could barely contain my feelings, but the little girl I was watching absorbed and grew from each encounter, approaching it slightly differently the next time.

What really struck me was how extraordinarily perceptive children are; they may not be able to contextualise or articulate experience in the way adults do but it makes them no less aware. It also makes quite a mockery of the 'keeping it from the children' approach that many parents feel bound to take from time to time. The experience made me realise how important it is to provide children with contained environments where they are safely able to explore all that it is to be human – particularly as we appear to become more litigious as a society, which drives an odd and unsupportive sterility into the environments we make for our young.

What an endearing and tiny human being I watched, who entirely blew away my former apprehension of childhood and also gave me the opportunity to give the small version of myself a much needed hug.

Does this inform my daily life? It most certainly does. Everyone I know was a child once. Sounds obvious when said, doesn't it?

Conclusion

I think it is clear from these moving and eloquent accounts that touch on maternal and paternal roles, as well as the internal child within each observer, how much emerges once one has become engaged in the observational task, undertaken for its sake rather than in order to embark on a psychotherapy training. In a recent paper by Birksted-Breen (2009) called 'Reverberation time: Dreaming and the capacity to dream', the author suggests that a sense of subjective time is created originally by what she calls the 'reverberation' between mother and infant, as an elaboration of Bion's concept of maternal reverie. 'It might also be called "reflection time", but this might suggest a more fully conscious process than what is involved' (p. 38). I continue to be impressed and also moved as to how the 'concentric containment' (Edwards, 2006) of the seminar leader and the group opens up spaces within an observation student's mind, to reflect on both the present and the past, the internal and the external, in what might be thought of as a dynamic reverberation that has its roots in the primal relationship between infant and caretaker, and the vital role of this in the unfolding of psychic life.

What I hope I have conveyed here, is that Infant Observation is not solely the province of pre-clinicians. It evidently has a place for anyone who is interested and curious to know about development, both of themselves and others. In a sense what these responses show is that in tracing what you might call the 'biography' of an infant, there is a chance for the observer to think about her/his own story, a kind of autobiographical revisiting, and an opportunity to think about the tasks we all grapple with: to make sense of ourselves and of the world, both personally and professionally.

Acknowledgements

Many thanks to those who have contributed directly and indirectly to this short paper, both students and seminar leaders, listed alphabetically here: Katherine Arnold, David Bartlett, Anna Blundy, Marie Bradley, Carol Hanson, Vic Roberts, Beverley Tydeman.

References

Birksted-Breen, D. (2009) 'Reverberation time, dreaming and the capacity to dream'. *International Journal of Psychoanalysis*, 90(1), 35–51.
Edwards, J. (2008) 'Splitting and projective identification'. *Journal of Infant Observation*, 11(1), 57–65.
Edwards, J., Arnold, K., Hanson, C., Ngah, Z., Oclander-Goldie, S. and Segal, B. (2006) 'Making connections: Teaching observational skills to non-clinical students on an MA course in psychoanalytic studies'. *Journal of Infant Observation*, 9(3), 221–32.
Grayling, A. C. (2002) 'On self-education'. *The Guardian*, 13 July.
Menzel, J. (Director). (1966) *Closely Observed Trains* [Motion picture].
Miller, L., Rustin, M., Rustin, M. and Shuttleworth, J. (eds). (1989) *Closely Observed Infants*. London: Duckworth.
Rustin, M. and Bradley, J. (2008) *Work Discussion: Learning from Reflective Practice in Work with Children and Families*. London: Karnac.
Spurling, H. (1998) *The Unknown Matisse*. London: Penguin Books.
Sternberg, J. (2005) *Infant Observation at the Heart of Training*. London: Karnac.

PART 2

ON CLINICAL WORK

Who shows a child as he really is?
Who helps him see himself from a distance
So he can set himself among the stars?
(Rilke, Duino Elegies No. 4, translated by JE)

What are we aiming for when we work clinically? If the work is any good at all then it should help individuals, whether children or adults, to find out more about themselves in relationship with others, and with parts of the self. In the clinical process the practitioner becomes a participant observer. 'Participation' is quite definitely not a limitation but an asset, as the tool of counter-transference in particular has become central in puzzling out over time 'what is going on' and what might benefit from change, as we help the patient to view events inside and outside the mind, from new points of view. So 'what is going on?' needs to be widened to include 'what is going on today?' Tomorrow may well be different, as may be different parts of one session. And the practitioner too needs to be alert to change in her/his own thinking, so that a 'selected fact' does not become set in a hardened mould that then turns it into an idea that is overvalued, precluding new under-standings and insights on the part both of patient and practitioner. What is essential here is the idea of an exchange, so that there can be an authentic picture emerging over time, not marred by omniscience and omnipotent thinking on either side. Clinicians produce a huge amount of careful work and thinking in the consulting room, and this can contribute to ongoing research about the efficacy of work with children and adults alike. The presentation and discussion of clinical material via the printed word as well as via the psychoanalytic seminar is vital, in order for us to share our discoveries and ensure that thinking does not indeed become ossified. 'Getting stuck' is a starting point not an end point if it is recognised and acknowledged as such: it can produce many new thoughts that aid all of our learning as we develop clinical skills, refine our tools and techniques, and then over time communicate these to those who will come after us on this demanding and always fascinating journey. The chapters presented here represent something of one clinician's journey, starting with an account of an intensive training patient. As Meltzer (1973) observed, each 'case' is a step along the way of the journey of the clinician too, who will learn things about her/himself as well as the patient, so at least the name of one participant in the process will appear on the finished published work. One works towards 'solid ground' which is the title of the first chapter here, but we should also perhaps be wary of when this 'solid ground' becomes too solid, impervious, preventing further growth.

Reference

Meltzer, D. (1973) *Sexual States of Mind*. Strath Tay: Clunie Press, p. viii.

CHAPTER 4

TOWARDS SOLID GROUND

The ongoing journey of an adolescent boy with autistic features

Introduction

Here I trace the development of thinking and sense of self in an adolescent boy whom I will call Joe, whose initial dread of annihilation and falling into limitless space became gradually modified as he grew more able to anchor himself within a space–time continuum and find his feet on what he came to call his 'solid ground'.

Time, according to my encyclopaedia, is:

> a concept that measures the duration of events and the periods that separate them. It is a fundamental parameter of all changes, measuring the rates at which they occur; it provides a scale of measurement enabling events that have occurred to be distinguished from those that are occurring and those that will occur. It appears intuitively to be flowing in one direction only, for all observers. However according to Einstein's theory of relativity this is not the case. The rate at which time passes (as measured by a clock) is not the same for observers in different frames of reference that are moving at a constant velocity with respect to each other. Thus according to the time dilation effect if two observers are moving at a constant velocity relative to each other it appears to each that the other's time processes are slowed down. In order to pinpoint an event in the universe, its position in a four dimensional space–time continuum must be specified. This continuum consists of three space dimensions and one of time.
>
> (*Macmillan Encyclopaedia*, 1988)

In a black hole, defined as 'a gravitationally collapsed object', time slows down infinitely. The boundary of the black hole is defined as 'the event horizon', and Stephen Hawking (1992) quotes Dante in his evocation of their magnitude: 'abandon hope all ye who enter here.' He does however go on to assert that black holes are not eternal. What I hope to show here is the struggle Joe went through in order to make at least a partial recovery from what might be thought of as gravitational collapse, to enter the space–time continuum of everyday life.

History

Joe, who was re-referred to the clinic when he was almost seventeen, was one of premature twins. Both were in incubators after the birth but Joe's sister was sturdy enough to be taken home after a few days, while Joe remained in hospital, not held, in an incubator for three weeks. When he finally went home he was, as his mother described him, stiff with terror; he refused the breast and had to be bottle-fed facing outwards. This was a violent and persistent turning away, and one can imagine his mother's difficulty in relating to Joe alongside his healthy twin. It seemed that it was very much due to his mother's determined efforts in Joe's babyhood that he did not withdraw in a more total way. Although his developmental milestones occurred normally, his echolalia and repetitive play became evident at an early stage: he was, as his parents described, 'obsessed' with hard objects such as keys and toy cars, and expressed fears of 'leaking down' that were perhaps related to fantasies surrounding early tube feeding. Did this process induce a feeling of helplessness and lack of engagement? Perhaps a baby's first sense of agency develops as he has to suck in order to get sustenance. When I presented Joe at the Tavistock Autism Workshop, Sue Reid talked of 'liquid states of terror' experienced by some autistic children, and perhaps it was Joe's constitutional 'primitive permeability' (Meltzer *et al.*, 1975) that plunged him into such a profoundly terrified state – he lacked the capacity to filter experience and so it bombarded him.

Joe received special schooling from nursery stage (he tested as ESN with an IQ of 50). Diagnosed as having autistic features, he had two years of intensive psychotherapy starting when he was six. With such a low IQ perhaps he would not have been taken on for treatment twenty years ago (Sinason, 1992). Therapy was felt to be beneficial, but after two years Joe appeared unable to make further use of it (a situation that was to be repeated in his later treatment). Then in late adolescence he himself made a request for further treatment, after he had fallen in love with a girl at school and his advances had been rejected. He called this subsequently 'my little breakdown'. At this stage he was still having great difficulties separating from his parents, was described as obsessional and as having inappropriate social boundaries.

Beginning

I arranged to see Joe for twice weekly sessions, but it soon became apparent that he would like more. We settled on three sessions a week as being a balance between what he would like and what my timetable would allow. My first impression of him was that he was slighter than I had expected and looked younger than his almost seventeen years. He had blond hair and walked in an ungainly stop–go way, as if being impelled forward and held back simultaneously, which reminded me of what one of Frances Tustin's patients called 'the undertow' (Tustin, 1986): a stubborn knot of forward and reverse thrusts that were to be enacted and re-enacted in his therapy. His characteristic movements of rubbing his hands desperately and flapping his arms to 'rid himself of the burden of accretions of stimuli' (Bion, 1967) became apparent soon after his treatment began. While at times he was gaze-avoidant, at other times he would fix me in an unblinking and consuming stare, which I came to understand as communicating his enormous need and demand for some sort of symbiotic union and his enormous fear of the claustrophobia attendant on such union. This also seemed related to ideas of adhesive identification as a desperate measure. Bick wrote:

> I began to see that an adhesive relationship was on the surface of the object and two dimensional while every separation and discontinuity was the

unknown third dimension, the fall into space. The catastrophic anxiety of falling into space, the dead end, haunts every demand for change and engenders a deep conservatism and demand for sameness, stability and support from the outside world.

(Bick, 1968, p. 485)

In Joe's first session he was able to outline to me in a graphic way the current embodiment of his catastrophic anxieties. He sat down and crossed his legs, saying immediately: 'I feel very anxious, that's why I've come, because I went to the doctor and he said it was all anxiety and I need help.' He then proceeded to elaborate a host of physical symptoms: pains in the head and all over his body, stiff shoulders, fear of having AIDS and a brain tumour. All this was accompanied by vivid body language as he squirmed and twisted in his chair, pointing to various parts of his body as he spoke about them. He looked at me piercingly and asked if I thought it was all anxiety.

The room seemed full of his fears and I acknowledged how hard it was for him to feel so anxious in so many different parts of his body. He seemed in that moment to be in what Frances Tustin (1986) calls 'a sensation dominated state', but a state that, far from giving him a feeling of sensuous enjoyment, filled him with terror and the dread of imminent annihilation. It made me wonder about Joe's response to the almost unbearable shock of being disconnected from his mother and also his twin sister at birth (what Tustin calls 'the power and energy crisis' caused by the mouth disconnected from the nipple) and being placed in an incubator where he may have experienced all interventions designed for his survival as persecutory. Perhaps tube feeding contributed to a feeling of not being actively engaged in the process of going on living? He described in this first session how his only escape from his anxieties was 'to sort of go into distance'. At this point he looked at me very intently and I had the feeling he both wanted to get inside me and wanted me to be inside his mind, but also feared it: that 'distance' might hold something dangerous.

Tustin (1986) says:

The first aim of treatment is to help the child to turn sufficiently from the excesses of his body-dominated world and to live over again the failed crisis of becoming a developing psychological being. The therapist's task is to heal the psychic break between mother and child.

It seemed as if the task would be with Joe, by way of what Anne Alvarez, in supervision, called 'minimal dose transformations', to recapitulate an area of failed infantile experience, the pain of which had recently been further exacerbated by Joe's experience of unrequited love. The task needed to proceed with painstaking slowness: time and time again Joe showed me by his lack of response how he absolutely could not take in my sometimes over-complex interpretations. I had to do quite a bit of unlearning in order to be open to being where Joe was, like a mother with a young baby, rather than half a mile ahead and probably up the wrong turning anyway. I needed to be constantly alert to Joe's wish to draw me into collusion with his autistic compulsion to repeat: to go over events in a circular way, in what Joseph (1989) called a '"chuntering" activity . . . a kind of mental brinkmanship in which the seeing of the self in this dilemma, unable to be helped, is an essential aspect'. As she says, the pull towards life and sanity is located in the analyst, while the patient is passive: 'the analyst is the only person in the room who seems actively to be concerned about change' (p. 128). The masochistic use of anxiety was a predominant feature in Joe's early sessions and I had to be constantly alert for the moment when an expression of real anxiety became drawn into a more perverse use.

Four weeks after therapy began and not long before the first Christmas break, Joe reported a dream – this was the only dream he ever told me about throughout his treatment. He described being on a train: 'everything's going real slow and I'm really small. I'm well terrified.' He did not seem to be able to talk further about it, but then said he often got the feeling of being very small in relation to objects in the room: 'There are big shadows and I'm well frightened.' He said he'd had this dream/fantasy 'for ever'. At that point he seemed to abandon thinking and wasn't interested in the idea of linking the dream with our relationship. When I commented on this sudden lack of interest, he then began to talk about an incident with a friendly policeman: he was not only persecuted by my attention but was pleasurably relieved that I would notice and care about him.

Yet, in the counter-transference I felt at this point a sense of profound hopelessness, which I was able later in the session to process for Joe with the idea that he found it hard to believe that we could make this slow train journey together and sort out the worries that threatened to overwhelm him. The slow train reminded me of the infinite slowness of time described as being endemic to the black hole. For weeks at a time I was left with a feeling of fragmentation and incoherence. This seemed impossible to convey in the writing up of his sessions; it felt as if the only way to do it might be to tear up pieces of paper on which were written his disjointed thoughts and spread them around the room. This mixture of 'minus K' (denuded understanding) and 'no K' (absence of understanding, things not able yet to be known) made me feel at times as despairing as Joe became later in his treatment, when he could bear to withdraw some of his massive projective identification and feel his own feelings. This projective identification may have been his way of desperately conveying his un-integrated state.

There was as yet no narrative thread: Meltzer *et al.* (1975) describe this suspension of mental life in the autistic child where 'the child is able to let his mental organisation fall passively to pieces'. They see the task of the therapist as being one of commanding 'or commandeering' attention like a magnet in order to reassemble the dismantled self. The question with Joe was how much had ever been coherent; as he declared himself 'I was born worried' – and how much he actively participated in a continuous process of dismantling. As Joseph said, 'there is a real misery which needs to be sorted out from the masochistic use and exploitation of misery' (Joseph, 1989, p. 128). It was a struggle for Joe and a struggle for me to 'keep in touch with meaning in different circumstances within the limits of one's own tolerance' (Meltzer *et al.*, 1975).

In many of the early sessions Joe seemed to 'sort of go off into distance' and I was left wondering how to bring him back. As Joseph says:

> when these lively parts of the patient remain split off it means that his whole capacity for wanting and appreciating, missing, feeling disturbed at losing etc, the very stuff that makes for whole object relating is projected and the patient remains with his addiction and without the psychological means of combating this . . . This means that with such splitting off of the life and instincts and of loving, ambivalence and guilt is largely evaded. As these patients improve and become more integrated and relationships become more real, they begin to

feel acute pain sometimes experienced as almost physical: undifferentiated but extremely intense.

(Joseph, 1989, p. 136)

Perhaps Joe's experience of falling in love had propelled him from what might be called comfortable masochism into a state of acute pain, echoing his earlier agony which became somatised. As our relationship grew and Joe was able to acknowledge his attachment, he also railed against me about the almost unbearable pain of his empty weekends, when all the members of his family went out and left him with the lonely solaces of a pizza and a video. For Joe, becoming alive was an often agonisingly painful business, and he frequently let me know how doubtful he was that it was really worth it.

In *Autistic States in Children* Tustin talks of a premature sense of 'twoness' – the infant becomes aware of separation from the mother too early: 'the insecurity of this precocious sense of twoness leads to pathological manoeuvres to reinstate a sense of one-ness' (Tustin, 1981, p. 78). Joe's refusal to look at his mother while feeding may well have been an enraged protest at being ripped away from all that he had been familiar with, life inside the womb with his twin sister.

Early work with Joe was very much informed by ideas of mother–infant interaction, as my supervisor pointed me in the direction of texts on child development to indicate how normal mothers of normal children claim and reclaim the attention of their babies in order to build up an ongoing sense of relationship, safety and meaning (Alvarez, 1992, ch. 5). Alvarez (2012) later went on to elaborate her thinking about levels of work with such children. In a very real sense Joe had not made the contact with mother's eyes and face as well as her breast. His preconceptions had not been met with realisations, but with something that must have seemed to him like a dark incomprehensible void that he evacuated wholesale. He had retreated into narcissism and autistic defences. It seemed as though it was my task to monitor each tiny change in his mood, go for the bits of feeling that came and went during each session and treat his smallest communications as if they had meaning. I came to understand that babies learn from pleasure and safety as well as from difficulty and danger; a state of mind that develops from what Trevarthen (1980) calls 'primary intersubjectivity'. Autistic withdrawal has a self-regulating as well as a defensive aspect, and I had to learn to respect that: the need a baby has to digest and recover.

I quote from a session some time after the first Christmas break:

He said, 'Mum says I've got a lot of work to do here and I shouldn't think about leaving, that's right isn't it?' I asked what he thought and when he didn't respond I said, after a few minutes, that it was hard for him just now to see for himself how things were. He said, 'I get confused – about the times', and I acknowledged how confused he was. He said, 'So I come here Monday, Tuesday and Wednesday, is that right?' I said I thought he was saying, as he'd said before, he'd like a Tuesday session too but we would stick to what we had agreed. He looked at his watch, looked up delightedly and said, 'Doesn't time go quickly when I talk to you!'

I said that he'd like always to feel good about me and being here, but then the time might go too quickly and he might feel too nice so he looked at his watch instead. (Not perhaps only a turning away but also a piece of self-regulation.) He looked reflective and then talked about his diminished fear of getting AIDS, but the wind blew at the door and he asked, 'What's that noise?'

I said he wanted to be sure we were safe in here and that this was a safe place to talk about his worries (interpreting the need for safety rather than only the persecutory fear). There was a long pause and then he said, 'I was worried on Monday because my face went numb on one side – did I tell you that? I try hard not to be worried but I can't help it.' I said, 'And you want me to try hard to understand your worries with you.' I asked more about the numb face, what he'd been thinking about, but he looked down and stopped talking. After another long pause I said, 'You got a bit worried there', and he said, 'Well it makes me feel bad talking about it.' I said, 'And the room gets full of your worries, it's hard to feel this is a safe place to think about them.' After more silence he said, 'I don't know why' – then broke off, then said, 'I'm *into* therapy now, I do feel better.' I said you feel better just now, not so scared. He talked about liking his previous therapist and the psychiatrist who assessed him (they and I had been 'prats' in the previous session) – he'd said hallo to Dr X at school. I said, 'And you like me a bit more now – you can be angry with Dr X and me and we're still there.' At this point his feet were very close to mine, there was silence in the room and a delicate feeling, fragile as eggshell, of things being OK. His foot moved nearer mine and he said, 'I've done well today haven't I?' I said I knew how hard he struggled, that he had some good feelings now. There were a few moments of companionable silence and he said, looking at his watch, 'I do look at my watch a lot, I must try to control it.' I said he was noticing more, now he felt there was some understanding between us.

Joe let me know early on in his treatment about his fear of being lost, lost in space, being swallowed by the black hole he used to imagine in the Tavistock car park, and that then became relocated under the sink in the cupboard of the room we used. He would stride up and down the room, flapping his hands and arms, hardly still for a moment, and then would open the cupboard door to take a quick peek before taking up his journey up and down the room again. As Alvarez pointed out in *Live Company* (1992) and as Joe himself demonstrated to me many times before I was sufficiently alerted to offer an appropriate interpretation, for a deprived, borderline or psychotic child it is necessary to use a different technique in interpreting. A different perspective with the holding out of hope needs to be offered to counteract the despair. Any interpretation of mine that talked of being lost or swallowed only exacerbated Joe's terror, and in one session I watched just such an escalation for some time before I had the wit to suggest that it was hard for him to believe he would be able to *find* me each time he came to the clinic, and to believe that Mum would be at home when he got there. His relief was palpable. For a child with a fragile ego the first task is to offer some necessary hope rather than to confirm despair. What Joe needed was help in scaling problems down: I had to provide a maternal sorting function.

Slowly, as I attempted to contain his distress and link together his feeling states, however disparate they might appear to be, Joe developed a sense of something stronger that was possible inside. He began to test the strength of the walls in the room by hitting them, to hang on the coat hook to test its endurance, and to have ideas about enlivening the appearance of our objectively very shabby room. When I commented on his having ideas to liven me up, that he felt very lively today and I should know about his ability to be creative, his response did not show a manic and omnipotent thrust. Before the first Easter break he was testing the strength of our link.

He got up and leaned on the window, opening it and saying, 'Some bolts are missing here – do people ever break in?' I said perhaps he was wondering if he could break in here over the holiday and get some of the sessions he felt I was robbing him of. He picked up the ruler from the table and started tapping the walls reflectively; I said perhaps he was testing how strong I was, if I could bear his wanting to break in and take something he felt was his. He laughed and began to walk up and down, saying, 'My Walkman's going to be really flashy. My Dad's got a BMW G Reg with a sunroof and my Mum's got a G Reg Mini with a sunroof.' I said I was to see him today as a smart flashy person with flashy parents. He said, 'No, they don't really have those cars, they're not rich. We're having the garden returfed and it's going to cost a fortune, we'll be really tight for money.' An acknowledgement of his potential for potency seemed to result not in omnipotence but in a realistic down-to-the-turf appraisal.

Joe liked music and his one ambition was to play the guitar like his hero Eric Clapton. In a session that had begun with Joe in a desperate state about being teased by his brother's friends at youth club, he used a rubber band first to think about the link between us and its power of endurance in difficult times:

He stretched the band over a splinter in the table and started to twang it. He began to play it, with high and low notes, making a sort of tune which sounded like the drone of a sitar, quite rhythmical and pleasant. He looked at me as he played, and was enjoying it. I said he was beginning to think about playing a tune here in therapy, with the high notes and the low notes, and he was enjoying the feeling he could entertain me. He carried on and I could sense that he was having an Eric Clapton fantasy as he made twanging guitar sounds. There was something very moving about this and his connection with me as the person entertained, his audience of one. It also seemed like a little child experimenting for the first time with sounds. Even when the band broke he held onto his mood of achievement and sat quietly saying, 'I could make a guitar, no, I could buy one.' There was some silence and he checked we had five minutes left. A car roared off powerfully and he imitated the noise. I said he was feeling powerful just now, that he could do things. He went to the window and looked out and said, 'I could ask Gran to buy me a guitar for Christmas.' I said he was really quite hopeful at the moment of buying a guitar and trying to play it, and perhaps finding other ways to please and entertain me. I thought afterwards too about a growing idea that he *could* make demands on his object, on Gran and on me.

It seemed that Joe was borrowing the identity of Eric Clapton, but in an anticipatory rather than an omnipotent way. Alvarez (1992) talks of these 'anticipatory identifications' as being an essential prerequisite of growth and development:

We need the psychoanalytic perspective to help us see the acorn in the oak tree, the baby in the child or the lost breast in the child's soft teddy. But we may need the developmentalists' and Jung's perspective to help us see the oak tree in the acorn, the man the child will become and *is in the process of becoming* ... a child more than any adult is filled with a sense of his future – provided of course that he is not severely depressed.

(1992, p. 177, emphasis in original)

Joe reminded me in this session of a toddler who needed a maternal object to contain in her mind the possibility of his eventual 'grown-upness'. In slowly emerging from a depressed and hopeless state, from limitless space into the defined space of a room with two people thinking together, Joe was beginning to be able to have a hope for the future.

Coming in from distance

As Joe's moments of real contact increased, he nevertheless needed frequent intervals for digestion and recovery. He would stare out of the window in a peaceful way, like a growing baby able to look out from the shelter of his mother's arms and to begin to have curiosity about the world and the people in it. 'Someone lives there', he mused as he stared out of the window. He also began to have ideas about others using the room, about me and what I did when we were not together. His frustrated curiosity fuelled further developmental progress. As he said when he discovered 'eff off' written underneath the couch, 'You wait till I get the bastard who wrote eff off in my room!'

In a session, about a year after the beginning of his treatment, he threw and caught the cushion, reminding me of Freud's grandson with the reel game – throwing away the object and getting it back – the idea of object constancy:

> He was exploring the puzzle of time, breaking the session into blocks of five minutes, and ten minutes, then ten and five. I talked about time going on and us going on within it, that he was interested in how things fitted together, the links between times and people. He went over to the window and looked out reflectively. After a while, he said with the sort of liveliness and ordinary curiosity of a young child, 'Where do you think the quietest place in the world is? Where there are no planes and doors and people and cars?' I asked where he thought and he said, 'In the country, I think.' He shut the window and rested his head against the glass, saying, 'So peaceful, so peaceful in here.' He came and sat down on the cushion again, looking around with real curiosity, and again it felt like a baby secure on mother's lap.

Gradually the idea of an internal space was being built up. As Joe slowly began to introject a containing capacity, so his perverse tendencies decreased to an extent:

> In one session he talked about Dad keeping him in order, reminding him of things 'That's what dads do, isn't it?' I linked it with our work and with me as a sort of monitor of his states and he said, 'Yes,' lapsed into silence for some time, took off his watch, tapped it and shook it. I said he was trying to find out things about me and how I worked. There was a lot more silence and I found my thoughts wandering. I said how hard it was for him today to keep his thoughts in the room. Later he started to make a timetable of sessions, saying, 'It's funny I can do this really well here, but not at school where there's a lot of noise.' He talked of the 'peace and quiet', looked at his work and said, 'It's a map – no in fact it's a contents page. I'll make a book, is that OK?'

It seemed as if the ideas of mapping his states of mind in the therapy had given him an internal space in which to start 'the book', a narrative that had begun in a formless and terrifying void but that could now move forward, although painfully and slowly, out of the abyss. As he announced to me rather grandly, 'I don't have keys any more, I have thought.'

In one session he told me about a poem he'd written about space, then could not remember it and felt hopeless. The next session however he shyly declaimed this poem, about a silver surfer in space, and I saluted his creativity and his memory, as well as the idea that he had things inside him, he was not alone.

It was agreed that we would have a review meeting with Joe's parents, set up at his request. Although this is unusual with a late adolescent (he was now seventeen), it felt appropriate to respond to his need and use the meeting to think about how he could develop a more ordinarily adolescent stance over time. His feelings about whether or not to attend the meeting fluctuated: finally he decided he would, and the decision gave him strength and energy:

> He snatched up a pencil and said, 'I'm going to write on my therapy room walls – can I?' I said he felt good at having decided, he wanted to make his mark, to shout out about how good he felt, but we should keep the walls clean; he had his paper in his folder to write on. He drew arcs with his pencil near the wall and repeated his request, and I acknowledged he wanted to make bold marks here. All right, I'll use the paper,' he said, and sat down. Then he looked round the room and said, 'This room's a bit of a mess, a bit bloody shitty.' We then had a sort of duet, with me saying, 'Mrs E you're pretty shitty not letting me write on the walls,' and him making further disparaging remarks about the room. He was laughing and enjoying this, the acknowledgement that I knew he was angry with me. He elaborated what he could do to improve this messy old room – remove the skirting, put wood-chip on the walls, remove the panels and put wallpaper up, carpet the floor. I said he was full of ideas and plans today – by this time he was walking round the room as he talked rather like someone giving a quote for work they could do. I said he felt really in command of this, that he could do a pretty good job on the room, on me and on himself. After a while he came and sat very close to me on the couch, compared times on our watches and then put his hand very close to mine to compare watch faces. They both said exactly the same and he was pleased. I said how pleased he felt that we could be here and have a conversation and agree about things. By this time his legs were very close to mine and he said, 'Can I go and get my radio?' I said we'd had a good chat but he wanted to be sure that he could get close and still feel safe. I said perhaps it was good to have a quiet time after being very full of ideas, so that they could settle down and become solid in his mind: the need to digest and recover.

In his journey towards what he came to call the 'solid ground' of his therapy – 'On solid ground' was a piece by a saxophonist he admired – there were frequent steps back as well as forward, as his claustrophobic fears overwhelmed him in what seemed almost a direct ratio with his engagement with me – perhaps inevitably so. In the session after the one just quoted he came in with his Walkman, which I saw as being simultaneously a way of blocking me out and also as an umbilical cord between us:

> He took the headphones off and put them round his neck, saying, 'You know, I like therapy. I'd like it to happen at home, we could sit on the sofa and listen to music, it helps me relax and get calm.' I said he'd like me to be around at

home so he could tune into me any time, like he could tune into the radio and find out about the weather. At one point he asked in a slightly anxious way, 'Can you read my mind?' I said he liked us thinking about things together but then it felt too close, as if I was inside his head and he didn't like that . . . A bit later he said, 'I really like therapy. I used to look at my watch all the time, didn't I?' (and he covertly looked at his watch). I said, 'You want to be sure we can keep a safe distance' (like a baby learning to modulate the intensity of his contact). He sat reflectively listening to the music, then talked about a song he wanted me to hear. He found it on the tape, stood up and played it. He said, 'This reminds me of therapy.' The words were something like 'she smiles he tells her she is like a flower' and the song mentioned something about their love. He stood quite close as I listened. I said it was a lovely song, he wanted me to know about his loving feelings, that therapy was important to him and I was important too. It did indeed feel moving, and I wondered how to handle it for him so he could have the feeling without being overwhelmed. He sat on the couch and said, 'I've talked to my Mum and my family about my emotional problem – I get nervous, anxious, embarrassed, claustrophobic' (an impressive list of feeling states). I said I thought he wanted to know it was safe to play the song and that we wouldn't get mixed up together.

Klein (1975, p. 173) advised, 'One should not underrate the loving impulses' that can help to mitigate hate and envy. I would like to quote from Reid's paper 'The importance of beauty in the psychoanalytic experience' (Reid, 1990), where she tells the story of little Georgie who, after a grossly deprived beginning, finally has in therapy 'the beautiful experience of being in mother's mind a loved beautiful baby'. She goes on to say:

> I think there is a deep-rooted fear that any 'confession' of a beautiful experience will be automatically met with words like idealisation and with attempts to suggest that we have missed what lies behind it. I think it is time to make love, beauty, pleasure and appreciation respectable concepts in the psycho-analytic work and literature. For without an appreciation of beauty linked to love there is no impetus to live life, to enjoy it and to seek and embrace experiences.
>
> (Reid, 1990, p. 51)

I think that in his struggle on the long journey from formless outer space to a defined internal space, Joe was able, as an adolescent, to reconstruct a vital infantile experience that he had missed, not so much because it had not in some ways been present, but because he had been too locked into a delusional 'oneness' to be able to experience the delights as well as the pains of 'twoness'. As Joseph says:

> If the patient has met up with no object in his infancy in whom he can place some, however little, love and trust, he will not come to us in analysis . . . we are not completely new objects, but, I think, greatly strengthened objects, because stronger and deeper emotions have been worked through in the transference.
>
> (Joseph, 1989, p. 164)

In a session not long before the second summer break we were talking about what he called the 'silly' part of his mind that undermined the 'sensible' part:

He held up his fingers and said, 'The sensible part's this big' (very small). I said at the moment the silly part felt quite large – perhaps, however, just now we were talking to the sensible part who wanted to work with me to get bigger and stronger and make more of a balance in his mind. He said, 'Yes, right. When I see someone I get right up close like this' (he came close to me and stared in a 'stupid' way into my face). He was half laughing and I said, 'It feels funny, but you know there's something wrong too.' He said, 'Anna won't go out with me. I said to them, "Look, me and Mary are twins too, and if I went out with you and she went out with John and got married and had babies would they be twins?" She said, "Go away" – why?' I asked him what he thought and he said, 'I got too close. I go up to girls and I say, "Will you go out with me" straight away [he came up and stared again] and they don't like it.' I said he seemed to be saying he knew he went too far and too fast, got too close too quickly. Perhaps he hoped he could practise this here with me and find out about getting friendly without getting too close and putting people off.

It was a constant struggle for him to achieve an appropriate distance and we worked hard at it: could he be with the object rather than be lost inside it? As we worked through this dilemma many times it became problematic for me when to make a direct transference interpretation that would be experienced as intrusive and when to leave interpretations in a transitional area so that he could have an experience without being overwhelmed by it. It was perhaps a question of the level of intensity of a transference interpretation: perhaps it was something I did not fully work out for myself and for Joe.

Time and the world of the watch

Like his Walkman, which seemed to embody both a defensive and communicative function, Joe's watch seemed to metamorphose during the course of treatment from an autistic object designed to block me out into something more transitional where he was able to work out many questions about 'going on being' in the world. As the therapy progressed, Joe became more aware of his 'chuntering' tendencies: 'I do go on, don't I?' This was sometimes said complacently and sometimes in a truly self-critical way. When I first suggested that he was 'using up life time' as Meltzer *et al.* (1975) put it, he was deeply wounded; but in a subsequent session he was able to say, 'I do these foolish things don't I?' experiencing real pain at getting in touch with this. What Meltzer *et al.* called 'autistic residues' became very evident in this tendency to 'go on' and he would follow the second hand of the watch round in a perseverative way that he had to be helped beyond. Just as he would sometimes quite mindlessly colour in something such as the letters of his name, he would fill time rather than use it.

Again I am reminded of the slow train and the infinite slowing down of time in the black hole. Gradually, as he became less autistic and rigid, he became able to string ideas and events together in a coherent time dimension, and at a review session his mother commented on how his understanding of time had improved greatly.

As Joe was able to step apart somewhat from his 'chuntering' self, he was able to discern patterns for himself. 'Things go in circles, don't they?' he said wonderingly. (I remember my three-year-old son making the same discovery.) He began to notice the difference between his digital watch and my sweep hand watch

– two ways of doing things. Events that had previously been placed outside the stream of collected and eventually organised recollection became linked. Session by session Joe seemed to take his place almost perceptibly within the rhythm of the universe – the 'white noise' of everyday life that Don Delillo refers to in his novel of the same name – the thousand and one noises of the world that surround us but do not ordinarily overwhelm us as Joe had previously been overwhelmed.

Object constancy became the jumping-off point for self-constancy: Joe gradually achieved a sense of his own continuity just as he was also achieving a sense of his own boundaries.

I would like briefly to describe a session eighteen months after the start of therapy to illustrate this:

> After an angry and disillusioned session on Monday, he arrived for his Wednesday session in a cheerful mood, with a watch someone had given him that needed mending. I took this up initially in terms of his wondering whether things could be OK today after his outburst on Monday. He sat close to me and was delighted our watches synchronised – we could get back together, there could be synchrony between us. 'How do watches tell the same time?' he wondered – as if he were really searching for a meaning, an ordering principle. He was looking at the watch happily, tapping it, whistling to himself, involved and serious, checking mine against it (the watch itself was working, it was the strap that needed to be replaced). I talked of the hands going round, like his sessions going round, and the rhythm of the week which we knew he liked. (This was just after the Easter break.) He pushed the buttons on the watch, reflective and slow, and finally he pushed one and a tune started to play. He was delighted and I linked it to his delight with the sessions starting up, the music starting up and his pleasure in the discovery that he had a part in this flow. He was talking about time in therapy and time in school – how they seemed to go at different rates, and I recalled his talking about wanting time to slow down a bit, he was getting older and knew he had some work to do. He seemed to be reflecting on our differences, and on ways in which we might be the same, back together in the same room.
>
> The session continued to fluctuate – at times he seemed obsessive and controlling, at times genuinely interested, like a toddler exploring his world. At one point he tried to put the watch in the key hole and attempted to turn it, and I said, 'You feel as if you're unlocking some secrets and understanding more about you and me when we're together and when we're apart, how it all fits together.' He went back to the watch faces and discovered my watch recorded seconds 'clockwise' whereas the lap recorder went anti-clockwise, and that there was a block shape on his watch face which also represented blocks of time. He got a bit manic, saying, 'This is great, this is wicked, I can use it to time things at school.' (I felt for his teachers.) After a while, I said it seemed the watch was so great it had taken the place of talking with me: I left him over holidays and between sessions and he'd rather have the watch he can control. He began to throw the watch onto the sill and retrieve it, saying, 'When you do this, it stops working I think.' I said perhaps he was recalling I'd stopped working over Easter, as if time stood still when we weren't together. He started to ask about the date – 'Is it the seventh? Is it Monday?' He finally got it straight and he was pleased, walked up and down the room and said, 'I don't need therapy.' I said I thought he was still thinking about the holidays, how he couldn't rely on me, then he wondered if he could rely

on me now, the watch seemed a much better bet. There were a few minutes to go. I told him this and he immediately said, 'I've got to go now, Harry [the driver of the cab] likes me to be on time.' I said I would stay till the end of the session – I thought it was important that he should have all his time. He said, 'Well OK, but I'll go anyway – OK?' (a bit anxiously). He did actually go a few minutes early. It was the first time he had managed to do this – he had felt too guilty before.

It was as if he had been able to leave me because he had internalised the idea of being able to throw away *and* retrieve his object, rather than fear losing it irrevocably – a vital step in learning to walk away from mummy, and further confirmation of object- and self-constancy.

Emerging narrative

As time for Joe became more comprehensible and he was able to take his place in the path of 'continuous becoming' rather than cling onto his autistic rituals as a protection against the bombardment of everyday life, so his memory improved. He became much more aware of his capacity to cut out by what he called 'being asleep', and spent one session berating himself for his failure to keep awake to reality. Finally, he was able to hear my suggestion that it was perhaps the very act of waking up which made him notice how much of his life time he had slept away: it was a painful realisation. All infants are in a sense born into chaos and Joe had, in his terror, split off chaos so that he did not meet up with and use the modifying elements present in normal mother–baby interaction, as the infant through containment and through enlivening is enriched and becomes himself. In his book *Awakenings* (1983), Oliver Sacks describes how patients who had been victims of the sleeping sickness encephalitis lethargica were awakened through the use of the drug L-Dopa and 'became startlingly, wonderfully alive'. Those who could retrieve no meaning fell back into a comatose state, while those who benefited in the long term were able to reinstate themselves in their own narrative. As Sacks says, 'I do not feel alive, psychologically alive, except insofar as a stream of feeling – perceiving, imagining, remembering, reflecting, revising, re-categorising, runs through me. I am that stream, that stream is me' (1983, p. 25).

As his therapy progressed, Joe's capacity to hold on to narrative for himself, rather than through the therapist as an auxiliary ego, became more evident. He talked more about music, and became interested in classical musicians. He asked me, 'Do you like Beethoven and Mozart?' He looked really excited and did not seem to be expecting an answer but to be listening. 'You can hear the silence in between, and then it comes in Da da da DA.' Just as the silences could now be perceived as part of the pattern, so he could trust in the continuity of going on being, and that he and I still existed in the silences between the sessions.

He checked the time on several occasions: dividing up what he'd had and what was to come in the session in a swift and accurate way. I said I was to see how well he could do this now. He went round tapping the walls, and I said he was getting a strong sense of time past and time to come, where he was in his session and where he was in his life. He was quiet a little, then said, 'So I've been here a year now?' I confirmed it would be a year to the exact date tomorrow. 'Oh wow, a year! That's amazing!' He slapped his palms together and walked up and down. 'So tomorrow I go to school.' I said perhaps he was saying he'd like to come here tomorrow to celebrate the exact date, to come for his therapy birthday. One year ago tomorrow he had been born into this therapy. He was silent, reflective again, and after a few moments I said how good it felt to him to be able to have the space here to think about that, to think about the past and the present. He was sitting on the couch very close, and he said after a pause, 'I'd like to see Mr C again' [his previous therapist], not that I don't like you or anything but I would.' I said he'd seen Dr X last week, he was thinking about his therapy with Mr C and his therapy with me, linking people up in his mind. It was important for me to know this, that he could like Mr C and Dr X as well as me, liking them didn't push me out.

He said, 'You know I was at school here, just up the road, I'd like to go back there.' He went to the window and looked out – 'It's that building there, isn't it?' I said he was thinking about the placing of everything today, buildings and things that had happened in his life, the story of Joe. He sat down again and was quiet, then said, 'I can remember a lot about it. They had a great big rope in the garden, we used to swing on it, and go carts.' He was quiet again, clearly seeing things in his mind. After a bit I said he really enjoyed that time and enjoyed remembering it – swinging on this strong rope was a bit like swinging up and down in his mind, linking together all the things that had happened in his life. This strong rope was a bit like his life which began in – 'July 1974', he said promptly – and he was remembering things that made up this strong life. A bit later he said, 'There was a brown door, it's still there, I can remember it really well.' I said, 'So well you could walk inside', and he shot me a smile and said, 'That's right.' I said he might also be talking about walking through the therapy door each week, and he could walk into his memories too and see what was inside his mind. He took his key out and looked at it reflectively. I said his memory was the key to putting all this together, opening the door and looking back into his memories. He went to the window and stared out again, and it felt indeed as if something was being delicately strung together in his mind. I said he was putting together the story of his life here – it was very important.

Ending

A year later Joe's therapy ended, prematurely in my view. We had been talking about ending some time during the following year, at his request, because I felt that, although there was evidently much more work to be done, it was also important to respect the independent adolescent voice in him. He was now much more able to get on with his life, to have friends, go to pubs, and generally enjoy himself socially, and this voice had been growing louder and stronger. A person like Joe would quite probably have frequent intervals of therapy interspersed with intervals of going it alone. We had a carefully planned weaning programme, which was then completely disrupted by external events to do with transport, which threw him into a state of total confusion. It became unbearable for him, try as I did to scale down his concerns. He insisted that he'd had enough, that he wanted to go and he wanted to dictate the timing. We had an emergency meeting with his mother and agreed on something that Joe himself thought he could manage, though I had many reservations about it which I expressed to him and to his mother. (In terms of timing this was very similar to his first treatment: with a concentration span of just over two years.) I had many concerns about my listening to a delusional omnipotent voice in the guise of a blustering adolescent; I feared he might land with a soundless bump back into some sort of hole, and lose the solid ground we had so painstakingly built together, because this ending was being acted out rather than being analysed in the therapy. He found it very difficult to come to the last few sessions and alternated between bravado, acting out by ordering the cab away, to saying plaintively 'I'll never find anyone like you,' which made me wonder about some wholesale re-projection of what I thought he had taken in. But he struggled as he always had done, and the last session was a moving testimony to his courage. He tapped the walls, jumped up and down on his 'solid ground', and lay on the couch with his legs in the air like a baby. At one point he looked at me very seriously and said, 'You know, you've got a good mind,' and I said I thought he'd discovered that he had a good mind. He was able to hear that we had different thoughts about the ending, he had thoughts about missing and acknowledged his sadness. He gave a pretend drum-roll on the couch to herald the end of the session, shook my hand solemnly and said, 'Carry on with the old therapy, won't you?'

Conclusion

In this account I have outlined the progress and development of Joe during two years of therapy and to link this with ideas of his gradually taking his place in the space–time continuum of everyday life, as it came to be symbolised for him through the rhythm of the therapeutic work. Session by session Joe seemed to take his place almost perceptibly within the rhythm of the universe and the thousand and one noises of the world that surround us but do not ordinarily overwhelm us as Joe had previously been overwhelmed. Events that had previously been placed 'outside the stream of aggregated and eventually organised recollection' became linked: as Meltzer *et al.* (1975) put it, via the thread of time on which are hung the pearls of recollection – and to this I would add the pearls of present collection and the pearls of anticipation. As Meltzer *et al.* say when describing a patient, Timmy, this was 'something akin to the cinematic photography of the blossoming of flowers, taken one frame every few minutes, in which the balletic unfolding and growth describes a pattern unseen by the waking eye'.

Acknowledgements

I would like to acknowledge the vitality of Anne Alvarez's fine supervision, which supported me on every step of the journey with Joe.

Note

1　A shortened version of this chapter was published in A. Alvarez and S. Reid (eds, 1999) *Autism and Personality*, London and New York: Routledge.

References

Alvarez, A. (1992) *Live Company*. London: Routledge.
Alvarez, A. (2012) *The Thinking Heart*. London and New York: Routledge
Bick, E. (1968) 'The experience of the skin in early object relations'. *International Journal of Psychoanalysis*, 49, 484–6.
Hawking, S. (1992) *A Brief History of Time*. BBC TV.
Joseph, B. (1989) *Psychic Equilibrium and Psychic Change*. London: Tavistock/Routledge.

Klein, M. (1975) *Envy and Gratitude*. London: Virago.

Macmillan Encyclopaedia (1988) London: Macmillan.

Meltzer, D. *et al.* (eds) (1975) *Explorations in Autism*. Strathtay, Perthshire: Clunie Press.

Reid, S. (1990) 'The importance of beauty in the psychoanalytic experience'. *Journal of Child Psychotherapy*, 16(1), 29–52.

Sacks, O. (1983) *Awakenings*. London: Picador.

Sinason, V. (1992) *Mental Handicap and the Human Condition*. London: Free Association Books.

Trevarthen, C. (1980) 'The foundations of intersubjectivity'. In D. K. Olson (ed.), *The Social Foundation of Language and Thought*. New York: Norton.

Tustin, F. (1981) *Autistic States in Children*. London: Hogarth Press.

Tustin, F. (1986) *Autistic Barriers in Neurotic Patients*. London: Karnac.

CHAPTER 5

YOU CAN'T MISS WHAT YOU'VE NEVER HAD: CAN YOU?

The challenges and struggles of single parenthood from a psychoanalytic perspective[1]

The issue of the growth of single-parent families has been in the forefront of political, social and moral debate in recent years. Children from single-parent families tend to be over-represented in clinic populations. Yet this state of family being may be no more potentially pathological than the nuclear family, which can become conceptually idealised. The aim of this chapter is to look behind the statistics and examine the impact on children of life in a single-parent family, to explore how this may be managed, and to look for potentiating factors that can enable good-enough development to unfold. Case material is used to illustrate the theme.

Introduction

The title of this paper is taken from the film *Secrets and Lies*, made in 1996 by Mike Leigh. The words are spoken by a downtrodden, exhausted middle-aged woman, who, when confronted with a grown-up daughter she had sent at birth for adoption, has to begin slowly and painfully to put together a fragmented history that had been dispersed both actively and passively over the years. She had never told her other daughter about *her* father. Did it matter? Clearly, as the film shows, it did, and it is by reorganising in the characters' minds the ruptured relationships that had so plagued their capacity to be that there emerges a firmer platform from which they can all move forward in a more coherent way.

I hope to be able to offer a framework for thinking about a state of mind and a state of family being that is not of necessity any more potentially pathological than that of the nuclear family, that can rather easily become conceptually idealised, but where, as the subtitle of the paper indicates, there are particular challenges and struggles to be encountered. Under the very label 'single parent' lie a host of family structures and family predicaments: from the family where father has never been known through degrees of 'lone parenthood' where fathers are not physically present but appear from time to time, or where divorce has institutionalised the family in terms of access orders and fixed rules of contact. In a sense, single parenthood as a concept can be seen as a continuum between these positions. I will not here be thinking about the impact of divorce, but will concentrate my attention more on the impact of the family structure which has not been deconstructed from a whole but has been from its inception in a sense a deviation from the culturally accepted norm. What impact does this have on the children? How can this be managed, and what are the potentiating factors that can enable good enough developmental growth to occur? I will first look in a general way at the prevalence of potential difficulties, and will later address these in terms of work I have been able to do with young people who have grown up in single-parent families.

Statistical background

The Office of Population, Censuses and Surveys in the UK (Haskey, 1994) found that, at what they called their 'best estimate', about one in five families with dependent children was a single-parent family, and similarly one in five children lived in such a family. This means that, in 1991 when the figures were collected, 2.2 million children lived in single-parent families, rising to almost 3 million in January 1998. These figures were those available when this chapter was first published as a paper in 1999. The Office for National Statistics' information reveals that there were nearly 1.9 million lone parents with dependent children in the UK in 2013, a figure that has grown steadily but not significantly from 1.8 million in 2003.

The definition of a one-parent family, used officially since 1971, was that adopted by the Finer Report (1974): 'a mother or a father living without a spouse and not co-habiting, with his or her never married dependent child or children aged either under 16, or from 16 to under 19 and still undertaking fulltime education.' The number of single-parent families had been rising steadily, and European Commission research in 1990 revealed that the highest proportion of single-parent households in the European community, running at 12 per cent, was in the United Kingdom. While earlier the figure had increased because of the increase in divorced lone mothers, by the mid 1980s the fastest growth was in single lone mothers. Ninety per cent of all lone parents are women. The 1991 Census showed that, in general, lone mothers were much younger than lone fathers.

The highest proportion of one-parent families occurred in the Inner London boroughs, and in Manchester, Liverpool and Glasgow, all major urban areas. In each of these districts at least three in every ten families were one-parent families, and in some the proportion exceeded 40 per cent. Lowest prevalence in the country occurred in Surrey and Buckinghamshire (two of the most wealthy counties in Great Britain) and the Western Isles, where population density is at its lowest.

Clearly there was a wealth of information to be distilled from the 1991 Census (and the last Census was done in 2011). In this brief outline I have not included features such as economic position, social class and ethnic grouping. What this necessarily short description demonstrates is both the complexity of the data and the escalating nature of a family structure in our society, which has cultural, emotional and psychological implications. We may as professionals observe how over-represented single-parent families are in clinic populations, and how much this shows the support needed to help families struggling through lack of emotional and financial support to achieve a better potential for growth and development. Later I shall turn to the subject of appropriate intervention, and describe work undertaken in community child guidance clinics and family centres.

Triangular structures

I want to move from the world of facts and figures into the more abstract geometrical world of structures and shapes, and particularly that of the triangle, in order to examine its relevance as a schema to underpin ideas about single parenthood. In a book about the intricate interweaving of Islamic patterns, Critchlow (1976, p. 45) describes the triangle as the first polygon: 'the minimal expression of an area, also symbolic of the minimal needs of consciousness; the knower, the known and the act of knowing.' He links this with what he calls the minimal description of our biological needs: ingestion, absorption and excretion. (And on a psychic level, these three functions also exist and underpin our considerations about psychic health.) He talks of patterns being, such as numbers, one of the fundamental conditions of existence, and as such a vehicle for archetypes and philosophical thought. As he says, 'what we take to be simple and "in the nature of things" has become profound to the point of our becoming oblivious to it' (p. 46).

In psychoanalytic literature the triangle has been a fundamental structure that originated with Freud's formulation (1923) of the Oedipal constellation of mother, father and child. The third point is seen as essential for there to develop a space for thinking (Critchlow's 'minimal expression of an area') and for separation and growth to take place. At the beginning of the infant's life, the mother–baby couple are protected by father. Gradually however father comes to take a more active role and presence. (Foetal research has suggested that father may indeed through his voice be an active pre-birth presence for the foetus (Tomatis, 1981; Prechtl, 1989).) The baby is then faced with what Kraemer (1988) in his paper 'The civilisation of fathers' called 'the facts of life as they are, rather than as the child believes or wishes them to be.' Winnicott (1971) talked of the 'progressive disillusionment' that needs to take place as the child has to relinquish the idea of being in sole possession of mother, and comes to accept the reality of the third, the other, and to be able from his own point on the triangle to perceive his parents as a couple. As Barrows (1995) indicated in his paper 'Oedipal issues at 4 and 44', this acceptance involves the linked concepts of knowing and being known (which again relates back to Critchlow's formulation). Quoting Temperley (1993) he noted that Kleinian and post-Kleinian analysts place a different emphasis from Freud's (1923) on the nature of the Oedipus complex: 'what the child has to accept is not primarily the prohibition of his incestuous wishes but the reality of the position in relation to his parents' sexual relationship' (1995, p. 86). Steiner (1996, p. 1076) also insisted that a true resolution of the Oedipus complex will come about by the parents' sensitive helping of the child: 'In my view, the classical description of the dissolution of the Oedipus Complex as a result of castration threats from the father leads not to a true resolution but to a psychic retreat based on grievance.' And, as in all psychic conflicts, this 'resolution' will need to be reworked and reworked throughout life, as our infantile omnipotence is challenged and rechallenged during the life cycle. Oedipus was grappling with what Narcissus failed to achieve: separation and a real relationship in love and hate with the other and others. As Segal (1989, p. 1) described it, the Oedipus complex has 'been recognised as the central conflict in the human psyche – the central cluster of conflicting phantasies, anxieties and defences'.

Freud (1905) was of the opinion that we are all forever tied to the fantasy and reality of our parents' intercourse; and that at a deep level we continually strive to overcome our unconscious outrage with our parents for having an exclusive relationship, and for having been responsible for our creation. While this may seem a question open to debate, it may be illustrated most graphically in work with children. When during a session with a single-parent mother and her seven-year-old only son, I commented on how hard it must be for her to struggle with her son's upbringing without the support of a partner, he shouted 'She has got a partner, she's got me!' For this boy there had not been the opportunity to struggle with the facts 'as they are' and he demonstrated his refusal to accept them in the way he refused to accept boundaries (and he had already been excluded from two schools), and in his identification with a 'superman' particularly shown as he jumped from inappropriate heights narrowly escaping serious injury. When his mother finally did enter into a new relationship he was angry and bitter, shouting in one of our sessions 'You've got a boy to sex you up'.

The pre-Oedipal triangle

Extending the notion of the triangle as the 'condition for learning', as Kraemer (1988) puts it, one may begin to consider the development of the capacity to think at all, which comes about through the infant's earliest experiences with other people and other minds. What Trevarthen and Hubley (1978) called 'primary intersubjectivity' is the beginning of this process. By being both a strong container of an infant's volatile states of mind, and by actively engaging in lively 'conversation' with him, a mother both helps him with his most primitive fears (Bion, 1962) and responds to his increasing overtures to develop his relationships in the world. This begins in the kind of ordinary but vital interchange as a mother soothes, calms and helps her baby to be contained in his own body and in his own mind, calming his agitated limbs and his fragmented thoughts. One could see this as a formation of two points on a line, the inter-subjective link that develops into secondary inter-subjectivity (Trevarthen and Hubley, 1978) when the baby is later able to pay attention to a third point, and join with mother in looking together at, say, a rattle, a teddy-bear or a bird. From the primary phase has developed the capacity to relate to the third point, and separation is beginning to develop. If a mother is depressed, or unsupported, it may be far less possible for her to offer her baby sufficient opportunity to move from two points to three. She may be overwhelmed by her own unmet needs or saturated by her own sorrow to the point where she cannot pick up the signals her baby emits. There may be a great difference between, say, a single-parent mother who is supported by her own mother and extended family so that she and her baby may benefit from other points, to a mother who feels alone and unsupported at this time. (This model also applies I think to later stages, if the trauma of a ruptured relationship causes a regression to a single line without external and perhaps internal points of contact. The child may feel overwhelmed, guilty and responsible for a mother who has withdrawn into her own sorrow.)

Myths and reality

So we have the idea of threeness as being developmentally important and this is the stuff of our work as child psychotherapists. How can this specifically be related to the 'twoness' implied in the single-parent family structure? In 'The myth of the one-parent family' (Johns, 1990) the author examines in some detail the way in which myths embody our conscious and unconscious strivings, and our defensive manoeuvres to outwit the truth: 'the facts as they are'. He discusses Robert Graves' notion that the function of myth is to answer life's awkward questions about creation and death, and to justify existing social systems. As Robert Graves said, 'one constant rule of mythology is that whatever happens among the Gods reflects events on earth'. We make our gods in our own image rather than vice versa, and they emerge in order to structure and render meaningful psychic life. They enact our conflicts to do with envy, murderousness, guilt and anxiety. Bion (1977) linked myths, and particularly the Oedipus myth, to the development of thinking itself, and saw psychoanalytic elements in myths that become the platform from which emerge the paradigms of psychoanalytic discourse. In linking this with his work with disturbed children and their families, Johns ponders on the defensive label 'one-parent family'. There never was yet, except in myth, a child born from one parent, and for every child born into this misleadingly labelled social structure there will be presented the struggle to understand and overcome ordinary developmental omnipotence without perhaps the necessary external figures to help and provide a good-enough reality in order to make tolerable the giving up of an omnipotent stance.

For every single parent too, there will be the struggle and pain associated with having to function without psychic and practical support, and to encompass in a satisfactory enough way the authority and the love that are both necessary in the bringing up of children. Just as the child may be tempted to deny his parents' involvement in his creation, so a parent with an unhappy history of relationship may be drawn between two poles in thinking about that relationship. Either all blame may lie with the absent partner or a falsely balanced view of equal responsibility may not facilitate the real working through of responsibility and justified grievance. Without that third point on the triangle, how does the child come to have an experience of him or herself, and be able to struggle towards understanding and the capacity to hope for meaningful adult relationships? Will a child without a father have an idea of what a father, or *his* father is, or is like? Is a father simply 'not mother'? Can a child get a true picture of his father through the eyes of his mother? (This is a particularly crucial question for boys, in terms of the need for identification.) I do not mean in any sense to indicate that a child in a single-parent family is doomed to struggle in vain and achieve partially or not at all the necessary integration of love, hate and ambivalence in order to achieve his best potential. What is clear is that many children within such a structure can and do achieve their potential, through the efforts of their remaining parent and by dint of drawing on their own constitutional capacities. Those fortunate enough to be born into extended and relatively close family structures can turn to alternative role models and feel supported to grow by drawing on the resources available to them. What is crucial is their own remaining parent's capacity to come to terms with their own story, and to offer coherence in potential adversity as a way forward. The research of Fonagy *et al.* (1991) with the Adult Attachment Interview demonstrated that the crucial factor enabling parents to parent appropriately is the capacity to reflect on experience, however difficult, to find a meaning in it, and move on with a measure of resolution and forgiveness. In this way, experience can be integrated through thinking and metabolised fruitfully in order to provide a coherent framework for further development. What became clear when he and his colleagues interviewed mothers and fathers in the last three months of a first pregnancy, was that parents' stance in relation to their own history was predictive of the attachment status of their children at twelve and eighteen months. Those individuals who were still hopelessly entangled in their past, or those who had become dismissive of early difficulty, were not able to provide a stable base for their children. So we can see that it is not so much adversity that presents a stumbling block but the way in which adversity is met and worked through.

The narrative gap

I want to extend this notion of narrative, which I suggest for a child in a single-parent family may be one of the most vital elements needed to make sense of the world and carry on. Main (1991) showed how early attachment patterns in children can later be traced to the developing child's ability to hold on to narrative and feel supported by internal strengths in later crises. What seems to be most vital, in cases where children and young people have not been able to achieve the necessary separation in order to move forward, is to find ways to offer the third point of view, to gain perspective on both the external and the internal situations. A young person may then feel that they can own their own narrative, both in terms of feeling potent rather than helpless, and being able to carry on their own story without too great an interference from their own or their parents' unconscious conflicts. 'Every family is a two parent family', said a Trustee of the Institute of Public Policy Research (Hewitt, 1996). It is how this notion may be internalised by the child in order to further his or her understanding that is at issue here.

In the novel Foe (1986) Coetzee reworks the story of Robinson Crusoe through the narrative of Susan Barton, who in Coetzee's version of the story was shipwrecked on Crusoe's island. The book is a multilayered reflection on narrative and who owns it. Susan Barton, struggling with Foe's desire to make the island story more dramatic than it really was, wishes to be 'the father to her own story'. Friday, who is mute, having had his tongue cut out, provides the unfathomable questions: how can we live, Susan Barton wonders, if we do not believe we know who we are and who we have been? She talks of the hole in the narrative that is Friday's story. She pictures this as a perfectly stitched buttonhole, only awaiting the button in order to fulfil its intended function. In a sense a child who does not have experience of both parents, externally and thus internally, may be left with a similar button-stitched hole, waiting for the button of the link with the other half of his being: in many cases the knowledge of a father and a linking up of identification with half of himself. This vital link gives him the opportunity to internalise both the couple he loves and the couple he hates, a combined parental object that carries the love and the authority to sustain his development.

So, in pulling together these two themes, what we are thinking about is the developmental necessity for the evolution of the triangular space, a space for thinking and a space where individual development is not compromised by the flooding in of undigested material from a parent's early history. In this space develops the personal story of the individual, or rather the story that the individual makes in order to gain coherence, link the button to the buttonhole, mother to father, in order to be fitted out for development in life in an integrated enough way. These concepts offer us a paradigm, what might be seen as a sine qua non. They do not however offer a magical solution to the continual struggles life offers, but rather a secure enough base from which to encounter them.

Some clinical examples

There are of course children and young people from single-parent families who do not for various reasons manage to achieve these developmental tasks adequately, and appear as referrals in child guidance clinics and family centres. Typical of these are two contrasting cases that appeared in a single week in a community child guidance clinic. Names and some circumstances have been changed in order to protect confidentiality.

Darren

Darren's school was concerned about him, and had been for two years. He was withdrawn and had difficulty making relationships with both adults and peers. He would spend long periods rocking back and forth and sometimes putting his head down on the table, which the teachers saw as a means of escape. He appeared unhappy, anxious, possibly depressed and would not talk about how he felt either at home or at school. Communication, when at all, was surly and sometimes disruptive, and he had a slight hesitation in his speech. He did the minimal amount of work, though he was an able boy. There had also been episodes of stealing. The school had discussed this with his mother, but until that point she had not acknowledged a problem. The three children in the family did not share a father, and there was no father resident. For a short time the children's names had been on the child protection register because of grave concern about neglect: the family had been isolated at the time, and mother had been 'hard on the children'. Mother felt Darren was different from her other children; she did not know how to handle him and was reported at that time finally to be keen for help.

Neil

Neil has a slightly different story. His mother had herself requested the referral because of his difficult behaviour during the last year. He had been disruptive and defiant both at school and at home. He denied there was a problem in either setting, and said he was happy. His mother was a single parent and Neil was the middle of three siblings. Neil's father did not visit and he had not seen him for three years. Father had recently had a new baby in another relationship. Neil maintained that he saw his father 'quite often'.

As can be seen from these two referrals, both are middle children, and have had somewhat different responses to their predicament. Darren has become withdrawn and out of contact, and clearly too in this family there are concerns about mother's capacity to manage at a minimum accepted level. It might be seen that in this family Darren carries the inability to grieve for loss and move on: often hesitation in speech may be connected with things that cannot be spoken about, and Darren, like the three absent fathers, might be seen to represent issues mother herself found hard to handle. Neil is more openly destructive and unhappy but denies he has a difficulty. It does seem however that he knows something about his father, although father's new family may be a tortured piece of knowing for him. In the event Darren's mother was not able to take up repeated offers of appointments (referral had been made by the school and the anxiety was clearly chiefly located there rather than in Darren's mother). Neil's mother, who had herself made the referral, was by contrast able to attend for some family sessions and gained some insight into the meaning of Neil's behaviour, as well as some much-needed support for herself.

Individual treatment

The cases of individual treatment below represent just two of the predicaments that may occur if a child comes from the 'single-parent family' constellation: one was a boy who was conceived at a party and never knew his father, the other was a boy who had sporadic contact with a father who lived abroad. I have described in a previous journal article (Edwards and Maltby, 1998) work done with an adolescent girl whose development was also compromised by the difficulties inherent for her in growing up without a father in the house. (I have not yet had the opportunity to work with a lone father and his family.) What these cases will show is the particular impact that their family situation had on each young person. As I emphasised earlier, being a child in a single-parent family is not a pathological condition, but can present a particular challenge to an individual, to which they will respond in a way determined by their individual psychological constitution and what they bring to their situation in terms of these factors. There will also be cultural issues to take into account, and it is vital to have a vertex that includes these where appropriate (see Maiello, 1999). In both cases described below, referral was made following difficulties around school attendance, which could be seen as a symptom of a more profound difficulty to do with separation and individuation, and the lack of the third point to help with this. These two cases were originally discussed from a different point of view in a chapter of a book about school refusal (Edwards and Daws, 1996).

Brian

Brian was referred to the clinic when he had stopped going to secondary school altogether in his first term after secondary transfer. He lived alone with his mother, who had previously suffered from an eating disorder, and Brian himself had been the product of a casual sexual encounter. His mother did not even know the surname of his father, and had not seen him subsequently. At the time of referral she had not seen this to be an issue of any importance. It was discovered in later work that Brian's mother herself had a history of difficult and inadequate parenting. Brian had managed to go to school in the relatively protected setting of a small primary school, but had found the task of emerging into the larger more uncontained environment of secondary school, where he was required to relate to many teachers during the day, and travel from room to room as well as subject to subject, in stark contrast to his memory of a nurturing primary experience with one teacher in one classroom, too difficult. If we relate this issue about separation back to the first crucial months in Brian's life with a depressed and unsupported mother, we could say that perhaps the primary task of separation had not been sufficiently negotiated in infancy, but this difficulty had remained latent until Brian was assailed by the impact of a large secondary school. He complained of headaches and stomach aches and stayed at home with his mother where they both slept a good deal of the time. Since his absences from school were attributed to minor illnesses it was almost a year before the severity of the problem was recognised. Brian was actually physically ill, but these illnesses were a symptom of his profound depression and despair. He had retreated into a hibernatory state with his mother, his primary object, and there was no father to offer him the energy to rouse himself from this lethargy, with which his mother unconsciously colluded because of her own unmet needs.

When we first met, Brian was silent in the presence of his mother, but was more able to talk to me later on his own. He had some insight into the current predicament, and said that he knew that he and his mother 'compounded each other's problems'. He also maintained firmly that he had 'never thought about' his father, and this remained his stance throughout the therapy that followed. Brian's defensive solution to his lack of a father was to refuse to acknowledge that there was a hole at all: a kind of annihilating denial that there had been two parents, even so fleetingly, at his conception. By the time the therapy began Brian was in a special unit, and he seemed to be in the grip of depressive illness. During the assessment his mother described staying up all night to ensure they made the morning times, because they both slept through alarms (and indeed it became clear that they had both ignored psychological alarms that might have alerted them earlier before the situation became so problematic). Brian seemed to function on the surface in an apparently articulate way: a kind of 'second skin' solution (Bick, 1968), but beneath this skin lay a mass of fears to do with separation and abandonment should he give up his anxious position as feeder and provider for a depressed mother. By acting in a paternal way towards his mother he usurped the father's role, but in so doing he denied himself the opportunity to be angry about his loss and this I think resulted in the draining away of his energy as he slept his life away.

In Brian's therapy two themes stand out. He drew a house with a skeleton structure that had no walls or roof, and I understood this both as the beginnings of something potentially stronger being built in his mind, but also an indication of an impoverished, semi-derelict internal world where he had been able to rely on no one. He found the idea of this internal exploration quite terrifying, although this latent feeling was usually masked by his accusations to me that he was bored and therapy was boring (while maintaining at the same time that he and his mother planned to buy a house in the road opposite the clinic). I think he managed to sustain his therapy in the early stages only because he incorporated it into his obsessive thinking about keeping to the same routes and routines. He described to me once how he had waited an hour in the snow for a bus that would take him by his usual route home, rather than catch another that would involve an adjustment in his route but get him home much earlier.

In the course of the last term of his three-term therapy, before he re-entered mainstream school, he made with great skill an anorak, which he brought to show me in its various stages. 'It's like a jacket, and not a disaster', he announced. I said I could see how proud he was to make something so difficult successfully, and not mess it up. He talked about the wadding that he would not use: it was to be a summer jacket (and we were approaching the summer break). 'The stripes from the inside go a different way, across and not down; it's not what you'd think', he said. I said I thought this jacket meant a lot to him, and that perhaps things too had changed quite a bit inside his mind and he had been able to do better than he thought, like going back to school gradually. The jacket and its symbolic equivalent seemed to be an appropriate and necessary defence for a boy who had previously lacked hope. As Alvarez (1992, p. 120) points out, a manic experience 'can signal the first glimmer of emergence from life-long clinical depression'. Brian began to be interested in the survival of the rainforests and the preservation of whales, who can communicate long distances under the sea. He began to connect, but in a covert way, with his anger, and drew spaceships in which the guns were concealed under retractable flaps. His mother also saw a worker at the clinic, and it was through this partnership that she was able to connect with parental strengths and make a separation between her own and Brian's needs. She made a new sexual relationship and started part-time work.

Brian ended his therapy abruptly, following a lively and angry session shortly after an apparently successful re-entry into school. He said I had never been any use, and I had never answered any of his questions. I had no recollection that he had ever asked me any. I think in the transference I became the absent father who had not been there to answer his questions about growing up. He left me rather than be left himself, and while this is only a partial solution it gave him the strength and energy to return to school.

In 'Precocious Oedipal fantasies and countertransference', Cancrini reflects on the effect of profound parental hostility on the internal world of the child:

> In the case of parents who love one another, the child's feelings – on all levels of the Oedipus Complex – are ones of exclusion, envy and jealousy. In the case of parents who hate one another, the child perceives the bond between them as 'a disaster'. He cannot think about it, and his life experience is one of disintegration and death. In fact, the experience of parents who hate one another and make their bond explode is especially dramatic for the child who is invaded by the conflict, and has no more space for himself. Moreover, he has no possibility of projecting his destructive impulses, and they rebound upon him with extreme violence. In such a situation a child is unable to enact any reliable identifications.
>
> (Cancrini, 1998, p. 430)

In cases such as Brian's, one can speculate that the internal picture is not one of destruction but rather of a void or of a blank screen, where projections can be thrown up but receive neither positive nor negative validation in terms of feedback externally or internally. For a young person such as Brian, the onset of adolescence with its tasks of reworking infantile conflicts and searching for an authentic identity in the progress towards the adult world is especially problematic, and the unanswered questions reverberated in a void. While I think I did become a psychic 'whale', picking up his sonar communications from a lonely internal space, the working through may well have to wait for another transitional stage, as it was less painful for him to make me the abandoned one. I think that a boy who has 'never thought about' his father might well need considerable help in thinking about how to be a father in his own turn. In their paper 'Will I be to my son as my father was to me?' (Tracey *et al.*, 1996, op. 192), the authors describe work done with the father of a premature baby in which he works through the pain of an abusive relationship: 'We saw this as the sensitive unfolding story of a father coming to life with his real baby as he came to terms with the birth of his psychic infant within, and struggled with old conflicts with his father.' For Brian, this much-needed working through would involve the painful acknowledgment of a void, and the reconnecting with buried unconscious anger. A father who unknowingly conceives a child may be felt most profoundly by the child to reject him, and in Brian this feeling struck at the very root of the idea of his father, so that no questions could develop and grow to the point where they could be formulated, although it was these very unformulated and inevitably unanswered questions that stood as my accusers in the transference. However, the strengthening effect of his anger in the transference towards me had helped him along the way at that juncture of his life.

Thomas

Thomas had become increasingly school phobic as he approached secondary transfer, and was referred to the clinic because of his nightmares and obsessive touching rituals. He had lived alone with his mother all his life, and she had been diagnosed as suffering from multiple sclerosis soon after his birth. Thomas had been conceived while his mother was travelling around the world: his father was someone similarly circling the globe, and they interconnected briefly. Unlike Brian however, Thomas did have somewhat of a relationship with his father, who was still travelling, but visited from time to time. The accounts I had via Thomas of his father was of a man who in his mid forties seemed still to be living out his adolescent fantasies, with fast motorbikes and a disconnected itinerant lifestyle.

Thomas' lifelong experience was therefore of a fragile mother without a father to help and support her. While consciously he seemed to have accepted his role of being merged with mother (with whom he was on first-name terms) in what could be described as a symbiotic union where they both even looked physically like two halves of one person, at an unconscious level he was terrified of this merging. He showed this when for the first year of his once-weekly therapy he played off-the-ground games and constructed dens in one corner of the room. I understood this as being in order to ward off contact with me as a frightening maternal object, projectively identified as being all-consuming, as Thomas himself also wished to intrude and take over. He spent sessions trying to play outside the therapy boundary by suspending objects over the window sill, attempting (and succeeding) in attracting the attention of other patients. It was clear that there was no notion of a boundary-keeper in his mind, no notion of a quiet reflective space. By getting rid in his mind of the idea of a father by taking his place, Thomas then himself feared takeover by a retaliatory and vengeful figure. It was difficult for Thomas to envisage a third position: he was either enmeshed or disengaged as a defence against this. For this child, the environmental difficulties of his infancy had prevented a working through of his ordinary omnipotence: his obsessive touching of boundaries could be seen as his own desperate attempt to contain himself.

Thomas asked me for 'miles of string', and he spent several sessions constructing elaborate webs in the room. He explained that he had made webs for as long as he could remember: that at first he made them in order not to get tangled up in them but then he had 'given up'. He got into his therapy web and deliberately wound its threads around his limbs. An entangling union like that between himself and his mother was all that he could envisage. I saw this as a kind of symbiosis, though not as in the scientific terminology, where both parties gain by the relationship. He both invited and dreaded this union, and he had nightmares about it. Bowlby (1973) described a similar incident with a nine-year-old boy who wound himself up in the window cord, saying 'See, I'm in a spider's web, and I can't get out'. Thomas told me the story of Robocop, a man who had been made into a machine: 'He was hurt so badly he didn't ever want it to happen again.' I said perhaps he was also talking about a part of himself that it felt very risky to allow to make any contact with me. It was hard for him to imagine that we could be friendly without someone getting trapped or hurt. For Thomas, a container swiftly turned into a straitjacket.

We talked about his heroes who were the macho stars of popular films. Thomas gradually began to be in touch with internal strengths that could develop once he had in therapy some experience of a relationship that could encompass dependency without overwhelming him. In the contained and consistent setting of the therapy room he came to appreciate what could be called a paternal part of me that could both strengthen the maternal and protect it against his own powerful wishes to take over. Meanwhile his mother received parallel support from a colleague. While initially she found it hard not to intrude into her son's therapy, over time, helped by the idea of myself and my colleague as a strong couple, she developed her own strengths and insights as she unravelled the problematic relationship she had had with her own parents.

Thomas made secondary transfer amid concerns among us all about his capacities to survive it, but he managed and has continued to do so. His therapy ended, but his mother continued to have support in order to help Thomas with the vital separation on his way to adolescence. There were inevitably questions that arose again during our final sessions about whether I could let him go, and in the penultimate session he announced that his wish-list for his birthday included a paint gun, goggles, camouflage, smoke grenades and a motor bike. I took this up in terms of his anxieties about me hanging onto him even though we had decided an ending date and were working towards it: would I let him go or would he have to put up a smokescreen, hit me and run? He was able subsequently to end on a note of sadness as well as hope, and what he took away was the knowledge that he could carry on his developmental path, without having to take care of his mother or be a premature adult. Again, triangular space for thinking provided new alignments, so that, with the idea of 'a notional couple', Thomas could be freed from the seductive web to achieve real growth.

The clinic couple

In both these cases, individual work with the young person proceeded alongside individual work with the parents, both of whom, for their own internal reasons, had previously denied the importance of a two-person relationship in bringing up a child. It is this absence of a sense of the internal creative couple that is at issue here, since, as I have already indicated, there are indeed many instances when a parent can make internal space for their creative counterpart, and also provide external opportunities for vital identifications to be made. For these two lone mothers, there was offered the opportunity both to think with their own worker and thus develop a less isolated and falsely independent stance, and to perceive the two clinic workers as a strong couple, working together both for the development of the child and also in partnership with the adult part of the parent's personality in the service of the infantile needs of the young person. While this scenario is an ideal one, and in many clinic settings there may well not be the opportunity for this parallel work to be offered, I think it is possible nevertheless to proceed, if the psychotherapist working with the child has a sense in her own mind of the strengthening presence of an other, a space for a father. In past years, as Rustin (1998) notes, the parallel work with a parent would have been carried out by psychiatric social workers. However, budget constraints and changes in the professional orientation of social workers have changed this picture, and child psychotherapists have had to think again about how to approach the question of work with a parent alongside the child's treatment. As the author points out, the intensive training in psychoanalytic work with children gives our profession a particularly rich base for this endeavour, and, in both these cases described above, it was the combined resource offered to the family that enabled the work to be done.

Conclusion

I have described two vignettes to illustrate ways in which a particular family structure may consciously and unconsciously impede development in a particular way. In these cases the absence of a father had implications on many levels to do with identification and an appropriate location in the Oedipal constellation. In each of these narratives, it can be seen that through therapeutic work there has been internal movement that has facilitated external movement, growth and development. As Feldman (1989) asserted, phantasies about mother and father can cause anxiety, defensiveness, and limit the capacity to think. As he says:

[I]f the anxieties associated with the phantasy of the parental couple are too great, then there will be a corresponding interference with the capacity for making connections between elements in the patient's mind, a process that seems to depend, in some essential way, on the phantasy associated with the conjunction of mouth and nipple, or penis and vagina.

(Feldman, 1989, p. 105)

And again, these early connections prefigure the narrative idea of the button and the button-hole: a conjunction that results in being fitted out to think and make links. It is vital for there to be the growth of an idea of a creative internal couple for there to be truly creative growth in the external world. By creating that 'minimum expression of space' that is a necessary precursor for thinking and for change, each young person was able to gain a different perspective and meet up with themselves and their objects in a different way. As my title queries: can you miss something you have never had? What I hope to have shown is that it is through this very acknowledgement of missing, and constructing internal narratives to restore coherence where once there was a gap, that developmental difficulties and delays can be helped, and developmental processes can be resumed on a firmer base.

Note

1 This paper was first presented at the Tavistock Society of Psychotherapists Conference 'Thinking Psychoanalytically' in Florence, August 1998. It also appeared in *Contrapunto* December 2000.

References

Alvarez, A. (1992) *Live Company*. London: Routledge.

Barrows, P. (1995) 'Oedipal issues at 4 and 44'. *Psychoanalytic Psychotherapy*, 9(1), 85–96.

Bick, E. (1968) 'The experience of skin in early object relations'. *International Journal of Psychoanalysis*, 49, 484–6.

Bion, W. R. (1962) *Learning from Experience*. London: Karnac.

Bion, W. R. (1977) *The Grid and the Caesura*. London: Karnac.

Bowlby, J. (1973) *Attachment and Loss 2: Separation, Anxiety and Anger*. London: Hogarth.

Cancrini, T. (1998) 'Precocious Oedipal fantasies and countertransference'. *Journal of Child Psychotherapy*, 24(3), 423–32.

Coetzee, J. M. (1986) *Foe*. London: Penguin.

Critchlow, K. (1976) *Islamic Patterns: An Analytic and Cosmological Approach*. London: Thames & Hudson.

Edwards, J. and Daws, D. (1996) 'Psychotherapy for school refusing children with separation anxiety'. In I. Berg and J. Nursten (eds), *Unwillingly to School*. London: Gaskell, pp. 279–94.

Edwards, J. and Maltby, J. (1998) 'Holding the child in mind: Work with parents and families in a consultation service'. *Journal of Child Psychotherapy*, 24(1), 109–33.

Feldman, M. (1989) 'The Oedipus complex: Manifestations in the inner world and the therapeutic situation'. In R. Britton, M. Feldman and E. O'Shaughnessy (eds), *The Oedipus Complex Today*. London: Karnac, pp. 103–28.

Fonagy, P., Steele, H. and Steele, M. (1991) 'Maternal representations of attachment during pregnancy predict the organization of infant/mother attachments at one year of age'. *Child Development*, 62, 891–905.

Freud, S. (1905) 'Three Essays on the Theory of Sexuality'. *S.E.* 7, 136–43. London: Hogarth.

Freud, S. (1923) 'The infantile genital organization'. *S.E. 19*, 139–45. London: Hogarth.

Haskey, J. (1994) *Estimated Numbers of One-parent Families and their Prevalence in Great Britain in 1991*. London: Office of Population, Censuses and Surveys.

Hewitt, P. (1996) *The Guardian*, March.

Johns, M. (1990) 'The myth of the one-parent family'. Tavistock Public Lecture No. 111.

Kraemer, S. (1988) 'The civilisation of fathers'. Tavistock Public Lecture.

Maiello, S. (1999) 'Encounter with an African healer'. *Journal of Child Psychotherapy*, *25*(2), 217–38.

Main, M. (1991) 'Metacognitive knowledge, metacognitive monitoring and individual differences in attachment organization during childhood'. In C. M. Parkes, *et al.* (eds) *Attachment across the Life Cycle*. London: Tavistock/Routledge, pp. 125–52.

Prechtl, H. F. R. (1989) 'Foetal behaviour'. In A. Hill and J. Volpe (eds), *Foetal Neurology*. New York: Raven Press.

Rustin, M. (1998) 'Dialogues with parents'. *Journal of Child Psychotherapy*, *24*(2), 233–52.

Segal, H. (1989) 'Introduction'. In R. Britton, M. Feldman and E. O'Shaughnessy (eds), *The Oedipus Complex Today*. London: Karnac, pp. 1–10.

Steiner, J. (1996) 'The aim of psychoanalysis in theory and in practice', *International Journal of Psychoanalysis*, *77*, 1073–83.

Temperley, J. (1993) 'Is the Oedipus complex bad news for women?'. *Free Associations*, *4*, 265–76.

The Finer Report (1974) Report of the Committee on One-Parent Families. London, HMSO.

Tomatis, A. (1981) *La Nuit Uterine*. Paris: Editions Stock.

Tracey, N., Blake, P., Warren, B., Hardy, H., Enfield, S. and Shein, P. (1996) 'Will I be to my son as my father was to me?'. *Journal of Child Psychotherapy*, *22*(2), 168–94.

Trevarthen, C. and Hubley, P. (1978) 'Secondary intersubjectivity: Confidence, confiding and acts of meaning in the first year'. In A. Lock (ed.), *Action, Gesture and Symbol: The Emergence of Language*. London: Academic Press, pp. 147–60.

Winnicott, D. W. (1971) *Playing and Reality*. London: Tavistock.

CHAPTER 6

ON BEING DROPPED AND PICKED UP

The plight of some late adopted children

The field of adoption has changed over the past years from one where there were babies available for many adoptive couples to one where increasingly the children who are needing adoption are those who have already suffered deprivations and difficulties in their families of origin, with disrupted attachments and a consequent traumatising effect of their early history on their internal worlds. Professionals working with these children, who have in effect been 'dropped', face the difficult task not only of placing them appropriately but of supporting their adoptive families. With the new experience of a secure base the original trauma may be reworked, and the new framework tested by these damaged and consequently often damaging children as they replay their feelings of being unwanted and unwantable. In describing once-weekly work with a six-year-old adopted boy, I suggest that the primary disillusion of his neonatal experience caused an internal catastrophe that was then reworked in his adoptive placement. This child did not experience what Winnicott (1971) called 'gradual disillusion' in terms of his belief that he creates the needed breast, and thus integration of love and hate of the primary object, but remained in a state of hyper-vigilance because of the deficits in his internal world. These deficits have been able partially to be addressed in psychotherapy treatment.

> Happy are those who lose imagination;
> They have enough to carry with ammunition.
> Their spirit drags no pack,
> Their old wounds, save with cold, can not more ache.
> Having seen all things red,
> Their eyes are rid
> Of the hurt of the colour of blood for ever.
> And terror's first constriction over,
> Their hearts remain small-drawn.
> Their sense in some scorching cautery of battle
> Now long since ironed,
> Can laugh among the dying, unconcerned.
>
> (Wilfred Owen, 'Insensibility')

In myth and legend there are several well-known cases of adoption. Moses was floated down the Nile to escape persecution, to be adopted in a strange land. Romulus and Remus also escaped persecution: they were to be drowned by an uncle, but were left on a hillside and, first, adopted by wolves and, subsequently, found by a herdsman. While the story of Moses had a positive ending, and he led his people to safety, Romulus and Remus had a less fortunate fate. After the foundation of Rome, the legend goes that Romulus killed Remus, ostensibly for laughing at the walls he had built, and the Rome of Romulus became a haven for adventurers and ne'er-do-wells. In this case one might think that the early experience of being abandoned had resulted in a persecuted state of mind that persisted into adulthood, in contrast to the state of mind represented by Moses, who was able to repair and save rather than destroy. In the case of children who are adopted, how can we ensure that they are able to achieve some integration of feeling, in order to be able to make satisfactory enough emotional and thus ordinary developmental progress? Like the seasoned (and we would now think traumatised) First World War soldiers in Wilfred Owen's poem, they have split off feeling: the original trauma has rendered the pain often too great to be borne, and their hearts do indeed remain 'small-drawn', with a resultant impoverishment of their emotional lives.

Oedipus and adoption

Perhaps the best-known case in myth of an adoption that had disastrous consequences is that of Oedipus, cast out by his parents because of a prophecy that he would kill his father and marry his mother, abandoned on a hillside and subsequently taken up by another couple but not told of his origins. Then, in an attempt to escape the prophetic shadow, he leaves his adoptive parents whom he believes to be his birth parents. Casting himself adrift from them, he returns 'by chance' to Thebes, his actual city of birth. Even before entering the city gates, he begins to enact the very situation most feared by himself and his parents, by killing the father he does not recognise. The Oedipus complex was one of Freud's core concepts, and has been of ongoing interest to psychoanalytic thinkers as a paradigm for some of our most central dilemmas. In a thought-provoking paper, Lupinacci (1998) reflects on the two couples involved in this tragic transaction: the parents of Thebes and the parents of Corinth. The Theban couple, in psychic terms, cannot bear the risk involved in bringing up this child, who may through his passion attempt to destroy their relationship (and this drama of the child who wants sole possession of mother to the exclusion of father is played out, particularly with a first child, with painful intensity in ordinary families). To save themselves, they expose Oedipus to certain death. The parents of Corinth accept Oedipus without question, and it is the love that Oedipus has for them that forces him to leave them, in order to spare them. However, as Dr Lupinacci points out, there then exists a split between the idealised couple of Corinth, who do not have to bear the murderous feelings of the infant, and the negative abandoning couple of Thebes, who split off and expel aggression and murderousness, which then returns with greater force. As Lupinacci observes, being an adopted child is a common childhood fantasy for non-adopted children when there is rage and anger against the biological parents: somewhere, the child reasons, there are my real parents who would not treat me in this way.

An adopted boy who had been badly abused in his original home had two contrasting memories that emerged in a therapy session: a flowered stair carpet and a frightening shape at the bottom which he thought had something to do with hanging coats. (He had in fact been found, nearly naked, shut in a cupboard under the stairs.) Whatever the reality on which these images had been based, however, I could simply take it up in terms of fragments, good and bad, safe and unsafe, that he was used to carrying around, trying to piece them together. We all have these Proustian images that seem to exist in an area between waking and dreaming, but for the adopted child with no idea of an internal couple who can link together inside his mind and help him think about his story, they can become persecuting and persistent. The non-adopted child in an ordinarily good enough home with biological parents has to struggle to unite the opposing ideas of loving and hating the same people. The process involves illusion and disillusion on the long road towards an adequate appreciation of reality. For the adopted child this task may be severely compromised by the facts of early history and the fantasies constructed around them. These may remain dormant and then erupt with great force when the child is finally placed for adoption and begins to have a sense of a secure base from which to express a rightful grievance. Are the birth parents bad? Is the child a bad child? Have the adoptive parents stolen the child from an idealised happier situation? It is sobering to note how the most abusive early situations can turn in the child's mind to something loved and lost in the face of the inevitable difficulties of fitting into a new family. As another child said to me, 'I just don't believe they did those things to me'. This was a child who had received substantial 'damages' from the Criminal Injuries Board for the treatment that had so damaged his beginnings with his birth parents. The often very violent repudiation of knowledge can, as with the myth of Oedipus, re-enter the mind in a similarly violent way, causing further splits because of the difficulty of integrating the facts and the fantasies in order to achieve a realistic and inevitably mixed picture, both of the birth family and the family of adoption. These conflicts may either persist as a factor inhibiting settling down, or they may re-emerge at times of stress, as in the case I describe here, where the stress of a new baby caused a resurgence of ancient griefs and grievances.

Some mediating factors

Research findings have indicated that children in long-term foster or adoptive care retain strong feelings for their birth parents and their siblings: these ruptured relationships may remain an internal preoccupation (McAuley, 1996) for years, and into adulthood. The development of new relationships in an adoptive family will inevitably be slow, and will be plagued by a resurgence of difficulties at points of crisis, as I have indicated. Research undertaken by Dr Miriam Steele at the Anna Freud Centre aims, by use of the Adult Attachment Interview, to help all those involved in the adoptive process better to assess an appropriate 'fit' between children and adoptive parents. The central question of the study is one that pre-occupies all those involved in this difficult work: 'How can we understand and assess the impact of previous adversities in a child's history on the new relationships that develop between themselves and their adoptive parents?' The interview, which takes the form of an elicited narrative account of parents' own childhoods, was found to be a strong indicator of the attachment status of biological children: secure, avoidant or ambivalent. It was found that it was not so much a difficult history in itself that made for either ongoing entanglement with the story or a defensive dismissal of its relevance, but the way that history had been able to be thought about and digested, so that the adult could look back with some measure of understanding and forgiveness, and make a meaningful assessment of the then and the now. The researchers hoped that, by the assessment through stories of particular dilemmas the child might face, they could find out something of the internal world of the child and their view of adults, both before placement and after periods of one and two years' adoption. By linking these findings with those derived from using the Adult Attachment Interview with adoptive parents, which may predict what their assumptions will be about the adoptive child and the prospective relationships they will make together, based on their own early experiences, vital new evidence will help in the placement and ongoing support for the adopted child (Hodges and Steele, 2000).

Telling the story: memory and thinking

We begin at the beginning. But for an adopted child, as I have said, beginnings have been painful, fragmented and often chaotic. With late adopted children, we all become used to hearing the stories of early lives fraught with instability, comings and goings, toings and froings, before events finally become such that the child is 'freed' for adoption. The slow unravelling of emotional ties (or their swift rupture) accompanies the inevitably (and necessarily so) slow external procedures. Inside the mind of the child, there may be huge uncharted areas of confusion and doubt. The 'Life Story Book', which is our adult way of helping the child to make sense of these confusions, may go some way to being a move forward, but may also inevitably leave untouched these uncharted areas of experience.

It is only during recent years that psychological research has shown that infants and young children are able to recall events in their lives. Freud noted that adults he saw had no recall of early life events and marvelled at 'this remarkable amnesia of childhood . . . the forgetting which veils our earliest youth from us and makes us strangers to it' (Freud, 1916–17). He thought that early memories were repressed, and that children retained images and fragments of events, but not coherent representations of past experiences. The subsequent observational and clinical experience of child psychotherapists and analysts over the years has put the profession very much in touch with the powerful but unconscious nature of early memories, and it is the verbalisation in the therapy of these that can bring relief, as I hope to show later in this chapter. Developmental research has now documented this early capacity to recall events. By demonstrating simple non-verbal sequences to children and infants over progressively longer periods it has been shown that, as early as thirteen months, the capacity to construct and maintain memories of specific events can result in recall over extended periods of time (Bauer and Hertsgaard, 1993). What was discovered to be crucial was the nature of the events, the number of exposures, and the availability of memory-jogging cues. The researchers talk of 'enabling relations' and by this they mean events that have coherence. We might, I think, extend this concept to include the enabling relationships that are available, or not, to render events meaningful for the child. For the child that begins life in an environment characterised by its instability, lack of continuity and often its potential for significant harm, where no enabling relationship is available to process events, it is not surprising that there remains an unprocessed swirl of unlinked fragments. This is in stark contrast to the experience for the normal infant and young child within a biological family, whose fears and phantasies are contained, transformed and returned in more manageable form through the reverie of its parents (Bion, 1962). This vital early experience forms the foundation from which thinking and linking can emerge, and learning and growth can ensue.

How can we, then, think about how to help these troubled and troubling children? I want to quote almost in full a letter written to the *Guardian* newspaper in April 1998, in response to a journalist's piece about government plans for children in care, by Andrew Cooper, then Professor of Social Work at the Tavistock Clinic:

> One reason for the breakdown of foster placements [and, I would suggest, adoptive places too] is the terrible intensity and complexity of emotional needs arising from the damaging family experiences which children will bring to any substitute care setting. Week by week the qualified social workers I teach bring cases of this kind for discussion; often they feel professionally isolated because they are the only ones prepared to recognise the depth of the child's suffering and disturbance, and the long-term impact of this on prospective carers. The idea of 'small family homes' creates a warm but illusory glow. Staff in such homes will need to be as highly trained and well-supported as anyone in the child care field, if this plan is to do justice to the children involved, and lead to better outcomes.

The message is unambiguous: we need across-the-board thinking, training and support, and we need to have an openness to the experience of damaged children that enables us to enable their carers to meet the demands they make. Being dropped is painful: being picked up gives the child the opportunity to cry. As psychodynamic workers, we have to recognize the need not only to offer help directly to the child, but to be available to consult to their adoptive parents and to the network where these themes may be re-enacted in the adoption process (Maltby, 1994; Obholzer and Zagier Roberts, 1994; Lanyado, 1999; Sprince, 2000).

Clinical example

Gary

The case I want to think about, that of a six-year-old boy called Gary, was the inspiration for the title of this chapter. It was Gary's inexorable development in therapy, from gently lowering himself onto the floor onto his head to headlong and reckless throwing himself or deliberately somersaulting onto his head, which caused me to think most urgently about the core experience of being emotionally dropped, not once but many times, during the course of a short life, and about the desperate state of the internal objects of a child who felt he had nothing more to lose.

It was the head teacher at Gary's school who suggested to his white middle-class adoptive mother that she should approach our family consultation service, because of behavioural problems both at school and at home. The head described him as a bright boy but restless and volatile, easily provoked and prone to attack other children, especially in the playground. When I met with the family, which comprised Gary's adoptive mother, her own son James (10) and her husband Edward, mother described Gary's ceaseless activity, inability to be in a group (he had been impossible to manage in local group activities), and the fact that he was apt to eat everything in the fridge at one sitting. He also wet the bed and there had been episodes of stealing. His adoptive mother was exhausted, but was also able to be helped through our discussions to be in touch with developments that seemed to occur after outbursts: tearing James's books and then learning to read; eating James's Easter egg and then learning to dress himself. In a sense his destructive envy of James, the birth child, had the effect of driving him forward, but it was this desperate driven quality that caused his carers later to be concerned for his sanity. Peter Wilson (1996) in talking about Winnicott's concept of 'the anti-social tendency' notes what he calls 'the mark of justification' in stealing. 'It's mine!' The child is seeking to right a wrong. Wilson (1996, p. 395) quotes Winnicott (1971):

> An antisocial child is a deprived child . . . in the psychopath and the delinquent and the deprived child there is logic in the implied attitude 'the environment owes me something' . . . he is searching in some way to get the world to acknowledge its debt.

Gary's birth mother had been a heroin addict and he had been born addicted and thus withdrawing from heroin himself as a result. In addition to the profound changes accompanying the normal caesura of birth, his first infantile experience was of enduring the pains and bewilderment of 'cold turkey' as heroin addicts describe their experience of withdrawal. In 'Children traumatized in infancy' (Emanuel, 1996) there is a description of a full-term baby on a special care baby unit who was being treated in the intensive care nursery for drug withdrawal. The baby, fourteen days old when first observed, was being treated with morphine and Clonazepam for the fits she was having. The observer (Mendelsohn) describes how the baby's twitching and shuddering seemed completely beyond any control: 'she suddenly gives a violent shudder and both arms are raised off the sheet, and she seems to be punching the air in front of her face.' Gary had been premature and had spent some time in an incubator before being taken home to a house where other addicts lived. In retrospect, one may postulate that for Gary time in the incubator had at least offered some containment. At 'home' he had been passed round members of the family and had been looked after for a while by maternal grandmother, who then took an overdose when Gary was in the house, because she felt at the end of her tether with the comings and goings of her daughter, who also had an older daughter by a different father. It was then that social services became involved, and Gary was taken into care; he was in a large foster-family where he stopped growing altogether and did not develop speech. The few words he did utter came out in a painful stammer. In her paper 'On childhood stuttering and the theory of clinging' (Klaniczay, 2000, p. 99), the author postulates that 'difficulties to do with the need for an object are central'. For Gary at this point in his short life there had indeed been no primary object for reliable identification, and the placement in a large foster-family must have induced further internal chaos in a child already bewildered and catastrophically confused. His adoptive mother was distantly related by marriage to his birth mother, and social services had initially been doubtful about the wisdom of her proposal to adopt him. Gary's prospective adoptive mother however managed to convince them, and indeed it has been in her care that Gary has begun to grow, to be extremely articulate (the stammer disappeared) and to feel properly held for the first time in his life. (In one of our sessions his mother described how she had been called to the house after the grandmother's overdose: Gary was hysterical and terrified, someone was trying to give him a bath, and, as she then said, 'he was falling apart, but I calmed him down and held him'.)

Family work

In the consultation service where I then worked we offered five family sessions in order to explore how much could be achieved by working with the family as a whole. The sessions might be spread over a period of several months. There may well have been enough change within this structure for the family to progress without further intervention, but we did also offer individual help according to resources available. (For a fuller account of this approach, see Edwards and Maltby, 1998.) Right from the first family session Gary (and his adoptive brother too) made it clear he liked having a space to think. His first act was to stick a drawing of himself on the wall. As the session progressed, he had the dolls fighting in the house, and there were crocodiles with teeth and fierce octopuses. The boys' mother said they fought a lot, and James said 'Gary laughs when I hurt him'. Gary's confusion and anger about his situation were evident in his communication that his real mother had ten children: he *could* go back to her, and then if he was naughty again he would be sent back to his adoptive mother. His adoptive mother had previously felt rather despairing at this rejection, but in the session, as we thought about both his guilt and his wish that someone should be punished, she was able to make some sense of the communication and empathise with *Gary's* desperation, and see that he was passing it on to her via the medium of projective identification.

As the meetings progressed, Gary settled down considerably, both at home and at school. His mother was impressed that he could tolerate her talking to me in the sessions, as usually he tried to interpose himself in a demanding and controlling way. At school he was still compulsively spilling out his story, and was finding changeovers to playtime and lunchtime problematic. We could link this to his anxieties about being dropped, and what happened in gaps, and mother then went in to school to ask for special thinking for Gary around these times, so he did not become, as she described it, a blitz or a whirlwind. Gary's play in the house revealed an internal world full of fighting, and a policeman had a fight with a bad baby, which we could link with his feelings that he must have been bad to be sent away by his birth mother. These sessions were helpful too for James, who could express some of his anger around being invaded by Gary and his difficulties. The family frequently arrived up to half an hour early for sessions, which I took to be a measure of the huge need for the thinking space. Gary's adoptive mother often looked exhausted, and there were difficulties with her husband, but he also attended some of the meetings. It was clear that our five family meetings would only begin to address Gary's predicament, and agreement was secured for weekly individual sessions, which have been funded by social services. The later theme of being picked up and dropped was already present in the family sessions, both in our thinking and in Gary's play. He would line up the soldiers and then knock them down in a manically triumphant rather than playful way as he and James played skittles: it was clear that he had identified with a powerful and controlling figure who would enact what he most feared, before it was visited on himself. His vulnerable self was heavily armoured in a suit of apparent invincibility, and I was to recall many times in the individual work what James had said about a Gary who laughed when he was hurt. As Wilfred Owen said, 'they can laugh among the dying, unconcerned'.

However, Gary was already making progress; he was calmer both at home and at school, less voracious and demanding. He was still wetting the bed though less frequently: in one session he drew a 'monster' (who looked rather like himself) who he said was 'weeing everywhere'. He stoutly maintained he liked wet beds.

He had started to draw what he called 'ghosts' on flimsy pieces of tissue, flitting them around my head, and I took this up in terms of thoughts and feelings that came and went, that he wanted to make sense of. It also made me think of Selma Fraiberg's work (1975) with deprived families, where what she called 'ghosts in the nursery', the parents' unworked-through difficulties, come back to haunt the next generation and sabotage the parents' capacity to parent. It seemed to me that these 'ghosts' of Gary's might well represent residues of his mother's difficulties, whispering and fluttering in the unconscious atmosphere surrounding him both pre- and post-birth. Certainly there had been intergenerational difficulties in Gary's family of origin that had affected his early life, and these 'ghosts', which seemed to me to be something to do with a transgenerational haunting, continued to appear in the individual sessions.

Individual therapy

Therapy began after the summer break. While Gary continued to stage interminable fights, 'mortal combat' where people were finished off, he denied anger, either with me or anyone else. But everyone in the play always ended up dead. My counter-transference feelings were often of boredom: when I said it was hard for him to think he could do anything else apart from killing, he stopped, surprised, and said 'But don't you like it?' In his mind he was confused with his primary object in an orgy of killing, of the kind described by Maiello (2000) which becomes cut off from original motives of anger towards the object and becomes mindless destruction, as opposed to aggression which implies an object relationship. He played and replayed scenarios where he was a 'big bad turtle' who was greedy and selfish, eating all the ice-cream, ordering pizzas loaded with numerous toppings. Issues about feeling abandoned emerged: Gary would lie on one of the soft chairs and lower himself slowly head first onto the floor. One of the small dolls would fly around the room and became called 'spider boy', then he would slide down a wall or a chair out into space, or into shark-infested waters, or be drowned in lava. I talked about a Gary who found gaps and breaks difficult, who then turned into a flying boy in order not to be a falling boy, and then killed off all the adults who might help, including myself, because he got into such a spin.

An unexpected event

Resources were such that it was possible for me to offer Gary's adoptive mother only monthly sessions herself. These were intended to support her work with Gary and to think through how to maintain the evident improvements in the world outside the therapy room, now that he had obtained a safe weekly space to begin simply to unload but hopefully eventually to digest some of his previously undigested experience. At one of these meetings his mother arrived saying that suddenly things seemed to have taken a turn for the worse. Was this part of the 'things get worse before they get better' pattern? The week before, Gary had had an outburst of uncontrollable swearing at school which had then been continued at home. He seemed much more unsettled again, and we thought around why this might be. At first we seemed to draw a blank. Then I asked mother how she herself was at the moment. She revealed that she had just had it confirmed that she was pregnant. While she was at first resistant to linking this with the swearing outbursts, she then said even the dog had noticed her lack of energy and was following her about! She was able then to think with me about Gary's feeling of guilt that people who look after him get tired (or even take overdoses as did maternal grandmother), and that he might be too much for them. We could then agree it would be important to be thinking about how to help Gary with this new turn of events.

A new character emerged in Gary's sessions: he was called 'Dynowrecker' and he was engaged in prolonged and bitter fighting. Occasional sad moments swiftly turned into contempt and self-loathing, and he would put himself in the bin. He was also concerned about me in an anxious way – 'you sound cross today' – and I felt he was monitoring my state of mind, as he was that of his adoptive mother, for signs that he had overstepped the mark and was about to be pushed out again. I think that this new-found feeling Gary had experienced of a place to be safe had stirred up all his old anxieties about being ejected from his mother's mind and the reasons for this.

As his adoptive mother's pregnancy advanced, so did my concerns about Gary. After the half-term break he zoomed back into the room and deliberately dived off a chair straight onto his head. He told me Mummy had a baby in her tummy, and that she would call it Nina. Then with no time for me to comment he zoomed off in a spaceship, leaving me with the tissue 'ghosts', telling me seriously 'they last a long time, you know'. I think in this way he was indicating the devastating remnants of his early trauma of being abandoned in an uncontained space, which returned to visit him as mother visibly grew larger with the baby inside her. During the next few months I was left on many occasions with the ghosts, while Gary and Mr Blobby went off in a space ship, hastily thrown together with a heap of chairs. Nina was chased by police, drowned, smacked and tortured. Meanwhile I was Sellotaped to my chair, forced to witness Nina's persecution. Different ways of killing babies were devised, and in many ways this seemed a helpful way of thinking about his murderous feelings so that they would not become enacted. In some sessions Gary's anger was cold and vengeful; in a way it had gone beyond anger to a state of vengeance cut off completely from links with better feelings. When I described his angry feelings as he talked of killing, he said, 'It's not about feeling, I'll do it'. Maiello's paper (2000) was helpful in thinking about a link that had not so much been actively broken, but never experienced, so that the nameless dread of falling for ever was not contained and became split off into mindless destruction, which in Gary's case was soon to become self-destruction. As Maiello suggests, 'Falling or dropping is not necessarily the consequence of hostile primary feelings, but may also result from the introjection of a weak link with the primary object' (2000, p. 5). As Maiello also points out, her thinking about deficit has been proceeding along similar lines to that of Alvarez (1998) in terms of links that have never been adequately forged. Gary started to threaten to swallow objects in the room, such as pen tops, and I talked to him about how I should be very worried about what he might do. I think he was communicating to me most urgently the sense he had of imminent destruction, and, as had become habitual, he would kill himself rather than be killed. He would leap dangerously from table to chair to table again, letting me know about a precarious and wildly veering emotional state where a second by second monitoring of the situation could even then barely prevent disaster. After many sessions I was left feeling exhausted as I attempted to hold on to Gary, both physically and emotionally, in order to contain his fragmented states of mind. I thought about the baby observed in the special care unit already quoted (Emanuel, 1996) as he would lie on the floor, writhing and shuddering.

The most concerning feature of this deterioration was Gary's increasingly frequent tendency to throw himself head first onto the floor, even one day as I was holding his hand to take him back to the waiting room at the end of a session. Unfortunately, when I told his adoptive father who was there to collect him, he laughed and made light of it. Gary himself had rubbed his head and said he wondered if he would bleed to death and all his brains would come out. Finally he was beginning to be in touch with his desperate internal plight. His adoptive mother was understandably extremely concerned about the deterioration, as he physically hurled himself from high places and was nearly impossible for her to contain at all at times in her heavily pregnant state, and she requested, with my support, a psychiatric assessment. While I felt that Gary's state of mind was directly linked to a resurgence of feelings of traumatic abandonment because of the pregnancy, mother herself feared he might be having a psychotic episode. (Again there featured here the ghosts of the past: Gary's mother had herself been mentally extremely unstable, and his adoptive mother linked his fragmented states with her fears of a repetition of this.) When a dissociated state changes and the patient is more in touch with his internal plight, work is vital but there may be the risk of suicide or suicidal attempts. In the event, the diagnosis by the psychiatrist, after some discussion with me, of 'ADHD but not needing medication' was a relief to mother, as it disconfirmed her worst fears, and she in turn was more able to contain Gary's panic. He settled down again, and, while I offered a second weekly session during the crisis, she felt she was able to manage. The sessions were still exhausting but did not feel so much on the edge of disaster. Gary could still move in and out of fragmented states, but seemed to be able to be more contained by my active technique. There was no question of my remaining on my chair holding Gary with interpretations alone: it was imperative that I follow him physically and link my interpretations to active physical contact at times of danger. In this context, I thought of the earliest interactions between mother and baby, where the physical interactions involving feeding, holding and cleaning are so intimately bound up with what the baby takes in of the mother, the good object being slowly built up in his mind (Bick, 1968).

On his adoptive mother's due date her husband brought Gary to his session, and this time he *accidentally* fell onto his head as he was holding onto a pillow. I was able to talk to him about shocks and how they made him feel he had been dropped on the head, but that it was important that we could think about them rather than him needing to hurt himself and become addicted to falling. He weathered the birth of his sister at home, but the sessions were again a whirlwind of activity, and he told me darkly 'my badness hasn't gone away'. Alvarez (2012) talks of the need with potentially psychopathic patients for the badness to be acknowledged but without condemnation. Gary was in many senses addicted to disillusion and pain, which in his case had resulted in characterological hardening and damage to himself.

As the therapy continued, Gary began to build spaceships where I had to steer from the back while he crouched at the front in a foetal position only to throw himself out violently and collapse in a heap on the floor. This was a significant development of an attachment relationship, that I took to be a re-enactment of his premature birth to a heroin-addicted mother. In the Francis Tustin Memorial Lecture (May 2000), Suzanne Maiello described work done with an autistic child who had been threatened in the womb by miscarriage. She talked of the foetus's sensitivity to tactile experiences and what might be engendered as the walls of the womb contract prematurely to expel the child too early into the world. One might speculate that for Gary, at a protomental level, there was even at such an early stage an impulse to hurl himself forward rather than passively wait to be expelled.

Later however there was a different birth enactment, where he emerged more quietly, 'with blood on my head', from under my chair. To quote Wilfred Owen again, while Gary previously wanted to rid his psychic eyes 'of the hurt of the colour of blood for ever', he was now beginning the slow work of integration of pain and guilt. In one session he called me 'Mummy' after one such birth enactment. I acknowledged this 'mummy feeling', the beginning of an idea of being held and not dropped. This seems to me not to be an illusion, but rather the first realisation of his previously unrealised preconception of 'something good'.

Trauma and attention deficit disorder

I want to include some necessarily rather brief thinking about Gary's ADHD diagnosis and its relevance to his early history. In 'Wrestling with the whirl-wind: an approach to the understanding of ADHD' (Orford, 1998), the author quotes research done by Perry and his co-workers in 1995. Their approach was neuro-biological, and it has now been proved that early experience does indeed have an effect on the development of neural pathways and later brain functioning. They note that the symptoms of ADHD are very similar to those that occur during trauma: the hyper-alertness, the need to act quickly, to live in constant expectation of danger to the exclusion of other thoughts. What they suggest is that in a critical period in infancy some children experience trauma that initiates an habitual automatic response, as though to external threat. As they grow up, these children are hyper-sensitive to threat and revert to 'action stations' in time of crisis. Babies may be exposed to frightening experiences that cause them to become habituated to feelings of threat. Perry's finding has been that children with ADHD have established neural pathways on the basis of response to threat and trauma. In other words, some traumatised children may develop ADHD. As Schore (1998) also explains, early traumatic events that result in excessive use of projective identification and then dissociation become imprinted in the right brain as primitive defence mechanisms that can potentially affect the regulation (or dysregulation) of feelings throughout the lifespan.

I think it is clear that, for Gary, his early experiences had indeed affected his habitual responses, and in his case he had attempted to avoid being threatened by threatening himself with danger and imminent destruction.

In his paper 'Precipitation anxiety' (Houzel, 1995, p. 65), the author postulates that:

> every object relation is established as a result of a caesura which creates a gradient of psychic energy. This energy gradient is experienced initially as a precipice, pulling irresistibly towards downfall and destruction. [And, as I have already postulated, Gary's premature emergence into the world withdrawing from heroin may indeed have felt like the most destructive and traumatic catapulting into life.] If the encounter with the object is to become possible, the gradient must be regulated in such a way that it can be negotiated with-out damage. Mental communication with the object enables this adjustment to take place: every time such communication is successful, it is as though a new level of stability is created in the slope down to the precipice. In this way, the self's advance towards the object is secured, and there is no danger of destructive collapse.

I think that Gary's earliest experience of being prematurely born heroin addicted to an addicted mother, of being in an incubator, unheld, and then in a chaotic home situation, had not given him the opportunity to experience regulation of the gradient: he frequently felt as if he were hurtling headlong into the precipice, and this profoundly felt anxiety was stirred up most painfully by his adoptive mother's pregnancy. By her own ability to be in touch with this through our work and by my efforts in the therapy to provide regulation and a space for thinking about chaos without sliding into it, Gary has indeed been able slowly and painfully to achieve a new level of stability, although this is still easily undermined by his terror of gaps and changes.

For a child such as Gary, there has been no illusion that he is in charge of the breast and the mother, but only primary disillusion as his hypothetical preconception of a containing maternal presence was not met by a corresponding reality in the external world. His experience could not have been further from the 'progressive disillusion' that Winnicott (1971) hypothesised as being needed for the baby to realise gradually the fact of separation and dependence on an external object that he both hates and loves.

Conclusion

What I hope to have shown is how the devastations that external circumstances have wrought on the internal worlds of late adopted children can then impact on their environment when they finally come to experience some safety, and how they can be most painfully vulnerable to change and development that may then cause similar feelings to reverberate in their adoptive families and in the professional networks surrounding them. Ordinary life events may then re-traumatise a vulnerable child. It is vital to be able to work with these upheavals not only to protect the children themselves and their placements but in order to prevent later resurgence of seemingly intractable difficulties, particularly during adolescence. It is our awareness as professionals of the ongoing issues involved for adoptive parents, at different moments in the developmental cycle of their adoptive children, that can facilitate the giving of time and space to consider the traumatic sequelae of being dropped, both externally and internally. A recent book (ed. Briggs 2015) addresses these issues from various perspectives.

Note

1   This chapter was given as a paper at the EFPP Conference, 'Internal Objects and Psychic Change', in Rome, October 1999, and was then published in a shortened version in *The Emotional Experience of Adoption: A Psychoanalytic Perspective* (Hindle and Shulman, Routledge 2008).

References

Alvarez, A. (1998) 'Failures to link: Attacks or defects?'. *Journal of Child Psychotherapy*, 24(2), 213–31.

Alvarez, A. (2012) *The Thinking Heart: Three Levels of Psychoanalytic Therapy with Disturbed Children*. London and New York: Routledge.

Bauer, P. J. and Hertsgaard, L. A. (1993) 'Increasing steps in recall of events: Factors facilitating immediate and long-term memory in 13.5 and 16.5 month old children'. *Child Development*, 64, 1204–223.

Bick, E. (1968) 'The experience of skin in early object relations'. *International Journal of Psychoanalysis*, 49, 484–6.

Bion, W. R. (1962) *Learning from Experience*. London: Heinemann.

Briggs, A. (2015) *Towards Belonging: Negotiating new relationships for adopted children and those in care*. London: Karnac.

Cooper, A. (1998) Letter in *The Guardian* (April).

Edwards, J. and Maltby, J. (1998) 'Holding the child in mind: Work with parents and families in a consultation service'. *Journal of Child Psychotherapy*, 24(1), 109–33.

Emanuel, R. (1996) 'Children traumatized in infancy'. *Journal of Child Psychotherapy*, 22(2), 214–39.

Fraiberg, S., Adelson, E. and Shapiro, V. (1975) 'Ghosts in the nursery: A psychoanalytic approach to the problems of impaired infant–mother relationships'. *Journal of the American Academy of Child Psychiatry*, 14(3), 387–422.

Freud, S. (1916–17) *Introductory Lectures in Psychoanalysis*, trans. and ed. J. Strachey. New York: Norton, 1966.

Hodges, J. and Steele, M. with Hillman, S., Henderson, K. and Neil, M. (2000) 'Effects of abuse attachment representations: Narrative assessments of abused children.' *Journal of Child Psychotherapy*, 26(3), 433–55.

Houzel, D. (1995) 'Precipitation anxiety'. *Journal of Child Psychotherapy*, 21(1), 65–78.

Klaniczay, S. (2000) 'On childhood stuttering and the theory of clinging'. *Journal of Child Psychotherapy*, 26(1), 97–115.

Lanyado, M. (1999) 'The significance of transitional phenomena in the therapy of two young children moving from long-term fostering to adoption'. Paper presented to the Fostering and Adoption Workshop and the 'Children in Transition: Finding and Sustaining Placements' course at the Tavistock Clinic.

Lupinacci, M. A. (1998) 'Reflections on the early stages of the Oedipus complex'. *Journal of Child Psychotherapy*, 24(3), 409–21.

McAuley, C. (1996) *Children in Long-term Foster Care: Emotional and Social Development*. Aldershot: Avebury.

Maiello, S. (2000) 'Broken links: Attack or breakdown? Notes on the origins of violence'. *Journal of Child Psychotherapy*, 26(2), 5–24.

Maltby, J. (1994) 'The contribution of a child psychotherapist to an adoption and fostering team'. *Fostering and Adoption*, 18(2), 31–5.

Obholzer, A. and Zagier Roberts, V. (eds) (1994) *The Unconscious at Work*. London: Routledge.

Orford, E. (1998) 'Wrestling with the whirlwind: An approach to the understanding of ADD/ADHD'. *Journal of Child Psychotherapy*, 24(2), 253–66.

Owen, W. (1963) *Collected Poems*. London: Chatto.

Schore, A. (1998) *Affect Regulation and the Origin of the Self*. Hillsdale, NJ: Lawrence Erlbaum.

Sprince, J. (2000) 'Towards an integrated framework'. *Journal of Child Psychotherapy*, 26(3), 413–31.

Wilson, P. (1996) 'Winnicott's clinical concepts: The anti-social tendency'. *Journal of Child Psychotherapy*, 22(3), 394–8.

Winnicott, D. W. (1971) *Playing and Reality*. London: Tavistock.

PART 3

THEORY, TEACHING AND LEARNING

The world is all within us, beloved.
Our life is taken up with these transformations
From inner to outer

(Rilke, Duino Elegies No. 7, translated by JE)

This section of the book recounts personal experience both of teaching and of learning about theory over the years. It is a privilege to be able to 'teach' and also to carry on learning about psychoanalysis. For the seasoned clinician, the return to primary texts can be vivifying and stimulating. If you look at the word 'theoretically', however, it is usually followed by some qualification – yes, theoretically, *but* in practice ... Theory that is un-anchored to clinical practice has its place in the academic world of psychoanalysis, but may tend towards what Bion (1962) called 'knowing about knowing' rather than true knowing that is felt in the bones and the heart, and that gathers meaning from both personal and clinical experience. Abstract concepts, for my understanding (and of course I am not alone here), do need to be related to concrete experience. The abstract concept gathers meaning only when it is a step along the way towards a unification of experience, much in the way Marx (1867, 2008, p. 11) described 'ascending to the concrete'. The ideal, he said is 'nothing less than the material world reflected by the human mind, and translated into forms of thought'. It is a two-way process, where the abstract and the concrete inter-penetrate as theory is indeed continually tested by practice. Thus theory itself may develop and grow, and this is the way in which the profession of psychoanalysis retains its vitality and extends the range of its scientific definitions. It is a dialectical method that involves both 'ascent' and 'descent', so that analysis and synthesis are closely interwoven. The living data of clinical work both feeds existing theory and is fed by it. Thus both theory and practice may change and grow over time. Psychoanalysis is not a 'dead' language: it lives and gives life to our clinical work, and may also be extended by it as it has been since its beginnings. The first chapter in this section uses Bion's model of digestion to illustrate this process, and I quote from a novel that had as its main character a university teacher whose own path had been created by this sense of growth and change: he like his students has a sense of discovery as they read texts together. A sense that 'when the subject lies at the centre of a much larger subject ... and one feels intensely that a pursuit of the subject is likely to lead – where, one does not know' (Williams, 2012, p. 41). We stand on the brink of a new world of teaching and learning, as more is enabled 'online', where students can pause, rewind, play over and over. But this is largely in the company of one. Where is this likely to lead? To repeat Williams' phrase, 'one does not know'.

References

Bion, W. R. (1962) A theory of thinking. *International Journal of Psychoanalysis*, **43**, 306–15. Later published in *Second Thoughts*, 1967. London: Karnac.

Marx, K. (1867) In *Capital: A New Abridgement*, (2008) Editor D. McLellan. Oxford: Oxford University Press.

Williams, J. (2012) *Stoner*. London: Vintage Books.

CHAPTER 7

TEACHING, LEARNING AND BION'S MODEL OF DIGESTION

In this chapter I use Bion's model of the digestive process, among other models, in order to think about how teaching of theory can be approached as a task and undertaken in practice. Beginning with the ideas of Plato, I discuss how new ideas may be best conveyed, and how psychoanalytic theory teachers (using the teaching of Melanie Klein's ideas here to make my points) may make what they teach acceptable and 'digestible' to students. I use some material from a theory group as well as a baby observation group, and conclude that in group teaching the responsibility for the taking on and elaboration of ideas – a process of digestion – is shared by the teacher and by the group. As psychoanalytic workers need to be able to 'manage uncertainty' in daily practice, this state of mind can usefully also be held by the theory teacher. The process of digestion will vary according to the composition of any group, drawing out different facets of understanding in both 'teachers' and 'learners', and may well draw on other vertices beyond that of psychoanalysis. These links will aid the process of digesting ideas, and will also be evident in the style, structure and content of this chapter.

Introduction

> But despite Walker [a class disrupter] it was a successful seminar, one of the best Stoner had ever taught. Almost from the first the implications of the subject caught the students, and they all had that sense of discovery that comes when one feels that the subject at hand lies at the center of a much larger subject, and when one feels intensely that a pursuit of the subject is likely to lead – where, one does not know.
>
> (Williams, 2012, p. 41)

The above quotation, taken from a novel about an academic who started out life on a farm, and then became 'consumed' by ideas, struck me as being apt in terms of the adventure that both learners and teachers embark on when considering theory. What is theory for? How do we teach it? In the training of clinicians, is it useful to apply Bion's digestive model to the process of taking on board whatever theory is needed? Can this then lie alongside living with the consulting room experience which is a *sine qua non* for clinical practice and technique to evolve? As Bion himself said:

> The analyst may make as many models as he chooses out of any material available to him. It is important not to confound these ephemeral structures

with realisations on the one hand or theories on the other. The model has a valuable function provided it is recognised for what it is.

(Bion, 1962b, p. 80)

By this Bion is indicating that we form models that derive from interactions during psychoanalytic sessions. Then abstractions from these models may result in the birth of new analytic theories, or may bring the realisation that the abstractions already fit an existing theory. He further asserts that models can be discarded if they fail in this purpose, but that if a model proves useful on a number of occasions it may be transformed into a theory. He also observed elsewhere:

> The view that psycho-analytic papers are to be treated as experiences which affect the development of the reader will not be subscribed to by all psychoanalysts. I do not contend that it is a matter of conscious choice determined by the reader's wishes, but that certain books, like certain works of art, rouse powerful feelings and stimulate growth willy-nilly. As everyone knows, this was so with Freud.
>
> (Bion, 1967, p. 56)

This chapter, then, is written in that spirit, and draws on the impact of subjective experience, as well as writers beyond Bion, Klein and Freud. It is couched in an informal episodic writing style, one that perhaps then results in what could be called a 'reflective essay'. As Bion observed (1967, p. 56), this may not suit everyone in our profession, and they may not 'subscribe' to it. Respect for difference is vital and the thoughts here may provoke further thoughts in the reader, or may not.

At its best, then, theory can offer inward sustenance for the clinician, while s/he gets on with the clinical business of each individual session with patients. That particular and unique situation of being with the Self, in all its many facets, and an Other, is then enabled, as it sits on well prepared soil, a platform of meaning as it were, made from the sustenance of theory, in order to grow whatever may be needed in this particular situation. How can this be conveyed to preclinical students, or to those recently embarked on clinical practice?

In this chapter I explore these questions via my own experience of teaching theory on various different courses at the Tavistock Clinic and elsewhere, where students are at different levels of understanding and experience. This chapter aims to be a kind of thought excursion where I am pulling together ideas from different points of view, in order to unpack any further ideas about how we teach, and how we learn to teach.

Points of view over the centuries

Does Plato have a place here? He was keen to unpack thoughts about teaching and learning. It seems appropriate to start with someone who was keen to impart ideas, in a dialogue that may be compared with that which starts internally, with one's internal objects, as one begins to unpack the thoughts residing in any psychoanalytic paper, prior to the project of communicating them to others.

In his *Socratic Dialogues* (370 BC) Plato (1946, pp. 219–87) sets up a conversation between Socrates and a student, Phaedrus, in which he explores the most effective way for written words to be communicated. He compares writing to painting, where 'the creatures of painting stand like living images. But if one asks them a question, they preserve a solemn silence'. So too with words, he insists:

> every word, once it is written, is bandied about, alike among those who under-stand and those who have no interest in it, and it knows not to whom to speak or not to speak – it has no power to protect or help itself.

Socrates then carefully lays out an argument that the written word cannot defend itself in mere dialogue with the reader, and thus cannot effectively teach anything worth knowing. It is only through back-and-forth discussion and rhetorical argument towards the working out of problems, he maintains, that true knowledge can be conveyed. In this way, he believes, the word can then be 'written with intelligence in the mind of the learner'. *Reading* mere *words*, in his mind, is akin to looking at a lake rather than swimming in it – or looking at a lake, and by so doing, thinking that now you *know* how to swim. Phaedrus takes his point (as he is designed to do): 'You mean the living and breathing word of him who knows, of which the written word may justly be called the image' (Plato, op. cit.).

Socrates' view of course does not take account of the countless thousands of auto-didacts who have, without the benefit of a thinking group, been able to come to some understanding of what they read. However, it does speak to the argument for a text being unpacked and truly 'understood' in the company of others. This is inevitably linked, for my understanding, to the task of teaching and learning about psychoanalysis in a group setting. Discussion can hopefully then result in what Plato via Socrates posits: thoughts 'written with intelligence in the mind of the learner' (Plato, op. cit.). If we do not aim to achieve this, in my view, we have not done the job very effectively.

So Plato is talking about 'the living and breathing word of him who knows' (Plato, op. cit.). Over 2000 years later, the analyst Ogden (2006) talks of 'the inseparability of an author's ideas and the way s/he uses language to express them'. He is referring to the author's way of handling her/his 'living and breathing words'. It was not enough, he said, 'simply to discuss a paraphrased version of ideas developed in an analytic paper, which is to lose touch with the idea that the paper is a piece of writing'. Here we have a strong articulation of the principle of studying primary texts, as well as paying attention to the way the author of those texts has expressed the ideas therein. Ogden offered the idea of reading a text aloud so that:

> it feels that we are not simply discussing an author's ideas, but immersing ourselves intellectually and emotionally in the way s/he thinks and writes – what s/he values/who s/he is, who s/he is becoming and perhaps most import-antly who we are becoming as a consequence of reading and studying together.

In other words, these ideas may then be pegs to hang your thoughts on, as you are in the state of becoming: a work in progress. This includes, as I have previously said, both teacher and learner. This is slow thinking, using primary texts, and anyone in the analytic profession learns over the years that this thinking is of the most valuable kind.

So how can one facilitate the development of this 'slow thinking'? My own view is that the transition needs to be made by the student, with encouragement from the teacher, from theory to practice, so that theory can then be tested by practice. In terms of the meta-development of psychoanalytic ideas, there needs to be a feedback loop in operation. This informs and changes theoretical ideas as clinical evidence refines or amplifies previous thoughts; or even overturns previously held and perhaps reified concepts. The conceptual equipment of psychoanalysis needs not to become ossified, but to have enough flexibility to encompass 'the new idea'. Psychoanalytic workers need to be able to 'manage uncertainty' in daily practice, and this state of mind can usefully also be held by the theory teacher: how will this particular group of students best become able to enlarge their thinking in terms of the theory being conveyed, so that it may occupy a meaningful place in their own future work (and life) experience?

The teacher of psychoanalytic theory and the problem of authenticity and 'validity'

This very naturally leads on to a consideration of one's own biases. In terms of teaching theory to clinical or indeed preclinical students, one's own predilections and attachments to specific theories as well as to one's own analyst, will inevitably have a role to play. While these ideas may seem self-evident, they are often not touched on in meetings thinking about how theory is taught; and at least in my experience, not many meetings of this kind take place in any case. This situation is now changing, however, I am glad to say.

In talking about the evidence base for the validity of psychoanalytic knowledge (and thus the theory that we teach), Hinshelwood (2010, p. 362) spells out how 'research confidence in clinical material has always been the basis of evidence in psychoanalysis'. Of course this firm linkage is a tradition that goes back to Freud, Klein and the other 'first footers' in the area. The generation of psychoanalytic knowledge is thus ongoingly recorded and amplified in the theory that we use, backed always by researches from the consulting room, and the theory that we seek to impart to future generations of clinicians. Of course there are arguments here about terms such as 'validity', and 'scientific research', but these are beyond the remit of what I am addressing here.

Theory and the 'good enough' feed

When teaching theory, the notion of feeding is always in my mind. Perhaps I share this in common with others doing the same job. However, when one is familiar with tried and trusted ideas based on one's own clinical experience over the years, one can run the risk of being too enthusiastic in imparting them, giving too rich a meal at one sitting – one has to be careful not to force feed. There will necessarily be anxiety on the part of the mother/feeder and the fed. This can also be observed as a dynamic between mothers and their young babies, and I will return to this idea later. But it is a sad baby indeed who is left on his/her own with the bottle propped up against a cushion – the human interaction is vital from the start. Theory needs to link to students' personal experience, including of course their analyses where relevant – plus current happenings that may offer useful pointers as to the universality of particular concepts, and work discussion/clinical work. As Barenboim and Said (2003, p. 33) said of music, 'the score is not the truth'. What they emphasised was that one does not do the same thing 'over and over again', but each time finds what is relevant at that particular moment, with the score as the text that is then open to some interpretation in the given moment. I find this notion helpful, and it links with what seems important when imparting 'theory' to a new generation of clinicians. I well recall the London riots of a few years back, when I was thinking with a group of students embarking on clinical work about the adolescent process. We had a Winnicott text to discuss. I brought in some of the sensational front-page pictures of the burning and the looting, and put them on the floor in the middle of the seminar room. My question then was, did these pictures help them associate to ideas they had been studying, about adolescent states of mind?

The role of the teacher

What are the demands placed upon the teacher, and what are the limits at work here? One needs to be mindful of course of the transference of the group and individuals within it to the teacher, and one's own countertranference feelings too, as one progresses towards the evolution of the group dynamic. At the beginning, what kind of internal object is Melanie Klein, for instance, for the student? This may be evident in group comments (as one beginning student said to me 'my social work colleagues told me to stay well away from Melanie Klein') or comments may need to be elicited by the seminar leader. It is vital to give space to these feelings in the group, and I offer up the idea to students that Melanie Klein, for example, like the group, was on her own learning curve: she was growing in her ideas and her thinking, which changed in the light of clinical work, and one hopes that this process of growing the self may also become effective in the group. I encourage one person to present so that pre-digestion is done by at least one other person apart from me. This is a time-honoured Tavistock tradition, at least in the Child and Family Department. I learned this first in the seminars of Gianna Williams on Freud in the 1980s, and she no doubt learned it from Martha Harris (Anne Alvarez, personal communication). I ask the presenter to arrive with questions, comments etc. and I encourage the idea of raising doubts and difficulties, as these will hopefully be learning points for the group. No question is too 'obvious', no question will be unimportant or irrelevant.

Often, as we know, one member of a group may voice issues that belong not only to that individual but to the developing group thinking. Sometimes I ask each student in the group (rather than just 'the presenter') to bring a question or a textual quote that has either struck them – or bothered them – and the latter, as I have emphasised, is an equally important issue. Being 'bothered', a state that disturbs a previously held equilibrium often holds the key to moving forward to new understanding, or clarifying previous understandings. As Bion said in *Second Thoughts* (1967) the turbulence of 'being bothered' usually denotes change. When someone becomes agitated or angry, this might be attributed to pathology, but might also represent a change from a previously held mental state to something new. (On a personal note I remember how 'bothered' was the whole student group when I was in training, taught by Arthur Hyatt Williams, as we struggled with Bion's own ideas.) In this respect I hope it is not stretching a point to call another of Bion's maxims to mind: the transformation of beta elements, unthinkable thoughts, or chaotic unprocessed thoughts, into alpha elements, available for real thinking, not 'knowing about' but 'knowing' (Bion, 1962b, p. 35).

When trying to understand how any individual moves from the un-thought area of beta elements to the area of alpha elements that are the first primitive thoughts, Bion made a link to the model of an infant depending on his mother to process unbearable and unthinkable thoughts, through her reverie, so that they may be then returned to him in more manageable form. The turbulence that may be either an individual or a whole group experience in a theory seminar will need similarly to be processed by the teacher, and rendered more manageable. Thus over time the student is enabled to amplify a theoretical text with her/his own experience, and if this is a subject of group discussion, it adds to the commonality of experience within the group. This continues a time-honoured tradition where theory and technique are closely and ongoingly interrelated in order for developments in thinking to take place. So there is of course a relationship here between the container or the seminar leader, and the contained, the student group. This concept of container/contained was first introduced in Bion's previously mentioned 1962 paper 'A theory of thinking' (Bion, 1962a).

The role of the learner

What I have found over many years of teaching is that it is vital to include the thinking of the 'learners' from the outset, and I would envisage a presentation that includes interactive input, from the beginning, from the participants, as I have emphasised. What I hope this triangular linkage between text, teacher and student provides is a central space within the room (equivalent to the physical space) where conversations can take place, and we can play with ideas, without wanting to reach a prescribed set of 'answers'. There will inevitably be anxiety in students' minds and also my own at the beginning. What I am aiming for is a space to think not filled up by me. This has links back to the feeding model, where the intersubjective space that opens up into a transitional space between mother and infant during feeding with solid food needs to be regulated by the mother, so that she is not forcing the pace in which the infant can take in what she is offering.

So then in this way students can take the juice out of the paper, break ideas down into smaller chunks, chew on them without having to swallow ideas whole, add whatever is needed in terms of their own individual learning 'speed' and their own experience into the digestive process, then discard what does not chime with them at the moment. To use the triangular notion again, we are thinking about a process of ingestion, absorption and excretion. Alvarez (2012, p. 56) talks of introjection as being 'the capacity to get what is being said', and she emphasises that introjection needs to precede more durable internalisations. This of course links back to Bion again, but also sideways to those working in the field of neuroscience, and the developmentalists. New neural pathways do indeed open up as we 'take in' new ideas and experiences, and the developmentalists have been able to capture such moments from the beginning of infantile life. The capacity to 'take in' involves both emotional and cognitive factors. This linkage is one that is beyond my remit to pursue in this short chapter, but is a fascinating and relevant one. Students may come back to the text later in the light of added experience, as of course do we as theory teachers over the years. We 'chew over' internally what we have taken in, and revisit it later. It is my experience that each time I approach what may be a very familiar text, familiarity has not bred contempt, but a different facet of understanding. It is important that an idea (however 'unpalatable' it may at first seem to anyone in the group) be given space and time in the mind before being discarded, if despite this, it still does not chime with where a particular person is at, at a particular time.

In a recent seminar discussing Melanie Klein's later thoughts about the Oedipus complex, there was a split in the group that I was leading. Was this concept credible and valid, or was it something that had become a psychoanalytic 'myth' that was adhered to in a semi-religious way? Could these ideas be tolerated, or would they need to be evacuated, spat out perhaps like unpalatable food? It seemed important to note the split, without labelling it 'resistance' at this point (although one might say of course that it was). Despite the split, we could agree in the group that the ideas remain, and can be revisited. As the mother of any baby knows, when the baby spits out the food, s/he means no, and it is usually fairly useless to force the issue.

Engaging the student in the thinking process

When one is faced with a group of students, how can one ensure that one engages them all in what is going on? Alvarez (2012, p. 30) mentions a paper I used to work from for many years in Child Development seminars. Feelings of efficacy, according to Broucek, the author of the paper called 'Efficacy in infancy' (1979), can be seen very early on in babies, and he gave them ways of using their kicking legs by rigging them up to a device to make bells ring; then calling their engagement and excitement 'almost an object relationship'. This he called 'efficacy'. If the mechanism was unhooked, however, then the babies would withdraw, and 'play possum'. There may be the same phenomenon happening in theory seminars, where those 'playing possum' have not felt that they can engage, or wish to engage, or dare engage, in what is going on. It is up to the teacher to be alert to the 'possums', and find a way of engaging them back into the ongoing thinking process. One student spent the whole year in one group not saying a word. The following year she came back, said she wanted to recapitulate the series, and she began to present and to contribute. She sent me a personal note later thanking me for the tolerance I had shown, in not forcing her 'before I was ready'.

So theorising involves seeing possibilities, establishing connections, asking questions. You need to stop, to ponder, to think again, to view any text from multiple vantage points. There is no marked road here (as there was not of course for the original thinker), and it will depend on the reactions of the group as to where this particular road will go, this particular time, in this particular year. Theory as I have already said seeks to use clinical experience to establish fundamental principles, to evolve concepts, and to link back again to clinical experience from where the concept originally came. While theoretical ideas may be thought of as governing principles, it is important that they do not become rigid and impervious to thought, a template that can then block out really 'digesting' and understanding. For theory to remain fresh for the teacher too, teaching ideally needs to take place in an atmosphere of openness and indeed playfulness. To link this back again to the mother–infant dyad and the first taking in of solid food, too much anxiety on the part of the mother may radically affect how or whether food may be taken in by the infant. In this regard too I consider that student 'feedback' – often seen simply somewhat cynically as something that is gathered solely for academic bureaucratic purposes, is vital, and its findings need to be discussed and incorporated in the onward journey of any seminar series. So the feeding metaphor goes both ways, and necessarily so.

Clinical work in psychoanalysis involves a specific way of being with the Self and Other in order to explore the human unconscious – no notes, no books. I envisage theory as a sort of benign circumference round the clinical space, alongside one's own internal objects, analysts, supervisors etc., to be consulted in one's mind if necessary – supporting the pure culture of the clinical encounter but not overloading it. If we extend this idea into the realm of teaching, the question then arises: do we need to teach differently for different levels of experience? I think one starts from group questions: and it was Bion (1990, p. 24) who exhorted his listeners to 'keep their questions in good repair'. This makes the seminar a place where the level is dictated by the group – it is helpful also to include one's own clinical stories but of course with an eye to confidentiality. Students tend to enjoy the notion that one has used these ideas to some effect, for thinking in the clinical setting, over time. It can add considerably to what might be described as a growing forum of meaning. Humour is also an advantage – not taking oneself too seriously as a leader of the group. I have a few anecdotes that may illustrate in a very simple way any concept that we are trying to puzzle out – for instance projective identification, the Oedipus complex or fusion. Poems too may play a part, as may films the students have seen that speak to the topic being discussed. This again is in line with an honourable tradition: in his *Brazilian Lectures* (1990, p. 41) Bion quotes the seventeenth century metaphysical poet John Donne to illustrate something about the transitional area between beta to alpha elements, from something not thought about, to something that becomes available for thought: 'the blood spoke in her cheek . . . as if her body thought.' Students too then also bring poems and sometimes write poems too – so that they are engaged in a way that enables the theory to take hold inside their minds. I have used film over the years, for instance, to illustrate schizoid withdrawal (Edwards, 2010) as well as the linked phenomena of mourning and melancholia (Edwards, 2014); I have used Renaissance pictures in order to elaborate complex ideas such as the Oedipus complex, where family configurations can illustrate the longings, rivalries and identifications talked about in theoretical texts, and sculpture (Edwards, 2009a), which can then help students understand such phenomena as projection and projective identification. They have shown themselves to be full of thoughts and ideas when such links are made. Theory can thus be seen to be relevant not only to our own time and place, but to previous eras, portrayed then but not elucidated in the way we are helped to do now with the benefit of founding psychoanalytic theoretical thinkers.

The link between theory and observation

This to my mind is a vital link in helping students move forward with their own learning trajectory. The tension between dependence, independence and the growth of autonomy that are at work during the process of development in education, in the minds of both the 'teachers' and the 'learners', is something that can be witnessed from the beginning of life in psychoanalytic infant observation, as mother and baby learn together about how to be, to manage relationship, to be truly alive and to thrive. I have been interested for many years how even 'non-clinical' students find that a two-year psychoanalytically informed observation of a baby or young child growing up in a family and wrestling with the problems entailed in being fully alive can both mirror their own struggles and help them understand unconscious processes in their own fields of endeavour. The baby is struggling to make sense of the world, both internally and externally; the mother is struggling to find out who this particular baby is and may become. Subjective dimensions open up back and forth from outside to inside in all involved in this process: in observer and teacher no less than in baby and caretaker. Lifelong learning experiences are made up of such moments.

This kind of observational research illuminates relationships and processes from the very beginning, and I suggest is also germane here in thinking about theory teaching. I would like to quote some material from an infant observation seminar in a preclinical year, looking at the function of the seminar leader, to illustrate this point in terms of its relation to theory, and to link this up with the notion of feeding and digestion of ideas over time. This material was used elsewhere in a more extensive form (Edwards, 2009b and see Chapter 2 here) to discuss Klein's seminal paper, 'Notes on some schizoid mechanisms' (Klein, 1946). I am aware of course that while some courses prioritise learning from experience – from infant observation for example – before students approach some of the more fundamental theoretical concepts underpinning what they are learning to do, for others in different courses they have already embarked on clinical work. This of course has an interface with the academic demands placed on the student on any particular course.

I had been reading Klein's 1946 paper on splitting one morning with a student group. These preclinical second-year students had struggled with doubts and anxieties about the complexities of Kleinian thought, and tended to approach reading assignments, such as this dense paper, with trepidation. They were half way through the year at this stage, and we were able to think back to the early stages of their observations, which had been done a year previously, and link those experiences with what Klein was describing. Individuals within the group offered some instances from their observations that might be seen to be relevant to this notion of primary splitting. One student voiced the thought that she wished she had known about this paper then, and others agreed. I responded by saying that maybe it was also important to think about the chance to have the experience first without wanting to put a label on it, which could be seen as a defence perhaps deployed in order to avoid the anxiety aroused by witnessing such extreme states. Working in this way enables the observer over time to develop the vital skill of being able to be both receptive and interpretive, which is the core need in therapeutic work with children (and also with adults), as Sternberg (2005) explicates so tellingly.

A baby observation seminar

That very afternoon, something occurred in an observation seminar that was germane to this question of linking practice with theory. I want to include it here as an illustration of how clinical work and theory form as it were an 'inseparable couple'. The excerpt from the seminar shows how a baby, when feeding, could move between two radically different states of mind, from a persecuted state where both milk and mother were seen to be hateful, to one where milk could finally become digested in a state of quiet communion. A baby called 'Lily' was being presented. The observer had hitherto not witnessed any difficult or extreme states during her observations, and felt the mother was a patient and thoughtful carer for her baby. The observer had never seen a nappy change, and had admitted when the group questioned this, that she was concerned to avoid 'messiness'. (I think this desire could be linked also to the wish for 'theory' to be a shiny idealised object, rather than something open to critique and debate. What might be called cognitive neatness is I suggest antipathetic to this project of unravelling meanings, dealing with loose ends, which might be seen as 'messy'.) In this observation, Lily screamed most of the time, and the observer said she felt as 'frazzled' as the mother clearly was. Father was away, and she was coping on her own. Lily screamed loudly with eyes shut, refused the proffered breast, and it was a struggle for mother to keep thinking under the hailstorm of her daughter's cries. The observer said the crying went on perhaps only for ten minutes, but it felt like an hour to her. Finally, the baby calmed, opened her hitherto tightly closed eyes, seemed to 'see' her mother as if for the first time, and settled into a feed from the other breast. It was then too that the mother was able to 'see' the observer.

When we thought about this (with the observer again looking somewhat 'frazzled'), a new dimension was added to the observation – it had been witnessed in the lived experience, written about, and then re-experienced in the seminar with the group. This again I suggest has links with reading theory on one's own, absorbing what is possible, and then re-experiencing it with the benefit of group thinking.

Although these were first-year students, I struggled internally with my 'theory teacher' Self in dialogue with my 'observation teacher' Self, about whether to introduce notions of splitting by reference to Klein's paper, which I had been thinking about with the second years that morning. I decided to do so; to go against what is 'advised'. We had after all first experienced the impact of the observation on the observer, as the baby moved from a state of mind where the breast was intolerable, to a state of mind where quiet feeding could again take place. I did not of course add to their load at this point in their learning path by mentioning Bion's theory of digestion, but this can be seen to be relevant in observations where babies take in milk in different states of mind, and either digest it or regurgitate it. The students in this group found the theory intervention helpful, it further illuminated what the observer herself had originally seen and we also had 'seen' in the seminar. What this illustrates I suggest is that there is always an internal struggle in a teacher, whether of observation or of theory, about how much to feed, and when. For learning to be transformative, it needs to be digested, just as concrete food does, in order to be used productively in the body. The leader has a responsibility to the members of the group, and they hopefully begin to feel this towards one another. It is in this way that members of any group, be it one majoring on theory or on observation, may be able to see the material with what one member of an observation group said of another, 'your new eyes'.

Transformative learning?

Other scholars, beyond the world of psychoanalysis share the purpose of transformative learning. I think there may be shared agreement here: all researches into the teaching process contribute to better understandings of the shifts in the learner's perspective of him/herself, in various ways, individually and collectively, cognitively, socially, emotionally, artistically, biographically and/or intuitively. I suggest that all of these aspects may be enabled to develop in the teaching of theory. These ideas, as I have formerly said, can hopefully be allowed to 'play' in the constructive and creative space not only within any teaching seminar, but in the world of 'the teachers' as we consider how we all continue to learn. In this way I think we may contribute to an enlivened understanding of how education in its best sense works, and how it may free the individual from the constraining bonds of previously received ideas. With this in mind in my own teaching endeavours, I frequently include aesthetic experiences I may have had myself in terms of a film, a play, a poem, that link with what we are discussing and the text we are critiquing. This encourages the students themselves to bring their own contributions, as I have said earlier. This is, it seems to me, one of the important points of group teaching, to link what is being studied to other 'ways of seeing'.

The proof of the pudding?

The proof of the pudding, so the old saying goes, is in the eating. What follows is of course not a general 'proof', and in each group setting different reactions will be evoked and expressed by group members. I use the metaphor here simply to extend the thinking around the digestive processes involved in taking on something new. This will be tempered by students' experience, their previous professions, their personal histories and their analyses, as well as their constitutions. How does the digestion process move forward? And how is the 'food' seen by the group? As in my quotation above of one observation seminar group, in terms of splitting both in theory and then on the ground as it were, the comments recorded below were elicited by me half way through the year of thinking about the work of Melanie Klein. I emphasised that the comments ideally should not be made to 'please' the seminar leader, but to further group understanding of how theory may indeed be ingested and incorporated – or not. I hoped that by this time there was enough feeling of safety within the group for this to be possible. I had talked to the students one week about this (we met fortnightly) and they came prepared with ideas about this for the next seminar.

The resultant comments were indeed varied. An art therapist said that the reading had deepened her understanding of her patients and given her a stability from which to understand her work further. Another volunteer said that she had valued the idea I had offered of 'sitting with' an idea rather than rejecting it immediately, and she could acknowledge her own resistances through doing this. A third said that there had been an oscillation between thinking the ideas 'brilliant' and 'not relevant'. One (very experienced) student said that reading the theory had made her feel 'de-skilled' – but then she found that supervision was a place where theory and practice could be brought together. (She had volunteered her own very helpful clinical examples during the seminar times.) One student said that when she started to think about putting pen to paper in order to write her essay, she had experienced an intensity of feeling: she wondered whether she had been 'corrupted' (her words) by Klein's 'brutal view'. There were many other comments, but what stood out to me was the student who talked of 'a foreign tongue' – she became upset and talked about the chaos she often felt in relation to the ideas we discussed. Later she sent me a message which she has allowed me to quote here:

> I have found the discussions and reading on Klein very thought-provoking. I don't know about you, but to me, when reading the material, it is not just an academic exercise; it's intensely personal too, because what she is saying, she is saying about persons and so this challenges me in lots of ways. Also, before it can become of use, I need to digest it and, like any rich meal, it takes time and cannot be rushed and sometimes, eating too much, too soon can make one sick or bloated! I attach a poem by Sujata Bhatt [this was about a poet writing in a foreign tongue] that has been on my mind lately in my experience of reading Klein. I think, amongst other things, it conveys a search for one's own tongue, not just the mother tongue that is used by one's community or the foreign tongue; and that this search involves some wrestling, within and without; like Jacob wrestling with the angel, one is never the same afterwards: there is a wound and a blessing. It feels like growth; it's just painful, at times.

I think it was important for this student to bring to the group the feeling of being overloaded with something 'too rich' (despite my best efforts to temper Klein's 'richness', in the way I have described above). I thanked her for her bravery in voicing something that no doubt others also felt. As theory teachers I think we always need to be mindful about what gets voiced, and what remains latent, in terms of the impact of 'the new ideas'.

Conclusion

My quotation at the beginning from the novel *Stoner* was chosen in order to illustrate something of the lively cooperative collaboration that needs to take place if 'true learning' is to evolve in a theory seminar. The protagonist of the novel, the eponymous Stoner, was a lecturer who felt initially drawn to – he knew not what – in a poem: Shakespeare's sonnet 73. Sonnet 73 is a meditation on separation and loss. This aroused his curiosity and his daring to take the next step, to leave behind his parents and the world of the farm where they lived. This was a huge leap for him. I realise in hindsight too that this example speaks to something at the heart of my own experience, which I have written about in a personal memoir (Edwards, 2015). We are asking students to make a leap too, in taking on 'new ideas' with an open mind, much as the infant opens her/his mouth for the new solid food that will be a replacement for the breast, which may be thought of as having been 'lost', but will also provide exciting new adventures in taste and in growing up. Mother is keen, even passionate, for the child to accept the new food, and the child's interest and passion is also aroused. Mother needs to ensure that her own passion is modulated, to suit the infant's rhythm in terms of timing and temperature. At its best, it is a benign cycle of reciprocity and cooperation. Passion can be contagious, and it is my suggestion that if we can teach with conviction and 'passion', this will be engendered in learners too. 'Thinking for oneself' is a state of being that can best be nurtured through this kind of reciprocal relationship, within a theory group, and it will hopefully remain 'experience near'. No two groups will be the same: the material studied will act as a stimulus to provoke the never-ending puzzling over difficult ideas, perhaps conflicting points of view, towards genuine understanding at a deep level. Student 'feedback' is vital in order to ensure that the teaching remains authentic and digestible. This is true learning from experience, which Bion (1962b) had flagged up as having its roots in the mother/infant relationship, both at a physical and also a psychological level. The responsibility lies both within the leader and within the group. This of course has ramifications beyond the world of theory teaching: lifelong learning experience is made up of such encounters between minds.

Acknowledgements

I would like to thank the many generations of students who have taught me to teach better over the years, and the course tutors who have given me the space to do the work.

References

Alvarez, A. (2012) *The Thinking Heart: Three levels of Psychoanalytic Therapy with Disturbed Children*. London and New York: Routledge.

Barenboim, D. and Said, E. W. (2003) *Parallels and Paradoxes: Explorations in Music and Society*. London, New York, Sydney and New Delhi: Bloomsbury.

Bion, W. R. (1962a) 'A theory of thinking'. *International Journal of Psychoanalysis*, 43, 306–15. Later published in *Second Thoughts*, 1967. London: Karnac.

Bion, W. R. (1962b) *Learning from Experience*. London: Heinemann.

Bion, W. R. (1967) *Second Thoughts*. London: Karnac.

Bion, W. R. (1990) *Brazilian Lectures*. London: Karnac.

Broucek, F. J. (1979) 'Efficacy in infancy: A review of some experimental studies and their possible implications for clinical theory'. *International Journal of Psychoanalysis*, 60, 311–16.

Edwards, J. (2009a) 'Seeing and being seen: Anthony Gormley's *Event Horizon*. Tavistock Scientific Meeting'. *Journal of Psychoanalysis, Society and Culture*, 68, 31–50.

Edwards, J. (2009b) 'Early splitting and projective identification'. *Journal of Infant Observation*, 11, 57–65.

Edwards, J. (2010) 'Teaching and Learning about psychoanalysis: Film as a teaching tool with reference to a particular film, *Morvern Callar*'. *British Journal of Psychotherapy*, 26, 80–99. A shortened version in C. Bainbridge and C. Yates (eds), (2014) *Media and the Inner World*. London and New York: Palgrave Macmillan.

Edwards, J. (2014) 'Sifting through the sands of time: Mourning and melancholia revisited via the documentary film *Nostalgia for the Light*'. *International Journal of Psychoanalysis*, 95, 791–9.

Edwards, J. (2015) *Pieces of Molly: An Ordinary Life*. London: Karnac.

Hinshelwood, R. D. (2010) 'Psychoanalytic research: Is clinical material any use?' *Psychoanalytic Psychotherapy*, 24, 362–79.

Klein, M. (1946) 'Notes on some schizoid mechanisms. *International Journal of Psychoanalysis*, 27, 99–110.

Ogden, T. (2006) 'On teaching psychoanalysis'. *International Journal of Psychoanalysis*, 87, 1069–85.

Plato. (1947) *Five Dialogues*, Everyman's Library no. 456. London and New York: J. M. Dent & Sons, pp. 219–87.

Sternberg, J. (2005) *Infant Observation at the Heart of Training*. London: Karnac.

Williams, J. (2012) *Stoner*. London: Vintage Books.

CHAPTER 8

BEFORE THE THRESHOLD

Destruction, reparation and creativity before the depressive position

Introduction

> The analyst may make as many models as he chooses out of any material
> available to him. It is important not to confound these ephemeral structures
> with realisations on the one hand or theories on the other. The model has a
> valuable function provided it is recognised for what it is.
>
> (Bion, 1962, p. 80)

It was at the beginning of the Renaissance that Western European humanity's quest
for meaning turned back to classical literature, and a re-acquaintance with the
Greek myths, where the gods are fashioned in the image of men. Freud, in his
inspired reframing of the Oedipus myth, united this ancient tale of adversity with
a psychoanalytic understanding of what Segal (1989, p. 1) called 'the central conflict
of the human psyche'. Klein indicated an earlier starting point for Oedipal striving
than Freud, locating its inception in the second half of the first year of an infant's
life (1946 [1975]). Segal suggested subsequently (1991, pp. 85–100) that Oedipal
struggles that result in a consciousness rooted predominantly in depressive
reconciliation are a *sine qua non* for any creative undertaking. As Bion (1962)
formulated it, Love, Hate and Knowledge are 'the three factors I regard as intrinsic
to the link between objects considered to be in relation to one another' (1962,
p. 93). Bion talks of K, or knowing, in relation to objects, both external and internal, in what he calls a 'commensal relationship' – a way of formulating Klein's
'epistemophilic instinct' (Segal, 1998). The complexity of this emotional experience
is given 'a system of notation' – in other words, a way of marking out of territory
involved in getting to know the other. The dialectical interplay of these elements
or essential experiences will, under adequate conditions, result in a realistic and
mixed picture of the self as well as of objects. In other words, to map Bion on to
Freud and Klein, the acceptance and internalisation of the parental couple, which
the subject paradoxically both loves and hates, allows the unfolding of knowledge
of the self in the light of the reality principle.

I suggest that while the achievement of the depressive position has been seen
as a necessary prerequisite for creative struggle, where reparative gifts are offered
to compensate for past destructive urges, creativity itself may also develop outside or before this 'position'. This does not diminish the importance of the impulse
towards reparation as part of the creative process. Using the myths of Ariadne and

Orpheus, I suggest a prior or perhaps parallel development. Just as the struggle with love and hate inside the mind sets in train the path towards self-knowledge, I suggest that doubt, which includes dread (perhaps 'named' dread), despair and uncertainty, together with hope, exist on a continuum that extends from manic, unreal hope to something more like Bion's faith in a good object, and are pre-requisites in the onward path towards creativity. Creativity represents a fundamental human endeavour not solely to do with guilt and the desire to repair, but also with an innate drive to participate in human discourse – what Grotstein (2004) has called 'the truth drive'. While Klein and Segal implicitly suggest a dialectic, there is a generally held view that does not encompass what I am articulating here. The latter might be formulated as a paranoid-schizoid type of creativity, which may need to precede the depressive position, and paves the way for it. The 'threshold' of the depressive position in some cases post-dates the subject's creative interaction with the environment. This involves both losing and finding, both of the object and within the self. This finely balanced dialectic begins in infancy, and continues throughout life, in social and cultural engagement, and in the production of cultural artefacts, from a child's first attempts during play to the products of adult endeavour.

By playing creatively with elements of the personality, which are precursors to the 'depressive position', deprived and borderline children may offer themselves the opportunity to move on. I have often had cause to ponder on the 'classical' notions about the roots of creativity. The work discussed here indicates something about a 'pre-position' related to the impulse to *repair the self* before reparation of the object.

As a rider to Melanie Klein's thoughts about 'states' and not 'stages', which have been so fruitfully taken forward by authors such as Britton (1998) and Steiner (1993), what I propose is a set of *not necessarily sequential* processes delineating the flux of the internal world externally in terms of creative acts. It is this very aspect of achievement in the real world that presents a continuum of creative endeavour from a work of art to the capacity to engage creatively in relationships inside the mind, and thus in the external world. Achievement in itself allays persecutory anxiety and reduces the need for omnipotent defences. I previously traced this oscillating spiral process through some of W. B. Yeats' poems (Edwards, 2003), connecting it with Ehrenzweig's theory about the process of artistic creativity. He says that ideas are projected in what he calls a 'manic' way into a creative internal womb or 'black hole' within the self, and chaos needs to be tolerated until meaning ensues. This requires courage, in order that the fragments can be borne without an escalation of anxiety that might cause the personality itself to fragment. This points the way towards the borderline between creativity and 'madness'. As Winnicott said: (1958 [1992, p. 150]): 'Through artistic expression we can hope to keep in touch with our primitive selves whence the most intense feelings and even fearfully acute sensations derive, and we are poor indeed if we are only sane.'

Mythic parallels

The myth of Oedipus with its tragic outcome has been fruitfully mined since the time of Freud by subsequent analytic thinkers, and I suggest there might be other aspects of the Greek pantheon where psychic truths about creativity could be expanded, linking this with work done with children who would be destined not to develop at all if we accepted that creativity only begins when the subject enters, or is on, the threshold of the depressive position.

When one reads a compilation of these myths, telling the story of Zeus and his quarrelsome family, one has the impression that all human predicaments were indeed attributed to these gods. I was drawn to the stories of Ariadne and of Orpheus, which indicate a forward trajectory into relatively unknown territory, via the labyrinth and the underworld. This is what every individual struggles to achieve, in the move beyond the parental space, and it may also symbolise the journey on which both patient and therapist embark.

The implication of this in ordinary development has not, I suggest, been sufficiently explored hitherto. The baby needs to forgive the mother during the process of weaning, and s/he turns to solid food, where the new tastes partly contain the representation of the lost object but also the challenge of new experience. This is a forward move, which is implied but not emphasised in Hannah Segal's formulations.

I want to consider certain aspects of these two myths in a similar way that one would use clinical vignettes to illustrate a hypothesis. This hypothesis essentially lies outside the realms of psychopathology, and yet may well also potentially include it, insofar as the subjective self may have internalised, or not, an adequate Oedipal constellation. This capacity may have been hindered by the environment as well as by internal factors, as indeed Klein (1937, p. 339) indicated:

> It is true, parents [or lack of parents] may have been lacking in love or understanding, and this would tend to increase difficulties ... if the child is not afforded enough happiness in his early life, his capacity for developing a hopeful attitude as well as love and trust in people will be disturbed.

Ariadne offered to Theseus a ball of magic string, so that he could enter the Cretan labyrinth with a tool to aid his return, having secured a pledge from him that she could return to Athens with him as his wife. At the heart of the labyrinth lay the Minotaur, the monster born of a union between Pasiphae, the wife of Minos, and the white bull of Poseidon. Theseus had vowed to destroy him. After the mission was accomplished, Theseus unaccountably abandoned his promise and Ariadne, leaving her asleep, broken-hearted and abandoned, on an alien shore that she had chosen over and above loyalty to her parents and her motherland.

I suggest that for Theseus what takes place is not integrated into the psyche; Ariadne turns from being a helpful good object into a persecuting one, imbued with his own projected destructive impulses. Thus he loses the opportunity to achieve what Klein called 'the true harmony of peace' by rebuilding the internal world. Ariadne becomes in a sense a 'failed object' as a reflection of his own failure.

In the second story of Orpheus and Eurydice, Orpheus, presented with a lyre by Apollo, even moved rocks with his sublime music. On his return from voyages with the Argonauts, he married Eurydice – the beginning of a new stage of development in terms of a united creative couple. But Eurydice then died of a snake bite. Orpheus was in despair and charmed Hades' ferryman Charon with his music, travelling to the underworld, where he secured a promise from Hades himself that Eurydice could follow him back to the upper world. The sole condition was that Orpheus should not look back during the journey. But on reaching sunlight, he forgot his promise and turned round anxiously to check that she had indeed been able to follow him. He lost her for ever.

There are alternative versions of this story, but the fact that this version has survived until the present day underlines, I suggest, a variety of possible unconscious meanings. There is the need to descend into an unknown, dark place in order to restore a creative link with oneself, and the danger of being drawn back through a lack of confidence in that same creativity. There is no marked road: the individual embarks on the journey in hope and doubt. If one makes a link with the myth of the labyrinth and the process of birth, this new journey involves the birth of the creative self, and will hopefully involve emergence into some 'light' after the lack of touch-points in a dark space, or as Ehrenzweig (1967) formulated it, the 'creative womb' within the self. There will be the struggle between doubt and faith in the reliability of the good object.

Limentani (1998) notes the twentieth-century's fascination with the Orpheus myth and suggests that it was the failure to work through Oedipal issues that caused Orpheus' reparative gesture to fail, and he lost his good object twice. While we might imagine different reasons for his turning round (greedy love and ambivalence being two of these), I suggest that it was doubt in his own creative capacities (his music) that caused him to lose his good object.

So as a starting point I want to think about the two myths as examples of tasks that both failed but for different reasons. One involved doubt in the goodness of the self (Orpheus' more depressive concern) and one involved doubt in the goodness of the object (Theseus' more persecuted stance). These doubts about self and object lie at the heart of our work, even perhaps prior to Oedipal concerns.

In the second of her classic papers dealing with the depressive position as an ego state in the psyche of the infant, Klein emphasises, 'in normal as well as abnormal mourning, and in manic depressive states, the infantile depressive position is activated . . . the child in his early development goes through a transitory manic depressive state as well as a state of mourning' (Klein, 1940, pp. 363–7).

In both these stories we have the notion of a young couple, united in a bond of love, setting out to discover something in a dark and problematic space. At the heart of Theseus' labyrinth lies something monstrous, the product of a union between a goddess and a bull, a 'combined object' of powerful fear that we could see as a projection of the child's hostile phantasies. One might think of the ball of string as similar to an umbilical cord that guides the subject back into hidden labyrinthine depths, and aids his return so that he or she is not lost in primordial chaos. In this case, what was brought back was a destructive impulse that then prompted dissolution of the link between the new couple. What began in hope and trust ends in doubt and despair.

In contrast, despair at Eurydice's death drives Orpheus on to descend into the realms of death to rescue the creative part of the self, in the hope that there can be a restorative link. Doubt overcomes hope in the final moments. Nevertheless what the story embodies is the impulse to move forward and create a new partnership with the self. With Orpheus, the doubt seems to relate to a part of the self, his music. His self-doubt puts him into a different relationship from Theseus to his good object, although in both cases loss ensues.

These myths remain so potent, I believe, because of this notion of a quest into the depths, which is a necessary prerequisite for creative acts to be won from the void. In the same way a child, particularly a deprived child, approaches his therapy facing the task of entering a problematic internal space never previously broached.

Although both these tales document failure, the important issue is that both Theseus and Orpheus made the attempt, risking extinction and annihilation. Deprived and borderline children come into psychoanalytic treatment with precious little internal reliance on good objects to guide them. Whereas we, as practitioners, have an idea of possible outcomes, they possess no similar understandings. They must take the plunge and enter dark and chaotic spaces, before there has been a notion about the destruction of good objects and the wish to repair them.

As Likierman (2001, p. 116) points out, if Klein's original ideas are considered (and they quite frequently still are) simply in terms of a 'move' from paranoid-schizoid to depressive, this oversimplifies the notion and leaves out important dimensions about continual movement that have been elaborated by post-Kleinian thinkers such as Bion, Segal and Joseph.

The psychoanalytic view

I want to return to Freud and his insistence that the need to create something exists in order not to become ill (1914). As he observes later, 'as a rule people fall ill because of frustration, of non-fulfilment' (p. 450). However, in his study of Leonardo, Freud (1910) suggests that the capacity for genius (and I would add for all our ordinary creative endeavours) is the ability to strike out on one's own without the need necessarily to derive authority from the past, while not disrespecting it either. In other words, there may be the need to put to one side, but with respect, the authority of 'the ancients', the parents, in order to move on to find what lies in the subject's own internal world as a result of a forward rather than a backward look. Frances Tustin, in describing her analysis with Bion, quoted his maxim that 'you do not need to be limited by your lecturers, teachers, analysts, parents. If you are there is no room for growth' (Mitrani and Mitrani, 1997, p. 7).

Klein (1929 [1975]) understood children's play in her consulting room to have links with profound unconscious phantasy, associated with parental figures, and came to consider that anxiety and guilt were the driving forces in the urge to symbolise. It is noteworthy that she also mentioned (but did not elaborate on) what I am exploring here, when she talked about *parts of the self* that the subject is driven to repair or restore. In one of her middle-period papers, when she was drawing together her previous thinking about the development of mental functioning, she emphasises that rejected aspects of the self, while they contribute to instability, 'are also at the source of inspiration in artistic productions' (1958 [1975 p. 245]) – and I would also consider this to encompass children's play.

It was Segal (1957) who wrote about the capacity to make symbolic reparation, a consequence of the working through of the depressive position, and the acceptance of the parental couple. She linked this later (1991) with creative productions in art and literature. Britton (1998, p. 32) emphasised that 'the depressive position and the Oedipus situation are never finished', and have to be reworked at different stages. As analytic workers with both adults and children experience, there can be fluctuations in one session between these different states of mind.

In a chapter examining what he calls 'existential anxiety' in Rilke's *Duino Elegies*, Britton (1998) describes Rilke's desperation when 'I prayed to rediscover my childhood; it has come back and it is just as difficult as it used to be'. His mother was still mourning the death of an earlier child during Rilke's infancy. Rilke was in fact a replacement child. Clearly, Rilke's anguished state pushed him almost to the borders of psychosis. Britton maintains, in order to remain within the creativity/depressive position paradigm that, 'to write as well as he did, Rilke had to be functioning in the mode of the depressive position' (p. 149). However, Britton goes on to say something rather different: that the writing was a *means* to move from a paranoid to a depressive state. I would like to underline that Rilke was in this respect similar to deprived and borderline children. He used the act of composing as a way to move from a predominantly paranoid to depressive mode, as the most deprived of our patients may also do. He called his writing 'a kind of self-treatment'.

When a deprived or borderline child has had a profoundly unpromising beginning, more because of deficits in the environment than primarily in his own constitution (although there is of course a dialectic between the two), there may continue to exist the preconception of a better object, but it requires constitutional resilience to turn to it and to use it without the envious impulse to destroy a good object previously unavailable. Regret for what was not available is of course very different from remorse, but, I suggest, also important. Whereas classical psychoanalysis addresses important concepts about the object, it has less to say, it seems to me, about recovery from the persecuting aspects that have caused damage to the self.

If there has been very little or no good experience externally, the infant/child may indeed feel internally that the lack is the outcome of his or her own hatred and aggression. This is not a realistic view, and may result in dissociation or over-identification with damaged objects. A move forward will involve the gradual integration of unsatisfactory objects, and it is important that the child has the opportunity to regret this, rather than feel guilty and be involved in what Winnicott (1958 [1992, p. 91]) called 'false reparation'.

In Rilke's *Sonnets to Orpheus*, Britton notes (1998, p. 162) that the poet demonstrates what could be described as his version of the depressive position. Here he can value his grief because he values what is lost, and *what he never had*. The inner void begins to transform into a container for thought, and by naming his losses he moves from paranoid-schizoid to depressive mode. This is in essence the same journey as that which takes place in the consulting room with child psychotherapists and their most damaged patients. When loss is acknowledged, but alongside gain, growth can begin. This involves acknowledging deficits not only, and often not principally, in the subject, but in the environment and the external objects. Creative play, or even play that at first seems to lack real creativity, can be a beginning, when there is certainly no capacity to acknowledge indebted-ness, or guilt, and often very little reason for the patient to do so at this stage. I suggest that in terms of psychic development the myths of Ariadne and Orpheus, which include references to being lost in the labyrinth and consumed by a 'black hole' beyond the river representing a separation between psychic aliveness and psychic despair, may often *precede* the myth of Oedipus. Creativity that is initiated in a more paranoid mode can gradually come more under the aegis of depressive concerns but may need, in order to remain 'alive', to revisit empty spaces not too saturated with guilt about parental objects. In other words there may be a split mode of functioning, where good has hitherto been only minimally developed.

Clinical explorations

Episodes of catastrophic anxiety denote pathological states, but what I suggest is that the creative act, in a child's most exploratory play or in adult endeavours, involves of necessity a leap beyond or away from previously known structures. This may either reproduce a potentially (although hopefully temporary) paranoid state, or occur within such a currently existing state. This is a state of fear, rather than of guilt. There may then follow feelings of safety and the beginnings of the building of a secure internal base. There is a fear of risk-taking embedded, I suggest, in the creative act; but risk-taking is a behaviour necessary for evolution to take place. We may be fortunate enough to have the internal support of our trainings and our parental psychoanalytic objects to help us; we have nevertheless to go forward on our own into a new space, in order for thinking to continue to evolve.

Clinical vignettes

Here I offer three examples from my own caseload over the years to illustrate emergence from the 'black hole', and the gradual move into something more depressive, but located still in general in a paranoid-schizoid mode. These are not of course full case studies, but extracts, used in order to indicate something about turning points 'before the threshold'. It is interesting to note, in terms of constant learning, how one revisits one's clinical practice as well as theoretical texts in order to think about current preoccupations. Whereas theory can elucidate clinical concerns, it may also, of course, be modified by it, as Bion's statement at the beginning of this paper intimates. What I hope this section will show is that creativity (here seen to be expressed in a poem, a story and the dawning of a new picture of the self in relation to better objects) can emerge and *result* in a more depressive integration, rather than vice versa, as in the classical formulation. Even in acutely split states, there can take place the building of an ideal object on one side of the divide that can then mitigate the more paranoid aspects of the personality.

Birth from a black hole

The first case involves intensive (four times weekly) treatment of a post-autistic adolescent boy, Joe, described in fuller detail elsewhere (Edwards, 1994 (also in Alvarez and Reid, 1999) and in Chapter 4 here). One's patients, as I have said, continue to have a life inside one's mind. When I was pondering on my current theme, material from his case, only tangentially referred to earlier, presented itself as being crucially involved here. It is perhaps sufficient to say that this boy, born prematurely as one of twins, where the healthy non-incubated twin went home while he remained in hospital, came into a second analytic treatment as a young adolescent. His first treatment as a young latency boy had been initiated when he was attending a small local school for children with behavioural and learning difficulties. This first treatment ended after two years when it became clear that having received some benefit from it, a break might be helpful so that he could integrate what he had received over time.

Joe re-referred himself as an adolescent, with the help of his parents, after an incident where he felt rejected by a 'girl-friend' (more in his phantasy than a real relationship) and had what he called 'my little breakdown'. His difficulty with relationships was still marked. He had a stated fear of black holes, those phenomena often appearing in work with patients on the autistic spectrum first noted by Tustin (1972). I hypothesised that his traumatic birth had caused him to evacuate thinking wholesale. He presented consequently as obsessive, having a compulsion to intrude into his objects in a way that resulted in inappropriate social boundaries. His family's hope was that after a pause in latency for developments to be consolidated, this second treatment in mid-adolescence (he was sixteen when we began to work together) might enable him to reconnect with the world in a more realistic and appropriate way. Hope was indeed a feature of the treatment from the beginning, but it resided in those around Joe rather than being something he could envisage in an ordinary rather than a manically unrealistic way.

From the beginning I was aware of Joe's intense gaze, which seemed like a desperate clinging to his object for fear of falling forever into the black hole:

> Joe described how his only escape from anxieties was 'to sort of go into distance'. At this point he looked at me very intently and I both had the feeling he wanted to get inside me or wanted me to be inside his mind, and also feared it. What he described as 'distance' might really hold something fearful and dangerous, paradoxically, about closeness.

As is frequently the case, in my experience, this first session contained in compressed form the core difficulties we would both be up against that would involve possible modification of modes of relating, particularly primarily adhesive and intrusive identification. I was aware that my task would be to reduce his persecution and build some hope – a state preceding the depressive position. His dread was too great; it was vital to help hope to grow.

A few months into his treatment he told me of a dream, the only one he ever related during our work. *He was in a train, which was slowing down, making noises as if it were going to stop: 'I was well terrified.'* I later hypothesised that this might relate to events just before his birth, before he felt catastrophically ejected from relative safety into the 'black hole' of life without his mother and his twin sister. It also reminded me of the infinite slowness described as being endemic to the astronomical black hole, where gravity collapses (Hawking, 1989). It was noteworthy to me that his initial shambling presentation, as if he might at any time somehow disintegrate, did begin to change as we worked together. This boy's positive preconceptions had not, in an actual sense, been confirmed by realisations. He had not been able to make that initial contact with his mother's eyes, her breast and her arms, and have a sense of himself being firmly held, in body and in mind. Later he managed to confess to me his profound fears about this black hole, an internal state of primordial chaos, space without the dimension of boundary and time. If I commented on this, he would only become more terrified and disconnected. I learned the wisdom over time of Alvarez's words (Alvarez, 1992). Rather than increase his terror by comments about this 'black hole' state, I learned, by seeing what my words could escalate, that the way to help him carry on thinking was to make suggestions about how hard it was for him to believe that he would *find* me each time he came to the clinic, and that he would *find* his Mum again at home. At first, I was the one who needed to provide some navigational signs that this black hole could be reconfigured. Later he was able to introject some measure of hope himself. Here is the helpful notion of an additional triangle, in relation to the self, where the subject balances the forces of doubt and hope in the evolution of creative space. For this boy this balance needed to *precede* ambivalence about his objects, and the path towards the depressive position.

Slowly, through a minute monitoring of his fluctuating states, and what Emanuel (2001) called 'courageous mindfulness', something less terrifying emerged. Joe came in 'from distance'. In one session, he arrived saying he had written a poem for the first time in his life. Shyly he stood in the middle of the room, looking uncertain and a little lost, took a deep breath and recited his poem. It was about a silver surfer, lost in space, but now joined to the mother ship by the breathing line. This seemed to be a very direct reference to his rediscovery in his treatment that he was connected, even though at times still adrift, to a thinking line that was being created between us. Later I connected this poem with Esther Bick's description of the newborn baby as an astronaut shot into space without a space suit (Bick, 1968).

For Joe, his actual birth experience had only exacerbated these terrifying early feeling states. My counter-transference at the beginning of Joe's treatment had been one of fragmentation and dispersal, reflecting this early primitive state. As the balance between love and hate slowly changed, and I am not suggesting that these were at this point integrated, so the capacity for creativity was building up, as his poem indicates. In a sense one might hypothesise this as the positive side of a predominantly paranoid position.

Linking this back to the myth of Ariadne and Theseus, Joe had discovered through our work together a thread or breathing line that could lead him forward from the timelessness of the black hole into ordinary life time. This initially rather fragile link had to be reworked many times, until the day when he told me that his favourite piece of music, by his jazz hero, was called 'On Solid Ground'. At last he had reached somewhere that had a time and space location. It was this treatment, in its vicissitudes and painfully slow developments, that initiated my interest in the chaos of mindlessness and possible ways out of it.

At the end of his treatment his parents noted how he had narrowed the developmental gap between himself and his twin sister, and a few years later he was living independently, an outcome they had previously not dared to hope for.

Desperate creativity

The second patient I want to talk about is a six-year-old adopted boy, who I will call Darren, prematurely born heroin-addicted to a heroin-addicted mother (See also Chapter 6 here). He was referred by his adoptive mother at the suggestion of his extremely tolerant primary school. He challenged all boundaries and needed almost constant one-to-one supervision. The school staff could sense that this was a boy who possessed a more than average intelligence, but who could not make use of what he was offered because of this puzzling behaviour. They knew simply that he had been adopted a couple of years previously. His older brother James, in his last year at primary school, often found Darren's behaviour an embarrassment, although he was also very loyal to him. Darren had, despite his chaotic presentation, an engaging personality, which I think was why the school was willing to persevere in the face of daily erosion of boundaries and routine.

Here again this was a birth severely compromised by external circumstances, with gross deprivation and abuse, that had resulted in a development of hyper-vigilance. The early fragmented nature of ordinary infantile experience had been further fragmented by external experience that held no meaning and much anxiety and fear. The word 'deprived' usually notes the disappearance of a previously better state. For this boy, privation had begun in the womb: there was nothing to mourn in terms of loss. He had been emotionally dropped not once but many times, and was predominantly in a persecutory state. Nevertheless, progress towards the depressive position was made through creative play – and it was his therapist too who had to struggle with the doubt that anything could be achieved in once-weekly work with such a damaged boy. But this was what could be managed by his adoptive family. After a series of very helpful family meetings, where James too could put his point of view about the ambivalence he felt, and I heard much more about Darren's early history (his mother had been a distant relative of his adoptive mother's), Darren's own evident settling into the space for thoughts, even chaotic ones, to be reflected on, was encouraging for all.

After a short time in his birth mother's chaotic house, Darren had been looked after by his grandmother. Grandmother was also in quite a desperate state, and after a suicide attempt while she was supposed to be looking after Darren, he was cared for in a series of foster placements, from the age of about eighteen months. Development slowed down, he stopped making attempts to speak, even stopped growing. Speech and growth itself started up again once he was in his new home and on the road to adoption, but this happened only when he was five years old. So much damage had been done in terms of prolonged privation of what he so clearly needed.

Treatment began with Darren himself being possessed of a manic hope that things could be dramatically changed. His idealisations soon broke down, however. He was one of the most challenging patients I worked with. What was swiftly gathered into the transference was all the anger, the pain, the disillusion and the hate that had accumulated in the terror and turbulence of his six years of life. I want to consider briefly how play, creative even in the throes of desperate destruction, enabled a lessening of Darren's acutely paranoid anxieties, although he could not in a 'technical' sense be said to have been functioning in the depressive position. Work nevertheless continued in the face of huge internal difficulties:

> After a session where he deliberately somersaulted on his head as I took him back to his adoptive father in the waiting room, he was able to be concerned for himself for the first time: 'I wonder if all my brains will fall out,' he said. Finally he was in touch with his internal state of terrified desperation. In the following session he literally leaped dangerously around the room. I took this up as a challenge to me to keep him alive; he settled down somewhat, and asked me to cut out a gingerbread man he had drawn in a previous session. He put the figure on his stomach as he lay down under a blanket in a 'house' he had made. 'I'm not going to die any more,' he said. I said we knew that gaps felt like dying to him. Things got terribly scary and he wanted us both to know how scared he got (an acknowledgement of the success of this massive projective identification). But now he had let me know about how he felt and we could think together about it, he could have a me in his mind to help him remember that we both did stay alive in breaks.

He was building up in himself trust in a good object who wanted him to live, as well as a sense of himself as someone who could stay alive, in spite of the warring aspects inside his mind.

In the next session, after trying to 'eat' the clock on the wall, which measured the minutes of his sessions, he asked me to write down the following story:

The Clock Machine

One day Mr Clock got out of bed. He had fried eggs for breakfast and then he made a machine. The clock machine could do everything about time. The time machine made a terrible mess. He threw the pens, he kicked the television, he jumped on the dog, he saw a clock and he ate it. But then he blowed up. And that was the end of the time machine.

We could link the ideas here to think about my role which he both hated and respected as time-giver of the session. He wished to devour this ambivalent object, and his own fears that his frustration about this would make him explode totally, feeling possessed inside, not of a black hole, a void filled with loss, but of a total chaos of catastrophe, a repetition of his own disastrous birth experience. This seemed to represent a turning point, linked to current external events. At this time not only was his mother pregnant, but his teacher too had left to have a baby. 'Time' was a persecutor, as the threatening inside babies grew ever larger. The 'inside space' was full of death and disaster, and he identified with a terrible internal mother. The story of the clock is one that represents all the chaos with which he had been struggling and continued to struggle. It is a disturbed and disturbing tale, but it is indeed a representation rather than an acting out of chaos. For the first time, form was being able to encompass chaos, in the presence of an object/therapist who could weather it, think about it, and help him begin to have thoughts about it too.

His sessions were always full of a manic and desperate creativity, often at the dangerous end of the spectrum. He fought with me, challenging me and bringing me to the edge of my capacity to manage him many times. Later, play became more symbolic, but spaces such as the dolls' house were transformed into arenas of death and carnage. And yet, as with the clock session, there was progress, even though for me as well as for my patient, it was often difficult to maintain hope. After we had sorted out his internal chaos, he could begin to think about his own destructive urges, but at a much later time in the process. Meanwhile he could use his own processes of often rather desperate creativity, to move towards some understanding of his self-divisions. Again we could see this as taking place in a predominantly paranoid-schizoid state, where, like Theseus, Darren had embarked on the task of confronting his internal monsters, and protecting himself from them. It was only after some of this internal chaos had been sorted out that he could begin to think about his own destructive urges.

The possibility of new development

The third vignette concerns a sixteen-year-old boy I will call David, referred to the family service by his GP because of depression (for which he was on medication), violent outbursts both emotional and physical at home, and social isolation. (This material is also used in Chapter 9, 'Ripples in mental space'.) He had a younger brother who reportedly also had difficulties. David looked older than his years, and his one stated role in terms of his peers was to be a computer games 'Grand Master', where he controlled tournaments and relationships from a high place in his mind. The work I agreed to undertake was done in close cooperation with his psychiatrist, but while she and I demonstrated this link very clearly, it was undermined many times by David, in a rivalrous setting-up of a competition in his mind between medication and therapy. Possessed of a higher than average IQ, and coming from a family where the intellect was idealised, there was a constant dialectic between genuine love of knowledge and its use in intellectual show-manship, to impress objects felt to be impermeable to underlying feelings of anxiety and doubt. The material quoted below comes from the third assessment session, and then six months into his once-weekly therapy, which lasted for two years.

From the outset I was to feel the full force of David's contempt, masking his feeling of being profoundly let down by unreliable objects. Teachers 'lost the plot about 200 years ago'; therapy 'is just a thing I do'. In a family beset by its own conflicts, the available internal space was saturated with negative projections from all sides. David's contempt for me lessened through the work, but could easily be exacerbated during breaks, and by difficulties with studies at school. He attempted to deny such difficulties by bluster and scorn. If he couldn't be top, then the subject lacked interest and rigour. He endeavoured to engage me in intellectual competitions.

Yet there was, too, a growing interest in the idea of a different way to approach relationships, even in the early stages. In the third assessment session, as he looked at the folder and pens I had provided, he recalled a picture he had drawn many years previously, of a unicorn who had been 'too busy playing' to join the ark. The unicorn stood on the cliff, with its calf, in the pouring rain, watching the ark sail away. When I talked about a missed opportunity, maybe a feeling of being furious with his younger self, but also lost innocence and possible feelings of abandonment, he talked only of his guilt. This seemed to represent not only a narcissistic reversal in the manner first described by Abraham (1924, p. 456), where the self is overwhelmed by inappropriate responsibility, but also an instance of Winnicott's aforementioned 'false reparation'.

David's therapy was frequently beset by his envious attacks on any understanding on my part. Any ideas I might offer were often met with a dismissive 'something like that'. After six months there was nevertheless a gradual emergence from an unseparated and violent enmeshment with his objects into a space that was less fraught, and a realisation that there were family difficulties as well as his own, which began to receive a more realistic acknowledgement.

In a mid-term session, he was reflecting on where he would like to be for the New Year. He had an image of standing by the ruins of the temple of Poseidon and looking out over the Aegean Sea. Rather than pursue associations to the ruined temple, which I feared from experience might lead to a bravura intellectual display, I commented on there being some hope at least around. He dismissed it – 'it must be the placebo effect' – but at the end of the session he told me about a novel he had started writing (and that he subsequently finished) – 'it's a love story'. This was something that while I linked to the transference, I did not comment on, because of the fragile nature of this new type of contact. I was reminded of Klein's manic-depressive woman patient, whose evident improvement could not yet be related to gratitude and dependence on a good object:

> There was very seldom any conscious confirmation of what I suggested. Yet the material by which she responded to the interpretations reflected their unconscious effect. The powerful resistance shown at this stage seemed to come from one part of the personality only, while at the same time another part responded to analytic work.
>
> (Klein, 1946 [1975, p. 17])

There were returns to persecuted states in David, and he would then be, as it seemed, consumed by the wish to denigrate me and the work we were doing, but there was more room after this session for a new kind of relationship to, and creative engagement with, better internal objects. One might think of this as a still narcissistic, but more potentially creative, part of the personality getting in touch with an object who could love him, but still in a predominantly paranoid-schizoid mode.

If we consider states of mind on a continuum from paranoid-schizoid to depressive, we might say that David had embarked on his own specific therapeutic task nearer to the 'threshold' of the depressive position. In terms of the aforementioned myths, David's 'music' (in this case his writing, and the developing interest in his therapy) could begin to be something he could trust, without having to look back in anger and contempt into an underworld of consuming anger both with himself and his objects.

Klein (1958 [1975, p. 245]) had, as I have already noted, talked about the need to repair parts of the self, fundamentally connected with anxiety about the self's destructive urges. So before this can be approached, there may need to be a setting aside of premature guilt, in the service of repairing a part of the self damaged by the environment.

What is needed is for there to be a setting aside of overwhelming depressive guilt, in order for the creative self to move forward. Guilt may need to be reduced, and, even in favourable circumstances, good internal objects have to be able to let the subject go.

Conclusion

Even in a relatively secure working through of depressive position anxiety, as suggested by Segal, I suggest that the internal parents need to be able to give space for the subject to examine the various contents of the internal world without casting too long a shadow over what results. This could be linked with Freud's (1917) memorable phrase about 'the shadow of the object falling on the ego', when melancholia rather than true mourning possesses the subject. One might think of a metaphorical *move* rather than a 'killing-off' in the drive towards creativity. This is needed for creativity to be tolerated in all its aspects, without the management of a great deal of depressive guilt.

If we accept the theory that we project aspects of ourselves into our work, then it seems to me that one needs to trust this process and follow the thread of thinking. This may involve times of feeling adrift and without compass points. It is this ability to cast off from safe water that can ensure that creative work can move on. If the 'entry into the depressive position' can be allowed, in a sense, to be an object in the background rather than foreground of the internal world, creative work can evolve.

In the cases of the patients whose material I have quoted above, about which I have thought over many years, something may begin that has never before been experienced, and ego capacities can be developed towards the integration of a sufficiently good object to *feel for*. This might be thought of as an opportunity to be able to repair the self to some extent, though in a predominantly paranoid-schizoid mode. Perhaps one might think of this as a kind of paranoid-schizoid creativity, responsible for splitting and protecting the very core of the self (C. Hering, personal communication). Klein (1958 [1975] talked about the impulse to repair parts of the self. What I have suggested here is that it is the self's building up of hope in the endurance of its creative capacity in the face of external as well as internal damage that may also pave the way for future developments.

References

Abraham, K. (1924) 'A short study of the development of the libido'. In *Selected Papers on Psychoanalysis*. London: Hogarth Press.

Alvarez, A. (1992) *Live Company*. London: Routledge.

Bick, E. (1968) 'The experience of skin in early object relations'. *International Journal of Psychoanalysis*, 49, 484–6.

Bion, W. R. (1962) *Learning from Experience*. London: Karnac.

Britton, R. (1998) *Belief and Imagination: Explorations in Psychoanalysis*. London: Routledge.

Edwards, J. (1994) 'Towards solid ground'. *Journal of Child Psychotherapy*, 20(1), 57–83. Also in Alvarez, A. and Reid, S. (eds) (1999) *Autism and Personality*. London: Routledge.

Edwards, J. (2003) 'The elusive pursuit of insight: Three poems by W. B. Yeats'. In H. Canham and C. Satyamurti (eds), *Acquainted with the Night*. London: Karnac, pp. 167–87.

Ehrenzweig, A. (1967) *The Hidden Order of Art*. London: Weidenfeld & Nicholson.

Emanuel, R. (2001) 'A-void: An exploration of defences against sensing nothingness'. *International Journal of Psychoanalysis*, 82, 1069–75. Also published in *Educational Therapy and Therapeutic Teaching*. Caspari Foundation. Issue 12. June 2003.

Freud, S. (1910) 'Leonardo da Vinci and a memory of his childhood', *S.E. 11*, 59–106. London: Hogarth.

Freud, S. (1914) 'On narcissism', *S.E. 14*, 73–102. London: Hogarth.

Freud, S. (1917) 'Mourning and melancholia', *S.E. 14*, 243–58. London: Hogarth.

Grotstein, J. S. (2004) 'The seventh servant: The implications of a truth drive in Bion's theory of "O"'. *International Journal of Psychoanalysis*, 85, 1081–101.

Hawking, S. (1989) *A Brief History of Time*. London and Auckland: Transworld Publishers.

Klein, M. (1929) 'Infantile anxiety situations in a work of art and the creative impulse'. In M. Klein (ed.) (1975) *The Writings of Melanie Klein, Vol. 1, Love, Guilt and Reparation and other works, 1921–45*. London: Hogarth Press, pp. 199–210.

Klein, M. (1937) 'Love, guilt and reparation'. In M. Klein (ed.) (1975) *The Writings of Melanie Klein, Vol. 1, Love, Guilt and Reparation and other works, 1921–45*. London: Hogarth Press, pp. 306–44.

Klein, M. (1940) 'Mourning and its relation to manic depressive states'. In M. Klein (ed.) (1975) *The Writings of Melanie Klein, Vol. 1, Love, Guilt and Reparation and other works, 1921–45*. London: Hogarth Press, pp. 344–70.

Klein, M. (1946) 'Notes on some schizoid mechanisms'. In M. Klein (ed.) (1975) *The Writings of Melanie Klein, Vol. 2, Envy and Gratitude and Other Works (1946–1963)*. London: Hogarth Press, pp. 1–24.

Klein, M. (1958) 'The development of mental functioning'. In M. Klein (ed.) (1975) *The Writings of Melanie Klein, Vol. 2, Envy and Gratitude and Other Works (1946–1963)*. London: Hogarth Press, pp. 236–47.

Klein, M. (1975) *The Writings of Melanie Klein, Vol. 1, Love, Guilt and Reparation and Other Works, 1921–45*. London: Hogarth Press.

Likierman, M. (2001) *Melanie Klein: Her Work in Context*. London: Continuum.

Limentani, A. (1998) *Between Freud and Klein: The Psychoanalytic Quest for Knowledge and Truth*. London: Karnac.

Mitrani, T. and Mitrani, J. (eds) (1997) *Encounters with Autistic States: A Memorial Tribute to Frances Tustin*. London and Northvale, NJ: Aronson.

Segal, H. (1957) 'Notes on symbol formation'. In E. B. Spillius (ed.), *Melanie Klein Today, Vol. 1*. London: Routledge, 1988, pp. 160–78.

Segal, H. (1989) 'Introduction'. In R. Britton, M. Feldman and E. O'Shaughnessy (eds), *The Oedipus Complex Today*. London: Karnac, pp. ix–x.

Segal, H. (1991) *Dream, Phantasy and Art*. London and New York: Tavistock/Routledge.

Segal, H. (1998) 'The importance of symbol formation in the development of the ego in context'. *Journal of Child Psychotherapy (Klein edition)*, 24(3), 349–57.

Steiner, J. (1993) *Psychic Retreats*. London: Routledge.

Tustin, F. (1972) *Autism and Childhood Psychosis*. London: Hogarth Press.

Winnicott, D. W. (1958) *Through Paediatrics to Psychoanalysis: Collected Papers*. London: Karnac, 1992.

CHAPTER 9

RIPPLES IN MENTAL SPACE CAUSED BY DARK MATTERS AND TWISTED TALES

Some reflections on memory, memoirs and therapeutic work

In this chapter, I am thinking about the issues of memory and the writing of personal memoirs, and how this impinges on our professional work. My title is drawn in part from the work of theoretical physicists who can hypothesise about the existence of dark matter by measuring the deformations it causes in surrounding stars and galaxies. What I suggest here is that there may be limitations in keeping strictly to disciplinary boundaries, and our professional lives may defy our efforts to box them in. The opening of doors to a more extensive world of ideas is often helpful, both for psychoanalysis and for the fields that it can illuminate and by which it can also be illuminated. I use the example of the publication and critical reception of my own memoir, *Pieces of Molly* to make links with our professional selves and our clinical work. I draw on the work of Freud, and other seminal thinkers in the field, as well as my own clinical work to illustrate the ways in which mental space and the memories within it can be contained and transformed over time, but also can be beset by both internal and external saboteurs.

Memory and dark matters

How do dark matter particles fit into a coherent picture of the universe? There is still much debate about this in the discipline of physics, and my linking of these particles with the 'dark matters' existing in the individual's unconscious is a metaphorical way of demonstrating how things we cannot see may affect the things we can see, and in a sense be measured as it were not in their own right, but by what they affect. As Bion averred:

> The analyst may make as many models as he chooses out of any material available to him. It is important not to confound these ephemeral structures with realisations on the one hand or theories on the other. The model has a valuable function provided it is recognised for what it is.
>
> (1962, p. 80)

In terms of this present chapter, I would think of the 'dark matters' as being thoughts and experiences that lie in the unconscious, or the subconscious, and that may sabotage or distort what finally emerges – the 'ripples in mental space'. Psychoanalytic workers are of course familiar with this, and we have our own analyses in order to manage our own 'ripples'. The 'memories' that patients bring, the 'memoirs' they have written about their lives, will be played out in the consulting room, and may well tap into parts of ourselves, despite our analyses. The transference will directly reflect past events, or the patients' experience and past interpretation of them, and be picked up in the counter-transference via projective identification. Of course this counter-transference needs to be examined for traces of one's own contribution to it – so our own analyses are a vital part of the whole project. Melanie Klein quite clearly showed how psychoanalytic work with her adult patients could subtly and even sometimes quite dramatically alter what they now 'remembered' (i.e. Klein, 1945). If one thinks of the etymology of the word, this 're-membering' can result in a reorientation of the subjective world, putting things together in a different way. New weight may be given to past events, or there may be a re-balancing of a past that has hitherto been skewed in a particular way.

In the process of writing, is one capturing new aspects of previously undefined areas of the self? As Harris Williams (2012, p. 397) has said:

> Psychoanalytic autobiography is seen as a mode of remaking the self – not omnipotently but through exploratory self-analysis, frequently following the familiar pattern of loss and rediscovery. It entails a special imagined relationship with the unknown reader, and a sense of being guided by a detached observational eye equivalent to that which Bion terms the 'third party' in a psychoanalytic situation.

I will say more about this later. What is key to the workings of the unconscious mind is the simultaneity of perspectives from which one can view one's emotional experience: the actual experiences one is having, both in the external and the internal world. So as Bion says, (1962, 1970) we can simultaneously view our experience both from a 'rational' as well as an 'omnipotent' point of view. This involves the intersection of time and timelessness. Experiences viewed through the lens of the primitive memory, unconscious and timeless, can render thoughts and actions indistinguishable. Maturity arrives when the interpreting subject can make a distinction between symbol and what is symbolised, as Segal (1957) first so clearly pointed out. Thus, there may be a conflict between the need to find 'safe' conclusions and make judgements that foreclose on true understanding, and the opposing need to eschew 'closure' in order to open up the possibility of fresh understandings, so that questions answered then result in further questioning, in terms of understanding of thoughts, feelings, dreams, memories and perceptions.

The nature of personal truth is always provisional. We seek to be as clear as we can in order to serve both ourselves and those with whom we work, both clinically and academically. It is often in reading about the lives of others in biography and also in fiction that we tap into our own deeper lives and thoughts.

Sigmund Freud was of course extremely interested in memory, his own as well as that of others. It is after all the stuff we work with. He conducted his own self analysis for several years, and regarded his *Interpretation of Dreams* as part of this endeavour. He became ambivalent, however, about the project, and declared self analysis impossible – but then in a letter in 1935 to the psychiatrist Paul Schilder, he suggested that even though 'in self-analysis the danger of incompleteness is particularly great', one might perhaps assert the right to 'an exceptional position' when no other analyst was available (quoted in Gay, 1988, p. 97). Freud's self analysis was a vital stage along the way, as he was building up his internal picture of the mind. His own dreams proved to be valuable signposts on the path towards self-knowledge.

Memoir writing

What psychological transactions does a person thinking and then writing about childhood make with her own childhood? In 'Creative Writers and Daydreaming' (1908) Freud considers that a writer uses aesthetic form in order to allow readers to view their own daydreams and memories through the lens of the writer's creative work 'without any self reproach or shame'. So, it becomes a shared enterprise, melding reader and writer at a subconscious level.

When I embarked on writing a memoir of my own early life, *Pieces of Molly: An ordinary life* (Edwards, 2014) I had these thoughts very much in mind. I also had certain pre-publication anxieties: people in the psychoanalytic profession very rarely raise their heads above the professional parapet, although we were all once children, and all patients. I had the support of my former analyst from the beginning, and also a senior analyst had a hand in editing the book, encouraging me to be less reticent about my professional identity – while also understanding the reticence as being pervasive in the profession, employed to avoid suggestions of narcissism under the surface reason of 'protecting patients'. (I published this work first under my family name of Gurney through an independent publishing company in order to differentiate it from the professional role.) As Britton (1998, p. 210) says in a chapter entitled 'Publication Anxiety', with reference to the complicated dynamics involved in professional writing, we are all concerned to bind ourselves to our ancestors and affiliates in writing clinical papers (let alone of course embarking on a route not usually taken in the profession of using one's own self as the object of scrutiny – in a sense researching one's own learning life, which will of course also be involved in the project of treating and teaching others). I was struck by the feedback I received, both from fellow professionals and those beyond the profession, where just this process that Freud mentioned seemed to be happening to readers of the memoir. We seemed in a sense to be joining forces at a subconscious/unconscious level. And so something I had embarked on for family reasons as a record of 'an ordinary life' did then become more than that: a shared enterprise with others, and of interest to others and their own subjectivities.

Reading memoirs and the evolution of triangular space

From Freud's first significant and foundational use of the Oedipus myth to illustrate psychological development and the development of the personality around acceptance of the parental couple with the subject as a third object outside the dyad, the triangle has afforded psychoanalytic thinking with a developed and still developing metaphorical image. In architectural terms, the triangle is the most robust building form and has also proved to be so in the field of psychoanalysis.

Melanie Klein, in her own engagement with infant development from the first hours of life, pushed back the idea of Oedipal struggles from Freud's four-year old to the infant of six months (Klein, 1945). Chief among those who have since elaborated and extended these ideas of an internal world originally connected as Klein suggested with the inside of mother's body is the psychoanalyst Britton (Britton *et al.*, 1989), whose development of ideas around subjectivity, objectivity and triangular space in relation to an internal acceptance of the primitive Oedipal situation are now central to thinking in this area. What he called 'internal triangulation' brings into being, he suggests, a third position in the mind, a notional triangular space for thinking to evolve. This is vital in order for the subjective self to have a relationship with an idea. Subjective and objective points of view can thus be correlated, as nodal points for this triangular space essential for thinking, the space in other words within the triangle. What might be called an internal spaciousness grows as the result of seeing oneself objectively as well as subjectively, in the Oedipal triangle.

What I would like to suggest is that in reading a memoir, especially a memoir majoring on childhood, reader and writer, as I have posited above, join forces at an unconscious/subconscious level. The reader projects part of the subjective self into the experience she/he is reading about, sees it from this 'third position', and extends the triangular internal space available for reflection about childhood in general and importantly about her/his own particular experience juxtaposed with the childhood being described by the writer of the memoir. As more than one commentator said to me 'this book caused echoes in my mind'. Early memories are revived later in life, I suggest, through reading descriptions of others' lives.

Before Freud, there was a general tendency to think of childhood, when it was thought about at all, as a separate and unimportant phase of life, a period of largely untroubled happiness (the sentimental Victorian view that was of course in stark contrast to working class conditions for children, which included child labour and prostitution. Dickens was notable in his documentation of these facts which were at odds with the sentimental middle class view). Through the work of Melanie Klein it became clear that ordinary children, without external environmental difficulties, go though serious conflicts, without these being necessarily pathological. Oedipal dynamics are at play in every life. For girls there is the 'Persephone dilemma' (Kulish and Holtzman, 2008) – how does a girl turn to men without leaving her mother behind? For boys there is the more straightforward route of turning to father as an object for identification as well as rivalry, and then turning back to the female as a sexual partner later in life, having been forced to renounce claims to mother. These Oedipal dynamics play out in each life and observing them where possible in the drive to negotiate them is a universal task. Each child has her/his own story. As practitioners, we too carry our stories into our work.

What lies behind the scenes we paint of our childhoods, our own as well as that of our patients and by extension our students? There is an interweaving of dynamics here. The writer Sebald (2001) tells how an inspired history teacher recounted the battle of Austerlitz with a capacity to get behind the painted scenes. 'All of us, even when we think we have noted every tiny detail, resort to set pieces which have already been staged often enough by others' (and I would add, by parts of the self in terms of personal history). As Sebald goes on to say, it is indeed quite a task to go 'behind' these pictures to discover something possibly hidden, and more deeply felt than the more available depictions can show. He reportedly said to one of his university students 'no-one should start writing until they are forty' (*Guardian Review* Letters, 27 April 2013): I take this to be an indication of how long indeed it takes to prepare a space that is less contaminated by one's own internal pre-fixed pictures.

For my understanding, the therapist's and the writer's task lies in good part in, like the history teacher, avoiding reconstruction that has already become a 'painted scene'; to go behind the now all-too-familiar (to the patient or ourselves) scenario to something that can be perceived, rescued, resuscitated and developed in a different way in the therapy, or in writing an account of one's own life. This has links with Emde and his colleagues' thoughts about transformational phantasy that overcomes fragmentation, and I will return to this later in the first clinical vignette (Emde *et al.*, 1997).

From another vertex, that of historical fiction, the novelist Mantel (2012) puts graphic words into the mouth of her protagonist Thomas Cromwell: 'What is the nature of the border between truth and lies? It is permeable and blurred because it is planted thick with rumour, confabulation, misunderstandings and twisted tales.' The 'truth' may lie deep in the unconscious, or be more available at a subconscious level, if only one can bear to look at it. As a sexually abused eleven-year-old patient of mine once used to say, with a wry smile on his face if I made a suggestion about his deeper thoughts – 'No – well, maybe. Perhaps I know it somewhere'.

Bion (1962) suggested that a sense of truth derives from combining different emotional views of the same object. Of course ambivalence is essential in moving towards at least a partly adequate appreciation of any situation, and in particular any subject's relationship to internal parents. This will involve struggling with Oedipal issues, as well as the mechanisms of defence deployed to evade reality: projection, denial, dissociation and splitting.

Creativity and psycho-biography

In the sphere of literature and art, there has developed, since the time of Freud, an increasing awareness not only of how psychoanalytic thinking can illuminate creativity, but of how creativity itself may illuminate states of mind within them. The territory has now been more clearly mapped, but as with the metaphysical poet's intuitive grasp of the value and richness of metaphor, like America's pre-Columbian existence, the land was already there.

In what must be one of the best known of his papers, Freud (1910) wrote a detailed reconstruction and then deconstruction of Leonardo da Vinci's earliest years. In this instance, he was keen to trace Leonardo's sexual orientation from his infancy and youth, and he did this by majoring on the 'vulture dream'. This was his first sustained venture into biography from a psychoanalytic perspective – it is of course important to note that he had already bravely taken his own self as subject before he turned to the subjectivity of others with an objective eye. Freud's study of Leonardo began an honourable tradition that has been extended in detail by subsequent thinkers such as Britton (op. cit., 1962) and Williams and Waddell (1991).

This has links too with the notion of the existing 'map' or template, and the need to set it to one side. It is striking to note, for instance, how the poet Keats' notions of 'negative capability', the 'capacity for submission' and 'disinterestedness', and Wordsworth's 'wise impassiveness', while speaking to their own project of writing poetry about the world with as much truth as possible, also foreshadowed Bion's maxims about learning from experience, being without memory and desire, and living with uncertainty, in psychoanalytic practice, in teaching psychoanalysis and of course any other subject. As Bion saw it, different forms of neurotic and psychotic difficulties represent struggles in dealing with truth. We all face these.

Many authors may interpret their findings by way of narrative distancing, or fictionalising their own characters. There is a greater distance between the self that narrates and the self who is the object of the narration, and I wrote in my own memoir both in the first and third person, describing a little girl I called 'Molly', in order to achieve some of this distancing through the adoption of both an internal and an external perspective. Most of my readers seemed to understand this and find it acceptable. As John Donne the metaphysical poet said 'Truth sits on a high crag, and he who would find her about must and about must go'. Bion (op. cit., 1962) was saying the same thing several centuries later. As we grow older, we take a different perspective on our lives.

Clinical examples of dark matters and twisted tales

I would like to add to these reflections by offering two short pieces of clinical material from my own caseload, illustrating something about how memories and the official 'internal memoir' can plague, overwhelm, deceive and thus prevent forward growth. While these are 'patients', the issue of the internal memoir can plague us all. There is of course the need always for the clinician to realise and acknowledge her/his own 'spin' on what unfolds in the consulting room. This will be linked to one's own theoretical frame, which through experience serves one well enough in trying to bring some more coherence to a patient's 'twisted tale'. This will also inevitably involve the practitioner's own subjectivity. This links back to Bion's thoughts about the functions of the models we choose, the theoretical orientations we find helpful, that need to be recognised as models rather than a reflection of ultimate reality. As soon as one puts words down to describe an encounter with a patient, it becomes 'an account' rather than ever being able accurately to transmit 'what happened'. This is an impossibility, and it is important to recognise that ours is only one version of 'what happened'. The first patient described here was asked by his mother after treatment ended (he was much improved and felt himself to be so) about his reactions to it. 'Well I don't remember much of what she actually said', he replied 'But I liked it because she always listened very carefully.' That in itself gives food for thought, and seems a decent enough conclusion to the work.

The first case involves an eight-year-old adopted boy whom I will call Jim. Jim had been badly abused in his original home, and he had two contrasting memories that emerged in an early therapy session: a flowered stair carpet and a frightening shape at the bottom that he thought had something to do with hanging coats. (He had in fact, as his huge file revealed, been found, nearly naked, shut in a cupboard under the stairs.) Perhaps too his own unconscious aggression made him fear he was the monster at the bottom of the stairs. Whatever the reality on which these images had been based, I could simply take it up in his therapy in terms of fragments, good and bad, safe and unsafe, that he was used to carrying around, trying to piece them together. Jim's 'painted scenes' were fragmented and threatening, lurking at the back of his mind, and ever-present.

We all have these Proustian images that seem to exist in an area between waking and dreaming, and I had attempted to pursue some of my own elusive areas in my memoir. We may indeed have no rational explanation for these, and may never achieve a full understanding of their meaning. For the averagely well-functioning adult (and therapist), living with this uncertainty can be tolerated, at least for most of the time. For the late-adopted child with perhaps little idea of helpful parents inside his mind to help him think about his story, the images can become persecuting and persistent. The 'ordinary' task of uniting the opposing forces of loving and hating in the mind may be severely compromised by the facts of abusive early history for the adopted child, and the fantasies that have been constructed around them. It is sobering to note how the most abusive early situations can turn in the child's mind to something loved and lost in the face of the inevitable difficulties of fitting into a new family. Jim said to me 'I just don't believe they did those things to me'. The unconscious 'dark matter' had produced uncoordinated and disturbed ripples in his mind. Jim had in fact received substantial 'damages' through the courts for the treatment that had so damaged his beginnings with his birth parents. This was an 'internal memoir' that was fractured and riven with contradictions in a more than usual way.

Jim was referred to me because of his difficulties making a relationship with his adoptive family, particularly his adoptive mother. He came to the first assessment meeting with his family, armed with, it seemed burdened by, a huge 'Life Story Book' that he solemnly placed on a chair. One of my first thoughts was that at least part of my work would be to help him slowly relegate this to the past, both painted scene and unconscious memory, in order to free the present and create a less contaminated future. Emde and his colleagues described what they called 'transformational phantasy' which overcomes fragmentation, as opposed to repetitive phantasy which traps the patient in a cycle of re-traumatisation (Emde *et al.*, 1997). This was also, incidentally but not without deep meaning, a direct link for me with my own history and my own analysis, where I too had been gradually able to turn to better objects.

Therapy began, and while he railed against boundary setting, he also seemed to appreciate firmness and my capacity to contain and think about his frustration. However, at times of breaks or when Jim felt I thwarted him he would return to a more autonomous and withdrawn state, and he built a castle with huge defences that could only later include a drawbridge that occasionally opened to let me in. 'My parents look after me; I stay well away from you' he said darkly. It was clear that by my taking the role in the therapy of the one who had abandoned him, he was able more to appreciate the love of his adoptive parents, and his adoptive mother appreciated this. This is the solution that therapy may offer: a facilitative split that precedes working through in a more coherent way. This is the way in my view that work with children can best proceed – while this may be my 'spin', it is also born of years of clinical experience. It was of course Klein who first insisted that it was vital to take up and interpret the negative transference alongside the positive. It is only then that there may be external changes that facilitate moving on.

Gradually, through a series of stories about a phoenix and a magic carpet, Jim was able to sort out his defensive use of magic powers from an ordinary healthy capacity to wish that things had been different. He was amazed when I endorsed his growing view that 'life now' was more important, rather than his obsessive concentration on chronically difficult life history, causing many ripples in himself and his adoptive family, from stories both known and unknown at a conscious level. At points during his session I found myself thinking of my own sessions with my analyst and spoke from that place of internal dialogue.

It was a year after work began with Jim that he was able to relax his guard, and a series of moving sessions culminated in his producing a powerful symbol. He was able to come out from his defensive hiding place and begin to believe that he could rework a difficult internal picture to make room for something new, and to turn to helpful external objects in the process. I too found his symbol helpful; as Meltzer (1973, p. viii) said: 'Every psychoanalytic discovery is a self-revelation, and every paper an autobiography. So, at least the name of one of the patients is revealed.'

He was drawing the cover for a book he planned to write. It was night-time in the picture, he said, and he drew a tree that had floating roots but no leaves. Then he drew some breast-like hills, with one in the distance, and a straight path to the distant hill. There was a fence on the hill, and I asked about it. He said it was to stop people falling off. The tree's roots were now within the nearer hill, and I talked about his feeling rooted here with a place to think. Perhaps we could think about sad things and happy things, without his falling off into space. (His growing awareness of being contained by thinking.) He was colouring the hills and then he drew a badger, saying 'it's sunset' (the whole sky was red) 'and he's waking up and coming out'. I simply commented on the badger emerging into the quiet evening, and the beautiful sky. 'Yes', he said, 'and there's a young moon coming up', and he drew it on the right hand side of the page, a thin yellow crescent hanging over the hills.

I think this symbol of the 'young moon' was a reworking of a projected part of himself that could abandon omnipotence as a defence against such a difficult early history, and begin a new cycle of growth and renewal. He had needed me to respect his working under cover of darkness for a long while before he could begin to emerge. This was a crucial turning point for Jim: not a flight from despair into idealisation but a movement towards something new. History cannot be changed, but what is possible is for the relationship to it to be modified, and for the ripples in space around unconscious memories, the 'internal memoir', to become less turbulent. The vital turning point for this little boy seemed to be reached with the symbol of the young moon (which had significance for both 'patient' and 'therapist' in this context). Although this is a comment made in hindsight (as of course is all transliteration of clinical work), it was as if two reveries had joined to make the symbol, the third, and I think this may be linked to Bion's concept of 'O', although this is beyond the scope of this present chapter.[1] This young moon seemed to offer a sign of hope and the capacity to change the relationship to unconscious memories, however deeply they remained buried.

David's unravelling of 'twisted tales'

The second vignette concerns a sixteen-year-old boy whom I will call David (see also Chapter 8 here), referred because of depression (for which he was on medication), violent outbursts both emotional and physical at home, and social isolation. David looked older than his years, and his one stated role in terms of his peers was to be a computer games 'Grand Master', where he controlled tournaments and relationships from a high place in his mind. Here, again is the theme of omnipotence used to defend against extreme helplessness. The work I agreed to undertake was done in close cooperation with his psychiatrist, but while she and I demonstrated this link very clearly, working as it were as a therapeutic couple, it would be undermined many times by David, in a rivalrous setting-up of a competition in his mind between medication and therapy. This was in a sense a replaying of the problematic Oedipal constellation in his family. This is a struggle, as I have said previously, that is played out in every family, and that I had discovered more about by writing about my own family.

Possessed of a higher than average IQ, and coming from a turbulent and difficult family where the intellect was idealised, there was a constant dialectic between genuine love of knowledge and its use in intellectual showmanship, to impress objects whom he felt were impermeable to underlying feelings of anxiety and doubt. This was for me personally also a recognisable trope: the push towards intellectual achievements to mask underlying uncertainties. This gave me warning that I could very easily be pulled into unhelpful dynamics. As Maroni observed in her review of *Pieces of Molly* (Maroni, 2012, p. 305):

Molly is not the first child with a narcissistic mother who turns to language and intellect for sustenance ... Molly's world becomes our world as she becomes both 'everychild' but also singularly her. The mark of a good book is the feeling of universality and recognition it engenders: oh yes, that's how it was for me too.

These difficult dynamics in David's family had created ripples in David's mind that made his ongoing life in the external world of school and his peers difficult for him to manage without an armoury of defensive weaponry, which also prevented anything better from reaching him.

From the outset I was to feel the full force of David's contempt, masking his feeling of being profoundly let down by unreliable objects. The negative transference was apparent from the beginning of the work. In a family beset by its own, often literally, violent conflicts, the available internal space was saturated with negative projections from all sides. David's contempt for me gradually lessened, but could easily be exacerbated as we approached breaks, and by real difficulties with studies at school, and he endeavoured to engage me in intellectual competitions. Because of my own early life, I had to be particularly aware of the very same tendency in myself. Yet there was, too, for David, a growing interest in the idea of a different way to approach relationships.

David's therapy was frequently beset by his envious attacks on any under-standing on my part. Any ideas I might offer were often met with a dismissive 'something like that'. After six months there was nevertheless a gradual emergence from an un-separated and violent enmeshment with his objects into a space that was less fraught, and a realisation that some of the difficulties that had appeared to be his alone, in fact originated in his family as a whole. This echoes the plight of many children and young people who think unrealistically that things are 'all my fault'. It is often problematic for such children, as it had been for me, to unravel their own unconscious aggression from the aggression in their environment.

In a mid-term session he was reflecting on where he would like to be for the New Year. He had an image of standing by the ruins of the temple of Poseidon and looking out over the Aegean Sea. Rather than pursue associations to the ruined temple, which I feared from experience might lead to a bravura intellectual display, I commented on some hope at least around. He dismissed it – 'it must be the placebo effect' – but at the end of the session he told me about a novel he had started writing – 'it's a love story'. This was something that while I could link to the transference, I did not comment on, because of the fragile nature of this new type of contact. Again, my own 'spin' on this was that one does often need to wait, acknowledge inside one's own mind that the transference is changing, but refrain from interpreting it, especially with adolescents who are usually resolutely turning away from contact with primary objects. This can be linked to Wordsworth's previously mentioned notion of 'wise impassiveness' – a state not always easy to achieve for the therapist. While such phrases as Bion's 'living with uncertainty' may become well worn from long usage, such phrases require constant vigilance in terms of how we practise, so that they do not rest in the area of mere phraseology.

While there were returns to persecuted states in David, and he would then be, as it seemed, consumed by the wish to denigrate me and the work we were doing, there was more room after this session for a new kind of relationship to and creative engagement with better internal objects. The 'twisted tales' from the family had lessened their impact, and the ripples in David's mind were becoming less turbulent.

Clinical overview

What I hope these two brief vignettes show is that when two people, patient and therapist, meet in the consulting room, both bring their own 'twisted tales' from childhood, events in their own current lives, and in addition the therapist brings her/his own theoretical orientation or 'spin' on what may transpire. So, one could conceptualise that, when working with children particularly, the therapist is having a dialogue internally with many 'pieces', including the child-self as well as the parental object self. Within this framework, which may hopefully be a flexible container rather than an inflexible constraint, something developmental may occur. Thomas Ogden (e.g. Ogden and Ogden, 2012) has been particularly open in talking about how his own reverie about something quite different at the time may help him understand the quality of 'what is happening' in a clinical session. Ultimately, one might also come to the conclusion that if there is improvement over time, this particular 'spin', be it Kleinian, Freudian, or any of the Independent traditions, has been at least partially helpful in assisting a patient to move on. I still recall the early days of my training, when a trainee older and wiser than me said he had come to think that 'cure' was an impossible ideal, unhelpfully idealising our role, and that 'mild amelioration' was a more sane and sober goal; which is in essence a reframing of Freud's well-known maxim about converting hysterical illness into 'ordinary unhappiness'.

As Hamilton (1996) discovered, all psychoanalytic practitioners wrestle with the ambiguous relations between various theoretical possibilities, their own and those of others, that encircle the patient/therapist encounter. As a self psychologist she interviewed said: 'I believe there is no statement that can be viewed purely intrapsychically. It is always a product of two subjectivities' (p. 179). Bion's maxim about living without memory and desire is an ideal, but one that is constantly bombarded by one's own and any other person's internal world of desires, unconscious memories and conflicting wishes, be they analysts, supervisors or patients. Ultimately 'what matters' will be intimately tied up with what each practitioner has found to work in the consulting room, as well as personal experiences with her/his own analyst, supervisors and colleagues. As Hamilton observes (p. 311) attachment issues between both patient and therapist and between her/him and close colleagues may (*I would say must*) pre-consciously occupy the psychoanalytic domain. These systems of attachment organise our professional lives and our theoretical identities, and will have at their foundation our relationship to our own childhood experiences. These memories may be then used to write a memoir, as I did, with which others resonated. There is now more interest in our own field in this, seeing it as a way to revisit experience and connect it with the ever-changing present.

Concluding remarks

What I hope to have done in this chapter is to make triangular links between ourselves and our work, via my own project of writing and publishing a personal memoir that then had a personal impact on others, both within the therapeutic profession and beyond it. The dialectic between what one has received from one's environment and what one makes of it, the core process at work in the development of infant and first caretakers, lies at the heart of what I have been thinking about in terms of memory and 'memoir', where possible deformations, 'ripples in space', may affect subsequent growth and development, and lie also at the heart of the ongoing process of emotional and intellectual development.

History, whether personal or general, has no plot; it goes beyond our control though we may wish to control it. The wish to capture the past 'the whole truth' remains unquenchable, but is perhaps inevitably always somewhat frustrating. As Edward Hopper, that consummate artist of the alienated and dissociated parts of ourselves, has said:

> What I most prize are all attempts to reconstruct the intimate sensations of childhood, any effort to make concrete those intense, formless, inconsistent souvenirs of early youth whose memory has usually long since faded by the time the power to express them has arrived, so close to dreams that they disappear when the hand tries to fix their changing forms.
>
> (Hopper, 1928, p. 7)

And as the poet Walt Whitman said, we are large, we contain multitudes – we contradict ourselves. This is essentially repeating what Montaigne had said much earlier in the sixteenth century: 'There is as much difference between us and ourselves as between us and others.' This gave rise to the title of my memoir piece about pieces. We need the help of our significant others to make sense of the world into which we are born – and that includes later worlds of learning, teaching and clinical practice.

The connection with different disciplines and the conversations that can take place between them parallels I suggest this crucial nature of 'other minds' in the development of the human psyche from birth, and those privileged to undertake infant observation may observe these processes *in statu nascendi*. This kind of close observation brings out the deepest unconscious feelings in the observing self, as I have written about elsewhere, even in those not involved in what are loosely known as 'the helping professions' (Edwards, 2009). Transformations in understanding may take place, in observation and in seminars where containment is practised, and reverie takes place. Melanie Klein described our first memories as 'memories in feelings' (Klein, 1957, p. 180): memories to do with the bodily care we received, and the satisfactions as well as dis-satisfactions that lie at the heart of every life. What is played out in every life involves struggles with loss and mourning, the Oedipal struggles to do with relinquishing fantasies of possession; the traversing of the long slow road from the pleasure principle towards the reality principle. The notion of a never-ending journey through life may have become a cliché, but I suggest it has become so because it does indeed embody a universal truth.

Our own emotional truths help us as we learn from our own lives as well as those of others, and this inevitably has an effect on how we shape our professional selves, as we learn from our analyses. Essentially, we live out experiences from our early childhood throughout our lives in all our relationships. We all have the wish and the need to make sense of our lived experience, both for ourselves and also to make sure we do not project, onto the lives of our patients or our students, aspects of our own lived or unlived experience. Inevitably, our own attachment patterns will come into play when we work with others. There are always internal as well as external saboteurs, and the enterprise is fraught with anxiety and difficulty, if it is approached in the spirit of being aware of the possible pitfalls. As a psychotherapist you develop what you might call 'the third ear' and that often has been first developed during childhood, where you sense meanings under 'words' as little 'Molly' in my memoir tended to do. To rephrase Henry James's *What*

Maisie Knew, there was a lot Molly did not know, and probably still does not. But others have found this a helpful reminder of our collective fallibility and frailty, and we are no worse for that. As Steiner (1985) said, there may be things we (as well as our patients) half know but choose to ignore, to 'turn a blind eye' to, as did Oedipus as he sat on his throne with his wife/mother.

Whether consciously or not, authors (and psychoanalytic writers), as well as patients, tell their tales, twisted or otherwise, from particular perspectives. In taking their own lives as their objects of knowledge, writers of memoirs nevertheless choose who and what to write about. They select from the multifariousness of human experience, imposing order on randomness, seeing what they choose to see or what their subconscious minds dictate, setting their stories within a selected frame, revealing subjectivity even as they seek to give an impression of objectivity.

I would like to end by quoting the philosopher Gadamer (cited by Rustin, 2011, p. 189, about conversations between differing points of view): 'To reach an understanding in a dialogue is not merely a matter of putting oneself forward and successfully asserting one's own point of view, but being *transformed into a communion in which we do not remain as we were*' (my italics). So, what one can hope for is a real dialogue rather than the clashing of separate monologues. In this respect, a good reader of texts such as memoirs lets her or himself resonate with the text, coming up with interesting new questions about the subjective self, which may then alter perspectives in a way that affects both teaching, learning and clinical practice, as I hope to have shown here. As Salzberger-Wittenburg, Henry and Osborne said in their book *The Emotional Experience of Teaching and Learning* (1983), learning inevitably takes place to some extent within a dependent relationship to another human being. It is vitally important for us to make internal as well as external connections in order to do our jobs as well as we can. We are subtly altered, if not sometimes transformed, by each clinical encounter we experience, as well as by reading and relating to the lives of others via autobiography and memoir.

Note

1   'O' grows out of the silence as practitioner listens to patient – a mindful space very much akin to Winnicott's ideas about potential space and to those of meditative practice, outside of quotidian awareness. These states exist as it were pre-verbally and then hopefully may become part of a shared clinical encounter. This links up for my understanding with Klein's description in her last paper (Klein, 1963), not published until after her death, where she talks about the 'longing for understanding without words'.

References

Bion, W. R. (1962) *Learning from Experience*. London: Karnac Books.

Bion, W. R. (1970) *Attention and Interpretation*. London: Karnac Books.

Britton, R. (1998) *Belief and Imagination: Explorations in Psychoanalysis*. London: Karnac Books.

Britton, R., Feldman, M. and O'Shaughnessy, E. (1989) *The Oedipus Complex Today*. London: Karnac Books.

Edwards, J. (2009) 'Teaching observation to non-clinical students: Further thoughts'. *International Journal of Infant Observation and Its Applications*, 12, 207–14.

Edwards, J. (originally Gurney, 2012 Matador) (2014) *Pieces of Molly: An Ordinary Life*. London: Karnac Books.

Emde, R., Kubicek, L. and Oppenheim, D. (1997) 'Imaginative reality observed during early language development'. *International Journal of Psychoanalysis*, 78, 115–33.

Freud, S. (1908) 'Creative writers and daydreaming'. *S.E.*, *1X*, 143. London: Hogarth.

Freud, S. (1910) 'Leonardo and a memory of his childhood'. *S.E.*, *1X*, 252. London: Hogarth.

Gay, P. (1988) *Freud: A Life for Our Time*. London: Dent.

Gurney, J. (2012) *Pieces of Molly: An Ordinary Life*. London: Troubador publishing.

Hamilton, V. (1996) *The Analyst's Preconscious*. Hillsdale, NJ: Analytic Press.

Harris Williams, M. (2012) 'On psychoanalytic autobiography'. *Psychodynamic Practice*, *18*, 397–412.

Hopper, E. (1928, July) 'Charles Burchfield: American'. *The Arts*, *14*, 7.

Klein, M. (1945/1975) 'The Oedipus complex in the light of early anxieties'. In M. Klein (ed.), *The Writings of Melanie Klein, Love Guilt and Reparation and Other Works*. London: Hogarth Press, vol. 1, pp. 1921–45.

Klein, M. (1957/1975) 'On Observing the Behaviour of Young Infants'. In J. Money-Kyrle and S. O'Shaugnessy (eds), *The Writings of Melanie Klein*. London: Hogarth Press, vol. III, pp. 94–102.

Klein, M. (1963/1988) 'On the sense of loneliness'. In M. Klein (ed.), *Envy and Gratitude and Other Works: The Writings of Melanie Klein*. London: Virago Press, vol. 2, pp. 300–14.

Kulish, N. and Holtzman, D. (2008) *A Story of Her Own: The Female Oedipus Complex Re-Examined and Re-Named*. New York: Aronson.

Mantel, H. (2012) *Bring Up the Bodies*. New York: John Macrae/Henry Holt.

Maroni, L. (2012, December) 'Review'. *Journal of Infant Observation*, *15*, 305–7.

Meltzer, D. (1973) *Sexual States of Mind*. Strathclyde: Clunie Press.

Ogden, T. H. and Ogden, B. H. (2012) 'How the analyst thinks as clinician and as literary reader'. *Psychoanalytic Perspectives*, *9*, 243–73.

Rustin, M. (2011) 'Infant observation and research'. *International Journal of Infant Observation*, *14*, 179–90.

Salzberger-Wittenburg, I., Henry, G. and Osborne, E. (1983) *The Emotional Experience of Teaching and Learning*. London: Routledge.

Sebald, W. G. (2001). *Austerlitz*. London: Hamish Hamilton.

Segal, H. (1957) 'Notes on symbol formation'. *International Journal of Psychoanalysis*, *38*, 391–7.

Steiner, J. (1985) 'Turning a blind eye: The cover up for Oedipus'. *International Review of Psychoanalysis*, *12*, 161–72.

Williams, M. H. and Waddell, M. (1991) *The Chamber of Maiden Thought*. London: Tavistock/Routledge.

PART 4

LINKS WITH THE ARTS

Just as someone stands on the last hill
Looking back to see the whole valley of life one last time,
We all stand, we watch, we linger,
That's how we live each day,
Saying our perpetual goodbyes

(Rilke, Duino Elegies No. 8, translated by JE)

Psychoanalytic thinkers have always been interested in the arts, and in making links with creative endeavours and the impulses at work in the internal world. Those working in the psychoanalytic field have drawn on culture and creativity in order to amplify and expand thinking about psychoanalytic processes, and mechanisms, as they have made their appearance in different cultures and different ages throughout history. The recognition of interdependencies is vital in this respect, whereas privileging one discipline over another is, I submit, a more questionable project. Can we indeed take our place alongside other disciplines, finding a place within the complexity of lived life, where new paths open up even as we walk them? Making sense of our human experience is a multifaceted and evolving study, involving existential aliveness to each moment.

Freud of course began this enterprise, with his thoughts about the Oedipus complex that began when he saw pictures by Italian masters of Virgin and child, and then notably he wrote about Leonardo Da Vinci (1910). Melanie Klein too was interested in the links that could be made: she wrote a paper 'On Identification' (1955) linking her ideas about massive projective identification and a character in a novel, If I were You, and she went on to write a paper that was not published until after her death on The Orestaia (1963).

Klein made references to literature in order to illustrate her theories: in 'Envy and Gratitude' (1957) she quotes Milton (whose Satan epitomised envy) and Chaucer, who named envy as 'the deadliest sin'. In the discussion following publication of his seminal paper 'The Theory of the Parent–Infant Relationship'(1962), Winnicott quotes Shakespeare's Hamlet describing the fawning Osric as an illustration of a 'false self' – 'He did comply with the dug before he sucked it' – surely the earliest piece of observationally derived description! (p. 256) .

If Freud had been able to have access to the plethora of films that are now so deeply a part of our culture, he would surely have found them another potent source for thinking about the unconscious and its manifestations. There exists increasingly a vast amount of psychoanalytic film criticism, and one of the following chapters on a film and its relevance for pre-clinicians adds to this growing body of work.

Understandably, however, many living artists and writers are somewhat sceptical of having their work subjected to psychoanalytic scrutiny. Early psychoanalytic ideas about the whole issue of creativity, which placed 'real' creativity firmly in a depressive position context (i.e. Klein, 1937; Segal, 1991), needed revisiting (see Chapter 8 in this book). As I point out, artists deemed central to our more recent heritage could not really be seen to have been functioning solely from a depressive position point, either in their art or their lives. It is vital for there not to be imposed on cultural artefacts a 'moral' dimension that this kind of thinking may tend towards, as Frosh, quoting Elliott (1997, pp. 94–5) observed. There are indeed challenges, as he said, inherent in states of mind generated in 'the paranoid-schizoid mode' that can make a vital contribution to creativity. I think there can exist a fine line between an artist finding work helpfully amplified by a psychoanalytic view, and a feeling that somehow one has become 'a patient'. The chapters in this section explore poetry and film in order to make creative links and offer others further thoughts about how the modern world too may be full of different ways to think about 'being here'.

References

Freud, S. (1910) *Leonardo da Vinci: A Memory of his Childhood. S.E.* 7, 125–44. London: Hogarth.

Frosh, S. (1997) *For and Against Psychoanalysis*. London and New York: Routledge.

Klein, M. (1937) 'Love, guilt and reparation'. In M. Klein (ed.) (1975), *The Writings of Melanie Klein, Vol. 1, Love, Guilt and Reparation and other works, 1921–45*. London: Hogarth Press, pp. 306–44.

Klein, M. (1955) 'On identification'. In M. Klein (ed.) (1975), *The Writings of Melanie Klein, Vol. 2, Envy and Gratitude and Other Works (1946–63)*. London: Hogarth Press, pp. 141–75.

Klein, M. (1957) 'Envy and gratitude'. In M. Klein (ed.) (1975), *Envy and Gratitude and Other Works*. London: Hogarth Press, pp. 177–235.

Klein, M. (1963) 'Some reflections on The Orestaia'. In M. Klein (ed.) (1975), *The Writings of Melanie Klein, Vol. 2, Envy and Gratitude and Other Works (1946–63)*. London: Hogarth Press, pp. 275–99.

Segal, H. (1991) *Dream, Phantasy and Art*. London and New York: Tavistock/Routledge.

Winnicott, D. (1962) 'The theory of the parent–infant relationship, contributions to discussion'. *International Journal of Psychoanalysis*, 43, 256–7.

CHAPTER 10

TEACHING AND LEARNING ABOUT PSYCHOANALYSIS

Film as a teaching tool, with reference to a particular film, *Morvern Callar*[1]

When the early analysts began their project of delving into the realms of the psyche and mapping out the territory, film was in its infancy. Now film is a major cultural reference point in our lives, and as such can be used in order to illustrate the inner worlds it so powerfully depicts, from a psychoanalytic perspective. Using a particular film, *Morvern Callar*, directed by Lynne Ramsay (2002) to reflect on the impact of the counter-transference, the feelings generated in the clinician or observer by what is 'projected', I suggest that film, with its capacity to communicate intense emotional and preverbal states, can make sense of certain key psychoanalytic concepts via a direct emotional experience.

I used this film for some years as an 'end of term' presentation for pre-clinical students at the Tavistock Clinic. My question was this: can film serve to convey something of the atmosphere that may be generated and experienced in a clinical session, to students who have not yet had this clinical experience? As we move on increasingly swiftly in terms of technology, what I suggest is that film may become part of our teaching repertoire as well as our increasingly thinking about the meanings implicit in films (i.e. Gabbard, 2000; Sabbadini, 2003). Can film indeed be used in a way as an adjunct to more theoretical and intellectual explications of the counter-transference, before students have the opportunity to have the experience in a controlled clinical setting?

I am considering this film in a particular way, in a sense, as it were, from a particular psychoanalytic vertex, but I am of course aware that we all bring our own associations to anything that we encounter – this is not a definitive view, and there are other ways it could be seen, even under the general rubric of 'psychoanalysis'. Indeed I think it is vital that we consider our particular views to be provisional, and open to question. Dogma is not helpful in order for us to encourage open-mindedness in those we teach, and the capacity to espouse Bion's still matchless advice about 'living with not knowing'.

So this short chapter has three facets. First, it deals with a possible method of teaching pre-clinical students about counter-transference through an experience engendered by a film, alongside other theoretical concepts. Second, it outlines from a Kleinian perspective the way a psychological mechanism vital in normal development may then be used when at a later stage someone is confronted with situations of trauma and loss that re-awaken earlier losses. Third, it addresses the above two points in terms of student reactions in a group situation, via a particular film, where the central character is seen in a particular way. What I hope to do is to offer pointers with the aim of finding ways to convey concepts and also importantly feelings to a student group.

This film on its release was given five stars by many film critics, but was also labelled as 'difficult', 'flawed' and 'obscure'. I think these very adjectives may give some clue to a work that goes beyond often-deployed filmic devices to give us something rather different and interesting that is, at least as I see it, an unvarnished re-creation on film of a state of mind we may meet in the consulting room.

The film tells the story of a young woman, Morvern Callar, who works in a supermarket in a small Scottish community. Her boyfriend commits suicide on Christmas Eve, leaving a note for her on his computer. Blood is seeping from his body onto the floor. The opening shots show her too, lying on the floor next to him, caressing his inert body, an expressionless look on her face. Already there is a strong hint of dissociation and cut-off communication. He has also left his just-finished novel, with instructions to send it to a list of publishers. 'I wrote it for you' he declares in a message left on the computer screen. This statement turns out to have a deeply ironical twist. 'Be brave'.

She opens his Christmas presents left neatly ranged for her on the floor: a leather jacket, a cigarette lighter, and a tape of music recorded 'for you' that will form the soundtrack to the film. She flicks the lighter on and off, quenching the flame with her finger, and the Christmas tree lights are left to flash on and off as a disturbing comment on the sudden end of a young life, on a day associated usually with birth rather than death.

In a director's statement, Lynne Ramsay's view is that Morvern defies all conventional expectations by going on to appropriate her boyfriend's novel as her own:

> just as a pragmatic means to escape the mundanity of her life . . . this is what makes her character so contemporary. Does it matter who wrote the novel? Is it worth more to a dead person than to someone trying to live life as best they can?

This view is somewhat in contrast both to the critics' comments on a 'difficult' film, and the confused and often rather hopeless state of mind engendered in many viewers, which seems far away from interpreting her gesture as one necessarily pointing to any notion of a robust and hopeful survival of deprivation. When I reflected on this dissonance, it seemed to me that it might be rather similar to that when in the consulting room an adolescent splits off all responsibility for an often worryingly delinquent act, and leaves the concern in the mind of the analyst. While I do not want to pathologise the director's view, it does seem to resonate with this phenomenon. My reading of the film draws on both psychoanalytic theory, and specifically on Melanie Klein's seminal work 'Notes on some schizoid mechanisms' (1946), and years of clinical work as a child and adolescent psychotherapist. While it offers a very different view from that of the director, it has helped me understand the critics' 'difficult' label.

In his introduction to *Psychoanalysis and Film* (Gabbard, 2000), the author describes what he calls 'seven time-honoured methodological approaches' to film criticism. The second approach he describes is that of seeing the film as a reflection of the film-maker's subjectivity (p. 4). It is true that Lynne Ramsay (2002) talked of an identification with her heroine, as did the actress who plays her, and both director and actress reportedly seemed to 'click' as collaborators on the project.

However, the category of criticism I wish to pursue here is to consider the film 'as a reflection of a universal developmental moment or crisis' (Gabbard, 2000, p. 5), and I want to link it specifically to the evolving struggle with loss, denial and resultant splitting documented by Melanie Klein (Klein, 1946, pp. 1–24) in 'Notes on Some Schizoid Mechanisms'.

In Klein's 1940 paper, 'Mourning and its Relation to Manic-Depressive States', Klein refers at the outset to Freud's 1917 paper 'Mourning and Melancholia', where he talks of the need to free the libido from the lost object and the necessity of reality testing. She suggests that normal mourning processes have close connections with early infantile processes, and goes on to outline the manic defences that then interfere with the secure internalisation of the good object and the progress towards the depressive position. Klein's subsequent 1946 paper, on which I propose to concentrate here, is one of her most important contributions to psychoanalytic theory. It shows us her first formulation of the paranoid-schizoid position. In it, she links Fairbairn's earlier use of the term 'schizoid', as she says in the paper, with her own descriptive use in previous papers of the word 'paranoid'. This is in order to describe a state that occurs developmentally in infancy, and may resurface later in life if it has been unresolved, remaining as a fixation point in the personality. As is well known, these infantile struggles are recapitulated in the developmental crises common in adolescence, after the relative stability of the latency period. What may resurface at a time of crisis may then harden into a pathological state.

In the film, after discovering her boyfriend's body, and lying for we know not how long beside it, caressing it, in a state of what looks like a mixture of shock, disbelief, grief and bewildered abandonment, Morvern puts on her makeup and goes to a Christmas party. She says, truthfully, that her boyfriend is 'at home, in the kitchen'. Before she goes, she takes some money from her dead boyfriend's pocket and whispers 'sorry'. Here then is the first hint of a propensity to steal, and to steal identity: she wears at the party a necklace with the name 'Jackie' on it – 'I found it', she says simply. Later, when Morvern tells her best friend Lanna 'he's left me', Lanna herself tells Morvern that she once slept with Morvern's boyfriend, but 'it was nothing really'. Echoes of Oedipal issues join with those of abandonment. After taking some ecstasy, Lanna and Morvern dance in a trancelike state, then end up in bed in a threesome with a boy at the party. Morvern is being unfaithful just in the way she feels her boyfriend has been to her, not only by sleeping with Lanna, but by his suicide.

In the early hours of Christmas Day, Morvern points out to Lanna the island in the mist 'where my foster-mother is buried'. Neither her foster-mother nor her psychic health seem to have survived. A misty, idealised view seems to be the only alternative to a reality that has become stripped of meaning: infantile hallucinatory gratification takes the place of real satisfaction with living objects. As Klein indicated, splitting is a key process in the formation of the paranoid-schizoid position, and an excessive flight into idealisation may hamper ego development (1946, pp. 7–8). The phone call Morvern almost makes to tell someone of her boyfriend's suicide is aborted when she answers the phone at the p-ublic box. 'I am sure she'll be all right' she reassures the caller, who is obviously anxious about somebody's whereabouts. The caller may be seen to represent someone who cares about his objects; the boyfriend who has abandoned her will become identified first with an abandoning object, and then with an object that becomes disintegrated because of her anger at the abandonment. We are not sure that *she* will be all right.

Morvern returns home, and sits down at the computer to read again the message 'I wrote it for you.'. There is a pause, and then she gets her fingers to work over the computer keys, purposefully changes the author's name on the novel to her own, and sends it to the first publisher on her boyfriend's list. In her 1955 paper 'On Identification' (pp. 141–175) Klein studies in detail by means of a character in a novel who morphs through several identities, the particular form of projective identification when a pseudo-identity is acquired by the subject, Fabian Especel, who is also unhappy and dissatisfied with himself and his lot. Klein describes him to be in identification with a sadistic part of the self first projected into an object and then reintrojected. She describes him as being 'ruled by ruthlessness', and Morvern's subsequent actions have the same quality of a relentless disregard for the object. She dispassionately disposes of her boyfriend's body by cutting it up, literally. She puts on a huge pair of sunglasses and strips down to her pants to do the job, with her walkman taped to her side so that she can listen to the music he recorded for her. The she buries the pieces, which she carries in a rucksack, in a shallow moorland grave. This could be seen as a concrete acting out of the phantasy of aggressively fragmenting the abandoning object (Klein, 1946, p. 8). Terror at resultant retaliation is defended against by cutting off feeling.

Before she begins her grisly work, Morvern puts a frozen pizza in the oven. She ignores the bell that tells her it is ready. When she takes it out later, it is burnt to a crisp. What she is now feeding herself is radically inedible, and one thinks of many other warning signs that have been ignored. In work with disturbed and disturbing adolescents, one is almost constantly preoccupied with signs, warnings that may at some point become disturbing actings-out. While Morvern works, she listens to a song that talks of sticking 'like glue' – an indication of a desperately dangerous adhesive identification with what she is doing. As Melanie Klein insisted (1946, p. 6), splitting or disintegrating of the object implies a similar fate for the ego. This splitting of the ego and the resultant states of fragmentation as seen in schizophrenic patients was to be the subject of later work by Bion, Segal, Meltzer and Rosenthal.

The song changes as Morvern finishes the work and sits back exhausted on her heels. The song ends by talking about being beyond right and wrong – a clue I suggest to a state that has been cut off from better feeling, indeed beyond any notions of consensus morality, as she has been traumatised by her boyfriend's destructive act and then terrified by her own retaliatory destruction. Yet somewhere inside her mind she may have the delusion that they are fused together in a radically delinquent state. As Klein suggested in 'The Importance of Symbol-Formation in the Development of the Ego' (1930), the ego's first defence against anxiety is violent expulsion (with the faeces, as she asserts, seen concretely as weapons) which has the dual function of being an attempt to relieve the ego and attack the object.

I was reminded as I have been previously with traumatised patients of Wilfred Owen's words about the results of traumatic happenings for soldiers in the First World War. 'Having seen all things red, Their eyes are rid/ Of the hurt of the colour of blood for ever' (quoted in Edwards, 2000, 2008). In other words, dissociation cuts the thinker off from unthinkable thoughts, pain is cut off from the person experiencing it. After the cursory burial of her boyfriend's fragmented remains, Morvern moves away from the shallow grave with a whooping shout, and then trails her hand in a little stream while watching the insect life moving in the earth; we think by implication, as perhaps does she, of the slow disintegration of her boyfriend's body. There has been a small clue implanted earlier (which only becomes clearer on more than one viewing of the film), when Morvern picks up a rotten carrot in the supermarket where she works, and sees a maggot slowly writhing within the rotting cavity of the vegetable.

With wordless power as she listens to the tape on her Walkman, she conveys the shock that has catapulted someone no doubt already multiply traumatised into a dissociated state, frozen so that mourning cannot take place. This henceforth constant soundtrack to her life highlights this traumatised state, where her head is filled with music to block thought.

This is a difficult, painful film, not because of contrived shocks or efforts to induce horror, but precisely because of the powerful way in which the actress conveys with precious few words, mostly banal, the disaffected state that is projected into the audience to process. We may be familiar with this state in the counter-transference that arises in work with profoundly deprived and disturbed adolescents.

There are hints that any return of feeling has immediately to be escaped, as when Morvern meets and has a sexual encounter with a young man at a Spanish beach resort to which she takes her friend Lanna, using the money her boyfriend left for his funeral. Just before they leave, there is a 'baking' scene in the kitchen of Morvern's flat, where, in a travesty of an identification with something nourishing provided by a good object, the girls throw flour around the room and at one another.

The light of Spain is a contrast to the brooding shadows of what she has attempted to leave behind in Scotland. The young man's mother has just died, and he is suddenly catapulted from the frenetic partying at the resort into a state of shock that occurs before the slower work of mourning. Here was a juncture where feeling could have been re-awakened: Morvern offers to tell him about her foster-mother's funeral when he asks her to stay and talk. But after a sexual encounter with him, which seems to defend against the death of a parent with its defiant and manic energy, giving them a sense of existing (they both bounce up and down the room, like naughty children), she escapes the threat of intimacy again, taking her long-suffering friend into the Spanish wilderness with her. 'What do you want?' demands Lanna, 'A planet of your own?' In a sense Morvern is already on a planet of her own, her own making, in her move from trauma to dissociation. Even the solace of the lighter her boyfriend left for her fails: it refuses to ignite. At this point too, she trails her hand in the dry dust of the deserted countryside, perhaps another reference to the decay that has happened back home.

The publishers, two fashionable young people unusually pursuing this unsolicited first novel, fly out to meet Morvern in Spain and offer her a huge advance. It is here that the disjunction between mask and reality seems to become inevitable and inescapable. Yet ironically it is here too that Morvern can admit that she works in a supermarket – citing her 'writing' as a way of getting away from the mundanity of the nine to five world. Her admission is seen by the publishers as witty and bizarre, and she seems to be fully captured by their projective identification of her as a quirky and also money-making proposition.

At the end of the film the friend, Lanna, who is after all an ordinary-enough adolescent seeking instant kicks but actually searching for something different, tells Morvern she should accept the 'pure crap' of where she is – a plea for the reality principle that needs to balance out the fantasy and 'fun' of adolescent mania at the Spanish resort, symbolised by the girl with smudged and rolling eyes in one corner of their hotel room. The boy Lanna met in Spain is coming to see her in Scotland. Morvern encourages Lanna to come with her, but her friend says simply 'everyone I know is here'. Morvern mutters 'I'm just going to the toilet'. This is the way, throughout the film, she has avoided saying goodbye. Children and young people who have experienced frequent changes of care leave situations before they are left, as a vain attempt to master their situation. With a large cheque for the stolen novel in her pocket, Morvern is last seen sprawled on a bench at a dark deserted station, waiting for a train, where the train tracks lead off the screen to an unknown future.

While this at one level may seem like a situation where there are 'no limits' to what can be achieved, this in itself is a boundary-less and ultimately terrifying proposition. The bleak station seems to be an indication of a profoundly lonely internal state; perhaps equivalent to what Klein describes as 'a kind of detached hostility'. As Klein points out 'the feeling of being disintegrated, of being unable to experience one's emotions, is in fact the equivalent of anxiety' (1946, p. 18).

One final sequence shows her in blank-faced fragmented strobe flashes at a city disco, which seems to emphasise not her freedom but her entrapment in a chaotic internal world, where she has lost any sense of her own identity. She has posted her door-keys back into the empty hall of the flat where she used to live, and the Christmas tree lights are still flashing. The sound track of music at the disco bodies out: dedicated as it says to the one I love. Her boyfriend said he wrote the novel 'for you' and she has taken this concretely into herself, to the detriment of her psychic health. This is a perversion of love, which then destroys one of the core elements of human functioning.

Who is Morvern Callar? At the end of the film she does not know, she is isolated and alone in a world of deluded pieces. While her boyfriend is actually dead by his own hand, she has pushed him to the outer limits of her own psychic world, to a place where redemption seems impossible. By taking over his novel she has ingested him in a poisonous, barren and ultimately completely hopeless way. She could be said to have committed psychic suicide, in order to defend herself from intolerable psychic pain. No hope remains, and there seems to be no lively objects left to whom she could turn, even in such a profound time of crisis. Inside her mind there exists a disaster zone. Her surname 'Callar' has some resonances with 'callous': and she has visited total destruction on herself and her whole internal world, with what seems like callous disregard. She has an internal sense of being unloved and unlovable, abandoned, wandering in a parched desert very similar to the one in Spain, to where she dragged Lanna, who is perhaps after all a friend in one sense, despite having slept with Morvern's boyfriend. 'You hate me, but it was just a fuck, not even a good one!' 'Shut up', says Morvern, 'he's dead'. He is literally dead, but she has also cut him out of her internal life. The notion of 'resilience' seems rather far removed from the actual internal picture here.

One could hypothesise here a scenario that would lead directly to psychotic breakdown. Strong feelings of omnipotence, as Klein said, can be deployed in order to deny psychic reality, but at a huge cost to the ego, which cannot split the object without itself being catastrophically split into pieces, or existing in danger of complete annihilation. As she describes, the anxieties of early infancy, characteristic of psychosis, drive the ego to develop defence mechanisms, and 'in this period the fixation point for all psychotic disorders are to be found . . . the anxiety of being destroyed from within becomes acute; the ego tends to fall to pieces' (1946, p. 7).

The audience, too, are left, in a state that is beyond hope or despair, seeming like a schizoid state in pure culture. This is something we may be forced to experience in work with distressed and disturbed adolescents, where depressive or reparative states seem to be in another country altogether. Despair is induced in the therapist rather than the patient, and this needs to be borne for perhaps a considerable time. Technically we may of course approach this impasse in different ways. We experience the despair and the adolescent may withdraw into what Steiner (1993) called a psychic retreat, avoiding pressure to engage either in external reality or the internal reality of painful feeling. There is a profound sense of being alone: no real intimacy is possible. The self has become completely detached from either helpful or malign objects, and floats in a void.

What I think the audience may find understandably difficult in this film is to find a way of relating to such a powerful schizoid state that pervades the action and leaves no room for the comfort of feel-good reactions. When Morvern leaves her sleeping friend on the Spanish road, for a minute the music bodies forth in the manner of a road-movie with a powerful life-affirming beat, but this is swiftly undercut. There are to be no happy endings here. We are left with the tinny sound heard from the outside of someone else's personal stereo, just as Morvern herself is cut off from the full spectrum of human emotions. There is no room for an easy slide into something more familiar and formulaic: this girl is in a desperate state and we are not allowed to escape it. It is an uncompromising portrayal.

Here is a state of mind where a young person has been pushed and has pushed herself to the furthest limits and beyond by earlier events only hinted at. One is invited perhaps to surmise that the death of her foster mother either caused or increased a traumatic break with reality, a defence that may have been entered into in order to escape a difficult beginning. Her boyfriend, along with his reported casual betrayal of her with a friend, had to be concretely cut up and disposed of along with any feelings about his death. Stealing his novel could be seen as an adhesive identification with a lost object and its creativity: a concrete way of possessing it and seeking to become it that denies the beginning of acceptance of loss and the onset of processes of mourning.

I have worked with this film for several years, with groups (with about twenty-five members usually) of non-clinical students who have come on to the Tavistock course from a variety of backgrounds in the 'helping' professions, such as teaching and social work.

By the time I show the film at the end of the third term in the year, the students have been exposed to a plethora of new ideas, new ways of thinking, and have struggled with acceptance and resistance, or a mixture of both, along the way. It is presented to them as a way of carrying on with thinking rather than as an 'end of term treat'. We view sections of the film in the student group, in a darkened seminar room, and we then explore what they think of the character's solution to the terrible traumatic loss (one can only hypothesise as the last of many) caused by her boyfriend's suicide? Is this simply, as the director thought, resilience? Has she simply followed her boyfriend's exhortation from beyond death to 'be brave'? Is it credible? Does the idea of massive splitting help? As I have explained, this has been a cumulative exercise for me in understanding the potential of the medium: I have not made extensive notes over these several years, and I will present fragments from the last showing alongside some student comments, not as 'evidence' that this works, but as a suggestion as to one way in which this kind of exercise could be viewed.

Many of the students have not previously seen the film. It is of course impossible to show it as a whole, and I picked several 5–10 minute excerpts from its unfolding in order to give at least some flavour of the whole. (I am of course already 'editing' their experience – and I do point this out to them.) There is no formal 'structure' per se to the discussion, and what emerges relies crucially on what is generated in any one group: how their own work experiences (and even at times their personal experiences) have resonated with what they have seen, albeit in a truncated and edited form. At the last showing, someone who was obviously deeply moved by the character's predicament, after there had been several minutes of silence in the group, described in detail Morvern's initial stunned but gentle caressing of the dead boy's body, as the Christmas lights relentlessly flash, and linked it with the flashing lights at the end of the film. Is she still looking for 'the one I love' or has she gone beyond that, as her friend Lanna said, 'to a planet of her own'? Another student then pointed out how well the words on the sound track songs seem to link up with the heroine's mental state.

Several students in this last cohort linked it to cases of their own in their different professions, where traumatised states and dissociation make those they work with often seem impossible to reach. One student talked of a whole family in just such a dissociated state, and felt that seeing the film and our discussion would help her bear what had previously seemed unbearable in her work, so that her understanding might help the family forward. Joseph (1975) talked about how, in psychoanalytic work with the patient who is difficult to reach, the concerned part of the self is projected into the analyst, who then can feel pressured to act out, rather than staying with the projective identification in order truly to experience the missing part of the patient. How can emotional understanding be offered when there is such a persistent drive to expel affect? In the family about which this student was thinking, an adolescent boy had become a persistent school refuser, engaging in anti-social acts, not within a 'gang', but as a social isolate. The student talked of his refusal to engage with her, and linked this to Morvern Callar's wish to run away to somewhere else – what Horne (2001) called the 'escapologist' cry for help from the disturbed teenager. Who will pursue the escapee? If nobody does, then there is the powerful risk of this experience being repeated at an unconscious level, as one of abandonment.

We thought about how Morvern might have been when she was younger, and when had the cut-off state begun? Given that her cutting up of the body could be seen at the far end of the spectrum in terms of 'an anti-social act', we linked this with Winnicott's notion of 'the anti-social tendency' (1984). He thought that behind every anti-social act lay a deprived child who thinks 'the environment owes me something'. Behind the deprived child lay an infant whose needs had not been met at the appropriate time. If anger at the absence of environmental provision gets fused in a deadly way with the most profound unconscious anger and wish to annihilate unfeeling objects who are feared in their own turn to be deadly, then the outcome, as with Morvern, is unsurprisingly very bleak. Several students then felt free to talk about younger clients, where they had felt unable to 'reach' the child, and where this view of the development of strong defences could then, they felt, be a beginning towards understanding those defences that, while in the first case perhaps necessary, may then harden into apparently ongoing impermeability. One student in particular resonated to the idea of the deprived child feeling that the environment was in his debt: she could relate it to a young adolescent she was seeing who seemed to embody that kind of defiant clarion call. It was this, among other reasons, the student then thought, could well have then prompted Morvern to steal her boyfriend's novel.

This film is based on a novel where perhaps more of Morvern Callar's background is fleshed out. As clinicians we would want to know more about it: though here we know two crucial facts. Morvern's early life has been so difficult that she has been fostered, one assumes successfully. But her foster mother has died.

There exists at least two views about when to read the often hugely heavy files that tend to arrive with the referral of cases such as that of the hypothetical traumatised Morvern. In terms of the book that preceded the film, I felt that for me to go back to the book in order to see what had been kept and what had been left out (as is usually the way when books are turned into film scripts) would not be relevant, although perhaps interesting, and would indeed be outside the aim of this paper. In a way one wants of course to know, but what I think gives the film its particular power is that the director leaves the spectator in the yawning void where feeling might have been before the push to traumatic dissociation, in an internal world perhaps peopled somewhere with victims and persecutors, but who are locked out and mute. This is a powerful example, I suggest, of the need to 'show', not 'tell'.

When the student group left after the end of the seminar, there was a sustained mood of quiet reflection that had been generated in the group discussion. Several came up afterwards to me in order to say something about the particular impact it had had, and what they would take away with them from the film and the group's reflections. One student said that it had given her a real understanding of the term 'counter-transference'; and that it was often hard to link what she called 'psychoanalytic technical words' with real understanding of emotional experiences. One remains aware of course that there will be many thoughts that need time to be developed in a particular individual's mind, to do not only with her or his own caseload, but in the internal world shaped by individual experience and phantasy (none of these students are in psychoanalytic treatment). Although many receive very little if any support for the difficult work they do, this course opens doors of understanding, and may then lead towards future training.

The length of the seminar is the usual one hour and fifteen minutes. During this time we see several excerpts, and spend the rest of the time in discussion, as I have already indicated, which is taken forward in the way that seems relevant and appropriate to the particular group. The thoughts below may arise in the discussion, or they may remain latent in my mind. Nevertheless they are the framework from within which I am working, and so it seems important to mention them in relation with the task as it has evolved over several years.

This film links in my mind with Britton's (1998) definition of 'truth-seeking' as opposed to 'truth-evading' literature (1998): permeated either with the wish to struggle with reality or to escape its privations, through fantasy and wish-fulfilment. Lynne Ramsay's previous film *The Ratcatcher* showed the troubled world of a pre-adolescent boy preoccupied by guilt. In this film by contrast the guilt has been disowned. In this way it stays with an entrenched internal position rather than drawing back to a meta-statement about change and hope. This is of course in contrast to Ramsay's 'director's statement', indicating a view of resilience and triumph over adversity. Stolen novel as passport to a new world of possibility.

I suggest that this is a reflection of the way in which schizoid states can be projected from patient to psychotherapist or analyst in the consulting room. In previous years, there have been at least one or two students who have majored on the hope, and who have been less able or willing to think about what this may mask. It then seems important to consider this seriously, and to see what it might mean. However, this kind of 'dead' presentation (or a kind of manic flight which cuts off other concerns) leaves the therapist with difficult, demanding and often mind-numbing work, where there is a balance to be maintained between containing frozen states while not becoming frozen oneself, and finding a way to cope with coming to life. Alvarez's (1992, 2007) thoughts about reclamation and levels of interpretation offer us ideas about this, how to link the fragments, what Bion (1962) called the beta elements, and move on. But when frozen dissociated states become more available, then begins an extremely painful process of integration and equally powerful resistances to this (Lechevalier-Haim, 2001). There are of course technical issues about timing and distance here that lie outside the parameters of this paper.

In spite of the director's statement, I think as clinicians we would think of Morvern Callar as being very ill. Klein's painstaking descriptions of the mechanism of splitting, which is facilitative for the young infant before integration can take place, do not really take account of something more radical, beyond splitting, as the subject proceeds to states of extreme dissociation. Here there exists no longer the capacity to project, because there are no live objects left in the internal world to receive the undigestible communication. Shock and outrage remain frozen in this non-feeling state, and there is no feeling self left to be projected by the traumatised person. In a sense one could say that the audience receives the feeling, not via projection, but because they can do so in their own right, they are still human (Anne Alvarez, personal communication).

Morvern Callar's state is one of shock and horror, way beyond what one might call 'simple' loss. Loss can only begin to be faced once there is at least some rudimentary platform of integration – in other words the beginnings of a negotiation of the paranoid-schizoid situation. If splitting has been followed by radical dissociation, then there is room for psychopathic elements to develop that are unfettered by any idea of better feelings, anywhere. As Maiello (2000, p. 5) suggests, mindless destructiveness may indeed result from envious attacks, but also if trauma is experienced very early and acutely, what may result is a more passive breakdown of the human disposition to create meaningful emotional links. There ensues an objectless state in the internal world.

I have thought elsewhere (Edwards, 2008) of ways to link theory and observation of psychological processes in a meaningful way that does not foreclose on true learning. How can teachers communicate theoretical concepts while also remaining 'experience near'? (Sandler and Sandler, 1994). I suggest here that seeing a film, participating in an emotional experience, and then seeking to link it with theoretical concepts may well bring greater understanding of the theory.

I think many of us may vividly recall our first experiences with patients, when the consulting room would be filled with the therapist's anxieties as well as those of the patient. While I think the anxiety of 'not knowing' never disappears, and nor indeed should it, in each case treated, it does become less overwhelming, and becomes one of a number of potentially informative psychoanalytic tools, via the medium of the counter-transference; an 'instrument of research' as Heimann (1950) first called it.

Psychoanalytic work involves a very specific way of relying on 'self and other' and 'self with other' observations. Reflexivity is built into the fabric of the work, which involves processing the ongoing and frequently shifting counter-transferences, discriminating their provenance in either patient as information via projection, or in the mind of the therapist separate from the patient's subjectivity. Bion (1955) talks of what he calls 'this most interesting problem' of how the patient imposes a phantasy and its corresponding affect upon the analyst. 'In the analytic situation, a peculiarity of communication of this kind is that, at first sight, it does not seem to have been made by the patient at all.' When we see a film, we are silent, unspeaking, and have the opportunity to experience something in a particularly individual way, even though we are in the company of others. I think by extension, we might find this way of experiencing to have affinities with what gets projected in the consulting room. If we consider this to be a valid link, then I suggest that working with film in this way may in a sense offer the student some proto-experience of the individual work in the consulting room, in a sense as a bridge towards later clinical experience, where the practitioner's mental space within the session, and indeed following it, is bounded by tenets and concepts of theory as by a flexible container, as Bion suggested. What he indicated was that learning depends on 'the capacity to remain integrated and yet lose rigidity. This is the foundation of the state of mind of the individual who can retain his knowledge and experience and yet be prepared ... to be receptive of a new idea' (Bion, 1962, p. 93).

I would like to end by quoting from Ogden's (2006) paper 'On Teaching Psychoanalysis'. He is of course talking of analysts in training, but I think one can extrapolate from what he suggests is order to reflect on how to introduce psychoanalytic concepts to pre-clinical students in a dynamic way. He talks about reading poetry and fiction as 'a form of ear-training': words create experiences to be lived by the reader. What I suggest is that film too can play a helpful role in re-creating painful, preverbal states and experiences, or, to paraphrase Ogden, 'a form of emotion-training' in how to think about bearing painful emotional states. 'In sum, teaching psychoanalysis is a paradoxical affair; someone who is supposed to know teaching someone who wants to know what it means not to know' (p. 1083).

Note

1   A more extended version of this chapter was originally published in the *British Journal of Psychotherapy* (2010) 26(1), and won the Jan Lee memorial Prize for the best paper in that year linking psychoanalysis with the arts. Also in Bainbridge and Yates (eds) (2014), *Media and the Inner World*, London and New York, Palgrave Macmillan.

References

Alvarez, A. (1992) *Live Company*. London and New York: Routledge.

Alvarez, A. (2007) 'Levels of analytic work and levels of pathology', paper presented at Association of Child Psychotherapists' Conference.

Bion, W. R. (1955) 'Language and the schizophrenic'. In M. Klein, P. Heimann and R. Money-Kyrle (eds), *New Directions in Psychoanalysis*. London: Tavistock, pp. 220–39.

Bion, W. R. (1962) *Learning from Experience*. London: Karnac.

Britton, R. (1998) *Belief and Imagination*. London and New York: Routledge.

Edwards, J. (2000) 'On being dropped and picked up: Adopted children and their internal objects'. *Journal of Child Psychotherapy*, 26(3), 349–67. Reprinted in Hindle and Shulman (2008), *The Emotional Experience of Adoption*. London and New York: Routledge.

Edwards, J. (2008) 'Early splitting and identification'. *Journal of Infant Observation*, 11(1), 57–65.

Freud, S. (1917) 'Mourning and melancholia'. *S.E. 14*, 327–60. London: Hogarth.

Gabbard, G. (ed.) (2000) *Psychoanalysis and Film*. London and New York: Karnac.

Heimann, P. (1950) 'On countertransference'. *International Journal of Psychoanalysis*, 31, 81–4.

Horne, A. (2001) 'Brief communications from the edge: Psychotherapy with challenging adolescents'. *Journal of Child Psychotherapy*, 27(1), 3–18.

Joseph, B. (1975) 'The patient who is difficult to reach'. In E. Bott Spillius (ed.), *Melanie Klein Today Vol. 2* (1988). London and New York: Routledge, pp. 48–60.

Klein, M. (1930) 'The importance of symbol formation in the development of the ego'. In M. Klein (ed.) (1975) *Love, Guilt and Reparation and Other Works 1921–1945*. London: Hogarth Press, pp. 219–232.

Klein, M. (1940) 'Mourning and its relation to manic-depressive states'. In M. Klein (ed.) (1975), *Love, Guilt and Reparation and Other Works 1921–1945*. London: Hogarth Press, pp. 344–69.

Klein, M. (1946) 'Notes on some schizoid mechanisms'. In M. Klein (ed.) (1975), *Envy and Gratitude and other works 1946–63*. London: Hogarth Press, pp. 1–24.

Klein, M. (1955) 'On identification', in M. Klein (ed.) (1975), *Envy and Gratitude, and Other Works 1946–63*. London: Hogarth Press, pp. 141–75.

Lechevalier-Haim, B. (2001) 'From freezing to thawing: working towards the depressive position in long term therapy with autistic patients'. In J. Edwards (ed.), *Being Alive*. London and New York: Routledge, pp. 89–101.

Maiello, S. (2000) 'Broken Links: Attack or breakdown?' *Journal of Child Psychotherapy*, 26(1), 5–24.

Ogden, T. H. (2006) 'On teaching psychoanalysis', *International Journal of Psychoanalysis*, 87, 1069–85.

Ramsay, L. (2002) Quoted in Momentum Pictures press release.

Sabbadini, A. (ed.) (2003) *The Couch and the Silver Screen: Psychoanalytic Reflections on European Cinema: The New Library of Psychoanalysis*. Hove and New York: Routledge.

Sandler, J. and Sandler, A-M. (1994) 'Comments on the conceptualisation of clinical facts'. *International Journal of Psychoanalysis*, 75(5/6), 995–1011.

Steiner, J. (1993) *Psychic Retreats*. London: Routledge.

Winnicott, D. W. (1984) *Deprivation and Delinquency*. London: Routledge.

CHAPTER 11

SIFTING THROUGH THE SANDS OF TIME

Mourning and melancholia revisited via the documentary *Nostalgia for the Light* (2011)

A film essay[1]

Film is of crucial importance in offering the opportunity to explore similar territory to that which the psychoanalyst studies in a different medium. The power of images and music together may create an extra dimension not possible with words alone. Viewing a film, as we normally do, in the darkness of a space shared with others, offers a specialised experience, partaking both of group and individual associations and states of mind. Associations to clinical material as well as one's own personal experiences are evoked. There are also of course issues about what of our experience we may project into film as well as what we may receive from the film and from the others with whom we share the experience.

Nostalgia for the Light (2011) is a documentary film by Patrick Guzman, one of Chile's foremost directors, set in the Atacama Desert in Chile, 10,000 feet above sea level. It immediately resonated with me and clearly with the original audience as a different way of thinking about the difference between mourning, melancholia, failed mourning and how to try to differentiate between these states of mind. This piece is not a 'film review' in the classical sense: much as a film editor might do, I have chosen to major on an overall theme. As is the issue with any 'review', a film interacts with the viewer's conscious and also unconscious preoccupations.

The opening footage shows the painstaking and laborious assembling of an old German telescope, iron wheels and brass cogs creaking and turning. The director explains that when he was young this was used to gaze at the stars. Guzman was always passionate about the skies, had learned the names of many visible stars by heart, and meanwhile he and his family lived 'a simple provincial life'. Chile at that time was, as he describes it, 'a haven of peace'. 'This old telescope that I'm seeing again after so many years reminds me of my childhood. One thinks one has left childhood behind,' he says, but of course as we know we never do.

The articulate and thoughtful astronomer interviewed in this film returns to this theme later: he talks of how the present does not exist – because of the speed of light 'we do not see things at the very second we look at them – we manipulate the past. The past is at the core of our work, in order that we can build a better future'. Perhaps it is important that we tolerate such paradoxes in the mind. We look to distant galaxies in order to understand our distant past, and to discover more about our origins as a species. 'We think we have answered questions and more arise', the astronomer says. 'In answering two we trigger four more.' This coincides with Bion's exhortation to 'keep your questions in good repair'. In this opening footage, the mechanisms of the old German telescope creak into place, the laboratory shutters are opened and the telescope lens is pointed towards the sky.

The film explores its theme from three main perspectives. There is that of the aforementioned astronomer: the unpolluted skies above the Atacama desert are the clearest in the world and allow astronomers to see the boundaries of our universe. There is an archaeologist: the Atacama desert is the only place to show up brown if one sees the world from space; it has absolutely zero moisture, and so archaeological remains are preserved in a way not possible elsewhere. And then there is a group of women still literally sifting through the desert sands to find remnants of their loved ones who 'disappeared' during the Chilean massacres of the Pinochet era.

So there are three strands: astronomers examine the most distant galaxies, archaeologists uncover traces of ancient civilizations, and meanwhile women sift the sand for the bones of their loved ones, murdered in the twentieth century. Guadelupe Marengo of Amnesty International stated in September 2013:

> It is not acceptable that 40 years after the military coup the search for justice, truth and reparation in Chile continues to be hampered. An amnesty law continues to shield human rights violators from prosecution, there are still long delays in judicial proceedings and sentences fail to reflect the severity of the crimes committed.

Nostalgia is a philosophical work, yet also profoundly rooted in painful particularity. The film touches on where we are now clinically with the ideas of depression, loss, mourning and moving on: a sort of meditation on the theme rather than an exercise per se in producing new ideas. This links with Wilfred Bion's idea of an open or empty 'unsaturated' space for thinking – the unpolluted desert; a space for cooperative mental intercourse, where there are no pre-digested conclusions, but where something, perhaps previously unknown, may emerge in the mind of a reader or viewer. And while the concept of 'mind' is somewhat concrete in itself, it is rather a process of mental energy with no fixed boundary. As teachers of psychoanalytic theory are aware, new thoughts on 'old' papers may emerge each year that one has the privilege of transmitting their central ideas to generations of students.

We may reflect that we travel under the skies of a vast area of knowledge that has grown and matured from the first thinking of Freud (and will never stop growing): we are, too, like archaeologists unearthing and linking past with present, in order to provoke questions and directions for the future, both for our patients and for our profession. As is of course well known, Freud himself was the first in the field to use this archaeological metaphor. All our knowledge and experience move us on as we extend our own clinical bases alongside the thoughts of others, those of our forefathers and mothers in the field, as well as those of our contemporaries. Between the realms of the skies and the territory 'under the earth' of everyday life (in the unconscious as we might say), are the women in the film.

This small band of women, courageous and indefatigable in their search for the bones of their loved ones, and yet bound by their own losses to a wheel of regret about loss and grievance, may be thought of as representing the dilemmas of patients, trapped in states of mind that seem to offer no way out, so that they endlessly rake over old coals. Lita Riesenberg, who was living in Chile at the time of the 'disappearances', said: 'This is the life of these women now . . . I have met some of them more recently; they cannot accept the present because they feel they would lose their loved ones for ever' (Personal communication).

'Nostalgia' is a term first coined by a Swiss doctor, Johannes Hofer, in a dissertation submitted to Basel University in 1688. It was meant to be used as a medical term to describe a depressed mood caused by intense longing to return home – derived from the Greek word *nostos*, the longing for home as portrayed by epic heroes such as Ulysses. But no *nostos* can change the fact that there can never be 'a return to the same'. In a book called *The Future of Nostalgia* (Boym, 2002), the author makes a distinction between 'restorative' and 'reflective' nostalgia. Nostalgia of the restorative kind concentrates on the *nostos*: returning to the lost home; reflective nostalgia on the other hand concentrates on the *algos* – the longing and the sense of loss – what Klein (1963) called 'pining'. Sohn (1983) attempted to differentiate between what he termed 'true' and 'false' nostalgia.

Central to this issue of nostalgia and the sense of loss is the notion of time. Freud (1915) noted that the unconscious is timeless. Jaques (1982) reminds us of the need to discriminate between 'objective' and 'subjective' time: the first is marked by measured uniformity of linear intervals, while the latter is irregular, dependent on multiple psychological factors. Linked to this is the notion of the impersonality of time, neither cruel nor kind, which carries us inexorably from birth to death. In a timeless realm, by contrast, one is locked into a frozen state outside time, with no hope of change or growth, a kind of existential depression that also locks the person so gripped into endless repetition compulsions. The subject is chained to traumatic events that cannot be psychologically represented (re-presented), in a way that facilitates moving on. The dominance of these conscious and unconscious thoughts reduces or completely negates the capacity for new emotional investments that might enrich the inevitable passage of time.

An adolescent patient came to me with a psychiatric diagnosis of 'post-autistic'. He had indeed emerged already from a profoundly autistic infantile state, after a traumatic birth and difficult early life, through some analytic work undertaken when he was in the latency stage. He continued to make progress. Whether or not one considers that autism can be successfully treated with psychoanalytic work, this young man did eventually live independently, which was an outcome his parents had never dared hope for. Through the work we did together, he finally managed to take his place in the space–time continuum, emerging from a 'timeless' space (Edwards, 1994a, 1994b). After nearly two years of intensive therapy, he arrived one day fired up by the opening bars of Beethoven's *Fifth Symphony* which his Dad had played at home. He said: 'You wait, then you hear da da da da – then there's a bit of a gap, then da-da-da-da again – then it starts!' He too had finally 'started'; had taken his place in the space–time continuum as defined by Einstein in which physical events are located, the three dimensions of space (height, width and depth) linked with one time dimension. He was now able to wait for the sessions and was held, as one is held by time, by their regular recurrence. But, as Einstein wrote in a letter to a bereaved friend (as if to provide some comfort): 'People like us who believe in physics know that the distinction between past, present and future is only a stubbornly persistent illusion' (Monk, 2012). This view is now orthodoxy among theoretical physicists.

Returning to Guzman's film, one might see this small band of women as endlessly locked into searching for the impossible – dry bones in the dry sand – sifting through their memories, raking the desert without hope of reconciliation, yet without the resources of 'truth' to enable them to move forwards. They might be seen as emotionally 'frozen' in the desert in a timeless state. This state could also be linked to a 'pre-depressive' state of mind that precludes movement until something can breach the 'threshold' of a defensive system (Edwards, 2005). The women have partially acknowledged the loss but remain in a 'psychic retreat' of illusory timelessness (Steiner, 1993). There can be no reconciliation for them without truth (these two must go together as events in South Africa have shown).

The director asks the astronomer, an articulate and profoundly reflective man in his thirties or forties, what he thinks of the searching women. His reply is that, while both his team and the team of women are searching for something in the past, there is of course one huge difference: 'After each night observing the past we can sleep easy, awake untroubled and begin again.' The women are looking for a past they may never be able to find. If he lost his own parents, he says, he would like to think he would search for them in the stars where he would imagine them to be. But these women searching in the vast expanses of the Atacama; how can one say to them as some people do: 'Oh, this is the past, enough is enough'? The past is at the core of the work of astronomy, he says, but these traumatised women still see those who arrested their loved ones in the streets. 'They will never find peace.'

It is clear that at one level these women continue politically, as is shown in the film, to keep the past alive, so that there should be no pushing these events under the carpet of time. They are situated as a painful reminder of events that were never acknowledged, and will never 'go away'. These will remain until truth, as far as it ever can be, is granted to them and the thousands like them, and not only in Chile, who experience the acute pain of loss without knowledge of what really took place, nor where the bones of their loved ones may lie.

Two seminal papers that lie at the heart of psychoanalytic thinking about loss are relevant here. Freud (1917) wrote 'Mourning and melancholia' in less than three months, early in 1915. Europe had embarked on the First World War (two of his sons fought on the front lines and he had been resistant to their going). This paper remains pivotal in the understanding of the unconscious working through of mourning and of melancholia. Both states are responses to loss and involve what Freud called 'grave departures from the normal attitude to life' (1917, p. 243). He describes melancholia as:

> a profoundly painful dejection, cessation of interest in the outside world, loss of the capacity to love, inhibition of all activity, and a lowering of the self-regarding feelings to a degree that finds utterances in self reproaches and self-revilings, and culminates in a delusional expectation of punishment.
>
> (Freud, 1917, p. 244)

As he further so memorably says: 'The shadow of the lost love-object falls on the ego' (p. 246). In other words, the object is berated for its loss although it is the subject who is consciously criticised. Mourning is seen as basically the same except for one crucial difference: 'the disturbance of self-regard is absent' (p. 247).

Klein's (1940) paper, 'Mourning and its relevance to manic-depressive states', was published twenty-five years later. She sees mourning as a 'depressive position' phenomenon. She stresses that earlier unresolved issues around mourning are reactivated in adult mourning, and the failure to recover from states of mourning is absolutely dependent on whether the depressive position has been resolved in infancy. She uses material from her own life following the death of her son Hans in 1932, and documents what she calls 'the passing states of elation', as well as profound pain, which are the other end of the swing between two poles following loss through death of a loved person. 'The ego is persuaded by the sum of the narcissistic satisfactions it derives from being alive to sever its attachment to the object that has been abolished' (1940, p. 127). Ambivalent states are experienced by both the melancholic and the 'normal' mourner, but become stuck and then displaced from object to subject in failed mourning. In the more 'normal' situation of mourning, equilibrium is regained with the passing of time, and the mourner is able to move on: as Klein says, he or she rebuilds the internal world 'which was disintegrated and in danger . . . he overcomes grief, regains security, and achieves true harmony and peace' (p. 153). This involves the passage of time, from the seemingly timeless agony of acute loss to acceptance of loss and the turning to other good objects, both internally and in the external world.

If one draws back for an overview, there remains a lifelong dialectic between time and timelessness, and to move from one to the other is inherent in the central work of accepting the reality principle, however painful this may be. Ultimately of course it links with our own mortality. We all have, as Bion (1962) averred, to tolerate the frustration of not knowing, but for these women in the film, this tolerance is not possible: there can be no movement or reconciliation for them without truth. (There were conflicting stories about these killings and whether the bodies had been disinterred from their original rough burial place in the desert to be dispersed either at sea beyond reach of any 'proof' of their having happened, or elsewhere in the desert.)

There were indeed reviews of the film that lauded the women for refusing to give up their search, without any thought given to the question of whether they were relentlessly raking over old coals. It is important that both points of view have space in the mind.

Over seventeen years thousands of political prisoners were massacred during the Pinochet regime. There is a long-shot of one of the women, starkly silhouetted against the pink beauty of the mountains and dawn sky, bent over the desert sand, stooping and standing over and over again, as she with the other women begins her relentless daily task. We see in her hands fragments that she can identify as insides and outsides of bones, by their markings and their levels of calcification. Her name is Vicky. She talks to camera of her brother's foot being found, still in his shoe, some fragments of bone, and some teeth, as well as nearly half of his skull:

> They finished him off with two bullets in the head . . . all that remains is what I can remember of his tender expression . . . Our final moment together was when his foot, still in its burgundy sock, was with me at my home. My mind was blank, I was in total shock. I got up in the night and went to stroke his foot; we were reunited. It was a great joy and a great disappointment. Only then did I take in that my brother was dead.

The state of timelessness may be either a frozen state where ongoing life cannot be contemplated, or may be the illusion of a narcissistic omnipotent state where the narcissistic self rejects anything beyond its control. In the frozen state, which I think these women inhabit (in spite of what some reviewers averred), it is the strength of love that makes them search in the present for these pathetic fragments of important objects/people from the past: a past that is perpetually remembered precisely because it cannot be re-membered. 'I want the bones so much', says another woman, Violeta, about her murdered husband, 'but I want him whole.' 'Reality' in this sense can either be a state of mind where one accepts loss and limits, but also a state where one may regain hope and possibility for the future. Time past, time present and time future, as T. S. Eliot and Bob Dylan among many others over the millennia have said, are inextricably intertwined. Time never moves backwards in reality; what has happened has happened, and cannot be undone, although as the attachment researchers showed us (Fonagy *et al.*, 1993) history is not destiny, and attitudes to the past can be reworked in order to move on to a less contaminated future. As one parent said to me about a broken relationship in the past: 'It took a long time for that one to become history.' And as the archaeologist in the film says: 'Memory has a gravitational force; it helps us to live in a fragile present. Those who have no memory don't live anywhere.'

So entering time is a sequential phenomenon where events unfold. This is a vital and basic necessity if the psyche is to remain healthy and able to think. Distance engendered by the passage of time is at the core of, for example, Proust's masterpiece. At one level one could see all our work with patients who are stuck in states of mourning or depression as being centrally connected with this resumption of 'temporality'. In this connection Green (2005) talked about two types of transference: the transference onto words and the transference onto the object. The first involves psychic elements being 'rescued' and converted into discourse (this is the consequence of attunement on the part of the object, as it is of course in the first primary relationships the infant makes within her/his world). This is intimately connected with the second aspect: that of the resultant transference onto the object. When thoughts become not only thinkable but speakable, they can become translated over time into personal history, re-created by the patient in the two-person relationship with the analyst. In a paper called 'A matter of time: Actual time and the production of the past', Scarfone (2006) makes a compelling argument for seeing consciousness itself as being inseparable from existential time and chronology. Object constancy and an ongoing sense of time may have been severely disrupted by trauma and disorganisation. In order for this transformation to take place there will *need* to be repetition in words of past experiences if this past is to become part of the intersubjective re-creation in the present between patient and therapist.

In the film, when asked whether she will carry on searching, Violeta says: 'For as long as I can. Even if I have doubts and questions within me I can't answer – did they really throw them into the sea? What if they threw them somewhere in the mountains?' She pauses for painful reflection here:

> Sometimes I feel like an idiot, because I never stop asking questions and nobody gives me answers. If someone told me the remains were on top of the mountains, then even though I'm seventy now I'd find a way to get to the top. It would be difficult, but hope gives you strength. Vicky and I have spent so many, many years searching. We set out full of hope, and come home with our heads hanging. Next day we pick ourselves up and set out again. But I told one of the researchers: 'I don't want his jawbone: I want him whole.'

As Hoffmann (2004) has discussed, far from leaving someone better equipped to deal with emotional life, actual experiences of persecution, by their indigestibly cruel nature, lend themselves to internal persecutory constellations, which Steiner (1993) has called pathological organisations; these may, in turn, promote further cruelty in the external world.

Towards the end of *Nostalgia for the Light*, two of the searching women, Vicky and Violeta, clamber up the iron ladder in the observatory and view the starry skies through the astronomer's massive telescope. We do not hear their reactions. There is music playing as they view the heavens. I thought this might represent a movement forward, to seeing their horribly painful memories from a wider perspective, in order to insert both themselves and these truly horrific historical events into an ongoing if terribly painful narrative, and move on rather than remain frozen and possessed eternally within it. Rilke (1923) wrote in his *Duino Elegies*:

Who shows a child as he really is?
Who helps him see himself from a distance
So he can set himself among the stars?

(Translated by JE)

In contrast to these women, the film shows how an architect who was imprisoned in a subsequently erased concentration camp in the desert went to remarkable lengths in order to pace out and record his prison, which he drew later in minute detail. This way of expressing the facts of his trauma had a therapeutic effect on him, as well as providing vital information that could not then be denied. Another set of imprisoned men viewed the star-filled sky secretly at night through an illicitly built telescope; this gave them huge emotional sustenance: 'We had a feeling of great freedom: we felt completely free, marveling at the constellations.'

Might one think about these solutions as being to do with more resilient character structures? While this may be so, it may be important too to give consideration to the different positions in a subject's mind. One either has the direct experience of the trauma, or is left waiting, as these women were, with the pain of the awareness of a physical trauma experienced by their loved ones inhabiting their hearts and minds. It is of course the lot of women, wives and mothers all over the often war-torn world to wait and to mourn, or to get stuck in the waiting and be unable to move on to the mourning.

The film shows a young mother, Valentina, who works at the astronomy laboratory, feeding her baby. She had been the daughter of 'disappeared ones' and had been brought up by grandparents who had had to reveal the address of their own daughter and her husband in order to save their grandchild. Although Valentina says she still felt like 'damaged goods' with 'a manufacturing defect', there seemed in her relationship to her baby also some hope of looking to the future, of the need to let the torturing past go, as well as gratitude to the grandparents who could be thought to represent recovered aspects of good lost parents. 'Stars must die', she says, 'and then others are born. Thinking about this at the laboratory frees me a little from the pain; I have the desire to progress.'

This film and the thoughts it engendered link to the clinical task of being able over time to generate an ongoing rather than circular trajectory of thought in traumatised patients, starting from whatever level their trauma may lie. Are they able to move forward and thus generate a new platform of meaning? Are they able to move onwards rather than dance round and round in pain and suffering? And are people trapped in states of melancholia suffering either from having cut off rather than repressed their history, or from being possessed too much by it? It is of course a matter always delicate to untangle, and it needs time and patient understanding of profoundly despairing mental states in order to work towards what Green (2005) described as 'transference onto words'. Lechevalier-Haim (2001), in talking of the long-term treatment of autistic children, observed that emotions only begin to thaw out after a great deal of time is spent processing them. As Ogden (2005, p. 65) in a chapter about Freud's 'Mourning and melancholia' said:

> The ambivalence in relations between unconscious internal objects involves not only the conflict with love and hate, but also the conflict between the wish to continue to be alive in one's object relationships and the wish to be at one with one's dead internal objects.

I have of course taken liberties in my 'viewing' of this film, from the perspective of psychoanalytic work, but I hope that this may produce more conversations about how we handle grief and trauma when patients come to us for help. I also hope that this piece may encourage others to see a film that, it seems to me, is a remarkable view from another vertex and discipline, of the perennial dilemmas to do with loss and recovery.

Note

1   This chapter was also published in *International Psychoanlayse, Behandlungsperspektiv* (2015) Edited Mauss-Hanke, Giessen, Germany.

References

Bion, W. R. (1962) *Learning from Experience*. London: Heinemann.
Boym, S. (2002) *The Future of Nostalgia*. New York: Basic Books.
Edwards, J. (1994a) 'On solid ground: The ongoing psychotherapeutic journey of an adolescent boy with autistic features'. *Journal of Child Psychotherapy, 20*, 57–84.
Edwards, J. (1994b) 'Joe: towards solid ground: an adolescent's request for a second course of psychotherapy'. In A. Alvarez and S. Reid (eds), *Autism and Personality*. London and New York: Routledge, pp, 57–83.
Edwards, J. (2005) 'Before the threshold: Destruction, reparation and creativity in relation to the depressive position'. *Journal of Child Psychotherapy, 31*, 317–35.
Fonagy, P., Steele, M., Moran, G. S., Higgitt, A. (1993) 'Measuring the ghosts in the nursery: An empirical study of the relation between parents' mental representations of childhood experiences and their infants' security of attachment'. *Journal of American Psychoanalytical Association, 41*, 957–89.
Freud, S. (1915) 'The unconscious'. *S.E. 14*, 166–215. London: Hogarth.
Freud, S. (1917) 'Mourning and melancholia'. *S.E. 14*, 239–48. London: Hogarth.
Green, A. (2005) *Key Ideas for a Contemporary Psychoanalysis*. London and New York: Routledge.
Hoffmann, E. (2004) *After Such Knowledge: A Meditation on the Aftermath of the Holocaust*. London: Secker & Warburg.
Jaques, E. (1982) *The Form of Time*. New York: Crane Russak.
Klein, M. (1940) 'Mourning and its relation to manic-depressive states'. In M. Klein (ed.) (1975) *Love, Guilt and Reparation*. London: Hogarth, pp. 344–69.
Klein, M. (1963) 'On the sense of loneliness'. In M. Klein (ed.) (1975) *Envy and Gratitude*. London: Hogarth, pp. 300–13.
Lechevalier-Haim, B. (2001) 'From freezing to thawing: Working towards the depressive position in long-term therapy with autistic patients'. In J. Edwards (ed.), *Being Alive: Building on the Work of Anne Alvarez*. Hove: Brunner Routledge, pp. 89–101.
Monk, R. (2012) 'Review: *Time Reborn* by Lee Smolin'. *The Guardian*, 8 June.
Ogden, T. H. (2005) *This Art of Psychoanalysis*. London: Routledge.
Rilke, R. M. (1923) *Duino Elegies*. Frankfurt: Insel-Verlag (Translation by Judith Edwards).

Scarfone, D. (2006) 'A matter of time: Actual time and the production of the past'. *Psychoanalytic Quarterly*, 75, 807–34.

Sohn, L. (1983) 'Nostalgia'. *International Journal of Psychoanalysis*, 64, 203–11.

Steiner, J. (1993) *Psychic Retreats*. London: Routledge.

CHAPTER 12

SEEING AND BEING SEEN

The dialectics of intimate space and Antony Gormley's 'Event Horizon'

> A time may indeed come when the pictures and statues that we may admire today will crumble to dust ... the value of all this beauty and perfection is determined only by its significance for our own emotional lives
>
> (Sigmund Freud 'On Transience', 1915)

In this short paper Freud offered a strong argument for the acceptance of transience, that we need to accept the passing and destruction of all things including of course ourselves ... Freud then goes on to say that the transience of beauty does not detract from its worth – 'transience value is scarcity value in time' – but it is precisely this very element that makes it more precious to us. In addition, one might wonder about Freud's own struggles with personal transience and the contrary wish to be remembered: a feeling that personal annihilation means the death of the capacity to experience the beauty of the world, which might make it paradoxically easier to accept its transience.

In May 2007 thirty-one life size iron male figures were placed on prominent buildings across London, in sites ranging from the Shell Centre and the National Theatre on the South Bank, to Waterloo Bridge and King's College, locations on either side of the river Thames. Their function was twofold: to be an installation in their own right, and to promote the sculptor Antony Gormley's exhibition 'Blind Light' at the Hayward Gallery, scheduled to run till mid August in the same year. All the statues were looking towards the gallery, from their various vantage points, as well as in some sense overlooking a whole section of the architecture in that region of London. They immediately became a talking point, and very soon a petition was being organised to send to Downing Street, asking that they stay in situ after the exhibition closed. This had already happened with a previous installation of Gormley's in 2005 called 'Another Place' on a beach near Liverpool, where despite a mixed reception by local people (some of whom 'decorated' the statues with underwear and other pieces of clothing, calling it 'pornography on the beach'), some of the figures did finally find a permanent site there in March 2007, looking out to sea as the tide came and went on Crosby Beach.

As is well known, Antony Gormley has been examining the potential of human form in sculpture for the last twenty-five years, with his own body as the medium for the investigation. He sees the body as a place of memory and transformation: 'I am interested in the body because it is the place where emotions are most directly registered. When you feel frightened, when you feel excited, happy, depressed, somehow the body registers it.' This has links with Freud's idea that 'the body is first and foremost a bodily ego' that emphasises the psycho-somatic connection from the beginning. Students of Infant Observation have the opportunity and privilege to observe the development of the infant's personality and the ego from the beginning, through the bodily ministrations of the infant's caretakers as well as their mindful reflection on the infant's own states of mind. These body/mind services remain embedded in the personality, as Melanie Klein averred, as 'memories in feeling'. Gormley has also said that he sees sculpture as an act of faith in life, in its continuity – which is a somewhat different view from that expressed by Freud on transience almost 100 years previously, although one might think that these ideas are not mutually exclusive either.

The sculptor said in a television interview that he uses his own body (which some have seen as being a narcissistic or an exhibitionist act), because it would be hard to ask others to endure the arduous process involved in making the statues. His view is that 'there are better ways of being vainglorious than making a few rusty, somewhat industrially produced clones that have no pretension to being idealised but just hang around' – hang around they may do, and they also hang around in people's minds, in a way that Gormley clearly intended, despite this somewhat disingenuous statement. Some commentators have seen these figures to be a depiction of the body as a lonely self, vulnerable in its nakedness, lost, looking out for a meaning that never perhaps arrives. This may indeed be part of the story. We are all perhaps looking for 'Another Place' – beyond the reality principle of our lives – some transforming truths that would ameliorate the pain of the human condition. In Freud's paper 'On transience' (1915) he describes his conversation with the young Rilke 'already a famous poet', who is struggling with the idea of transition and transience:

> The idea that all this beauty was transient was giving these two sensitive minds [*that also of Lou-Andreas Salome, Rilke's companion*] a foretaste of mourning over its decease; and since the mind instinctively recoils from anything so painful, they felt their enjoyment of beauty was interfered with by thoughts of its transience.

Cities now account for 50 per cent of the world's population. By locating his figures overlooking one of the world's great cities, did Gormley articulate for us all a sense of searching, of looking over the 'Event Horizon' for something that we may not be able to begin to know about in words? Might this be a search for meaning, or conversely a search to evade the pain of meaning? Bollas (2000) talked of city architecture and its 'play with life and death': that buildings enhance the inorganic spaces they inhabit. In these figures presiding over the cityscape, there seemed to reside some juxtaposition between thoughts of life and death, of flying and falling.

The title 'Event Horizon' for the installation intrigued me. The catalogue notes to the 'Blind Light' exhibition explain that the term is used to refer to 'the body of the observable universe'. The term 'Event Horizon' was one first used in theoretical physics, to describe the surface of a 'black hole', beyond which the inward pull of gravity is so overwhelming that no information about the black hole's interior can ever escape into the outer universe. Inside the black hole matter has collapsed to infinite density – and the question is, where lies the 'point of no return' at which any matter or energy is doomed to disappear from the visible universe? The event horizon is a kind of surface or 'skin', covering this bizarre and terrifying situation where space and time cease to exist. Gormley's stated project is that his 'silent witnesses' are designed to create uncertainty about the work's dimensions – 'Beyond the figures you can actually see, how many more are there that you can't see?' I offer an additional view here, and investigate whether there is anything to be gained by looking at unconscious processes, in terms of seeing and being seen.

Black holes, it is thought, may form as the result of a massive star collapsing at its 'death'. It was Frances Tustin, a brilliant and insightful child and adult psychotherapist, who first noted these phenomena in work with autistic patients, and linked them with catastrophic feelings of being separated and unprotected, indeed with no sense of a protective 'skin'. These ideas have links with Esther Bick's notion of the newborn infant : it was she who, at John Bowlby's suggestion, initiated seminars on Infant Observation at the Tavistock Clinic, as a prerequisite for psychoanalytic training in work with children. The infant at the beginning feels to a large extent fragmented, experiencing mother's physical and psychological holding as a kind of mental skin holding his primitive self together (1968). The psychoanalyst Bion (1959) elaborated the idea of the way this holding and 'containment', in which the caretaker receives the projections of the infant's terror and attempts to understand them, then returning them in a more digested form, allays fears of disintegration and falling apart. Houzel (1995) in a paper called 'Precipitation Anxiety' describes what may happen if the psychic as well as the physical gradient is not managed in a way that ameliorates the terror of 'falling into the world' – and it is significant that midwives in some cultures still talk of 'catching' the baby as she is born. Observers of infants may witness many such moments in the early weeks of an infant's life, in the course of an ordinary day, where change and fear of absence or of being uncontained, one might hypothesise, stir up the anxieties experienced around the profound moment of being born: that 'caesura of birth' as Freud had called it.

While Tustin talked of 'autistic capsules' in the personality, Ogden (1997) then went on to reflect on what he called 'the autistic contiguous position', a universal mode of generating experience that he sees as part of the normal daily human repertoire functioning as a respite from bombardment: what he sees as being a buffer against the daily strains of being alive.

As Klein (1959, p. 248) averred 'the process of birth and the adjustment to postnatal situations cause the baby to experience anxiety of a persecuting nature'. She went on to write, in her last paper, unpublished till after her death, that 'phantasies never stop playing a great part in mental life'. Loneliness, she thought, could never be completely eliminated. And it was Winnicott (1965) who maintained that isolation is a necessary condition for psychological health – an essential component in the experience of living and reality testing. He saw the individual to be, in some fundamental and important sense, 'an isolate, permanently unknown, in fact unfound' (p. 183).

Linking these thoughts about the terror of falling, and the isolated nature of our existence, with the Gormley installation, the question then arises: might the figures have been looking into the black hole (some of them indeed looked down) or beyond it? Were they sentinels warning of danger, or might they have delineated in people's minds the borders between survival and an infinite fall into the void?

We have in essence several themes here: that of transience as opposed to continuity, that of being 'above it all', looking towards an unknown future, and the opposite idea of 'falling', or being held to prevent the fall, in what we might think of as a reciprocal holding gaze. Winnicott (1989, p. 199) observed that 'successful' analyses 'enable patients to abandon invulnerability and become sufferers'. I wondered whether these contrasting ideas of suffering and denial of pain might be latent in the minds of those looking at these imposing figures on the skyline. When I visited the area I was struck by the impact of the figures, and the differential reactions to them. Did they represent Superman, or Everyman (and where does this leave Superwoman, or Everywoman?), safety or danger; might they be seen as parents, either benign or critical, or as fellow members of the naked human race? They looked out, and we looked at them – they did not watch us watching them, their purpose was to be seen by us, and yet they may also have conveyed the effect of being onlookers, or over-lookers, as they stood on the various buildings around the Thames. From the earliest eye contact and exchange of gaze between the infant and the caretaker, looking and being looked at are vital components in the establishment of personal relationships. What cultural function might these statues be seen to have performed at an unconscious level? Might they represent conflicts between differing aspects of our internal reality, and internal object relations?

In order to think more about this I decided to interview people, both adults and if possible children, as they were in situ on the South Bank, where they could see the statues grouped around the horizon, in the hope of at least finding out a little more about the issue. This of course can in no way be seen as a scientific research project in the usual sense. I had no formal 'justification' for pursuing this line of enquiry. I am also aware that interviewing processes present one with a different set of methodological problems from the ones to which I am used as a child and adult psychotherapist. The work of the psychotherapist is contingent on core concepts such as transference, resistance, free association and play, involving the patient's deployment of defences to ward off painful ideas about separation, separateness and loss, shown over time within a defined and regular space. I wondered however whether I might at least find some clues to my questions. 'Certainty', as Freud said in 'Moses and Monotheism', 'Is unattainable' (1939, p. 27 fn): and my modest goal was to find out something more from a psychoanalytic vertex about the same question that Gormley himself posed – what do his audience make of his works? As he observed:

> You could say that there are two very discrete and almost oppositional places where a sculpture belongs. One is physical, in a landscape or a room, and the other is in the imagination of the viewer, in her/his experience and memory. They are equally important and in many sense the work is there waiting— almost like a trap—for the life of the viewer to come and fill it, or inhabit it. And then once 'captured' the art—or its arising—inhabits him or her . . . how an object is interpreted or experienced by the viewer is none of my business at all.
>
> (Gormley, 2007, p. 44)

Bollas (2000 op. cit.) talked of cities as 'holding environments'. He describes what he calls 'the spirit of human endeavour' which needs representation in the built environment and goes on to say 'we may consider the ways in which a psychoanalysis of the built world could lead to a psycho-spiritual representation of human life' (p. 28). It became evident during the interviews that the 'built environment', often experienced by people in big cities as being impersonal and forbidding, may certainly benefit from the humanising presence of works of art created by sculptors such as Gormley, who respond to deep human needs and by so doing offer different facets for interpretation and enjoyment, giving people as it were an 'inner city' that is more manageable.

The interviews

I had prepared in my mind a set of questions to act as starting points to the interviews, or conversations (as I preferred to call them). This did not mean they would provide a rigid protocol to be followed, but that they would hopefully allow for a more flexible flow if this proved possible, but with an inherent containing structure. In practice, as conversations unfolded, not all the questions necessarily came up each time. Nevertheless what I hoped (and this was achieved in some cases) was that there might be a sort of 'surprising the unconscious' as people developed their thoughts – perhaps somewhat similar to Gormley's idea of a 'trap' where the art and the individual mind come into a particular relationship. Several people thanked me for the conversation, saying that it had indeed allowed them to put words to what they had been experiencing, at least in a preliminary way.

I had ten questions as a framework for whatever might emerge:

1   What were your first thoughts when you saw the figures?
2   What do you think they might be doing?
3   How do they make you feel?
4   Would you like to be up there with them?
5   What might you say to one of them?
6   What might he say to you?
7   Do you think they are exhibitionist?
8   Does it bother you that there are no women?
9   There's a petition to request that they stay – would you support that?
10   Would you miss them if they go?

The fifteen interviews as a whole were variously of mixed composition, with some family groups, some couples, some pairs or groups of friends, and a few individuals. Group conversations inevitably had their own particular dynamic, where one person's response might provoke either agreement or the offering of a different point of view, towards an interesting and more complex picture. One Dutch father of a nine-year-old boy who spoke no English at first translated my questions and the boy's responses, and then became so interested that he started to elaborate his own views directly to me, without translation for his son. This then became a feature of the boy's further responses. It was interesting at this point, when I managed to include the boy again by asking him what he thought the figures might say to him, he said, tellingly I thought, 'I would have nothing to say to them, and there are so many people here, why should the figures bother to speak to me?' He became animated again when I asked what he thought of the figures staying on the buildings (his father had thought they should not stay). 'I'd like that', he said in a lively tone, 'then the whole town would be the museum, not just inside!'

I found the experience of being able to have conversations with people in quite a free-flowing way, nevertheless defined by the questions I had in mind, to be in itself an interesting and dynamic experience. As one might expect, the eye and mind of the beholder holds individual meaning, both internally and externally, and these meanings are complicated and many-faceted. Unconscious meanings may be less clear, but some of the ideas expressed in the conversations here may be suggestive. I will summarise many of the fifteen 'conversations' and concentrate on just three in order to elucidate the issues of seeing and being seen.

I made a hesitant beginning, and for the first conversation, with a family group, I forgot to switch on the recorder. Luckily my training enabled me to recall afterwards how the family had responded, for the most part positively, to my request. The adolescent daughter was enthusiastic, and likened the figures to 'guardian angels'. Her mother was not sure, but she said they gave her a 'funny, friendly feeling', and then she wondered how they would feel up there in their own silent world. She felt they would not communicate with her. The father agreed, but said they gave him an added sense of perspective.

A cheerful and young French couple were enthusiastic, comparing them to gargoyles on French churches 'just looking down, checking and protecting'. A group of people on a day trip to London were very vocal. 'We come from the Angel' as one woman proudly said. 'They're just looking into the distance, no, they can't be looking at me, but maybe they're just observing us, like Dr Who [sic] or Angels in America.' One of the older men said they made him feel reassured, while another found it hard to enter into the idea of communication at all: 'I'm not used to talking to inanimate objects – well I think they should stay, they're good as lightning conductors at least.' A younger woman took up the idea of watching, but in a less benign way – she felt she wouldn't want one too near, peering into her living room, a bit like a peeping Tom. There seemed to be some messages here about my own presence, and as I thanked them and turned away, the man previously quoted said 'well a politician might canvass them – or are you Mrs Gormley?'

At an adjacent table sat an elderly man, his physically disabled wife, and their middle-aged son. They were keen to talk. The woman said:

> Anything that makes you look up and out is brilliant – they make you look further than you normally would, they are for instance on the other side of the river too – they make me smile but I might find them threatening if I was in a glum mood or with weather like yesterday (monsoons!) – I hate heights, but I would say 'Stay there for a long time, looking as far as you can see' – they might say 'come up and join us' [which seemed like a hopeful aspiration, for this disabled older woman].

Her son said 'I like them a lot, it's good to look up and not have your head always down – I'd like them to stay, I'd like them maybe to turn round and look in different directions too, change *their* perspective.' His mother said 'You can't be sure they are looking at this space', and her son rejoined:

> Maybe they're saying there go another bunch of tourists, wonder what they're saying about us! It works both ways – they add a lot. It's the opposite of *Blind Light*, looking inwards, and at gallery walls, this is about looking *outward* at the whole environment – it gives an expanded view, it definitely changes your perspective.

A young Italian woman, who was sitting alone with a guidebook and a map, seemed keen to share her thoughts:

> They're strange, you feel there should be a group of people underneath saying 'please don't jump' – they're on the edge: in a way it's quite comical – it's an unusual way to look down on us – it's strange to be looked down on like that,

weird, I'd say 'Don't jump!' too. I think they should stay, everyone can see them taking over parts of London – I'm an art student on a summer course at the Slade. The way Gormley works with space is fantastic, interacting with it, and he takes sculpture to a whole new level – London is such a big place you can easily feel faceless, get lost, [she had her map open on the table] and he has taken it over and made his presence felt.

I approached two laughing middle-aged women, who looked as though they were thoroughly enjoying their day out. They welcomed me and made space at the table for me to sit down. After I explained what I was doing, they launched into their own conversation about the figures with no further prompting from me:

There's a feeling of being watched, yes, but they're not intimidating – it's good for kids, great fun – the stance of the figures isn't threatening, they're standing with their arms open and sort of loose, you might see some people on rooves, security people, with guns, but these are gentle watching presences.

The second woman agreed:

That's such a good point, really thoughtful – I see them all the time because I live quite near here, it feels like fun, they're part of our environment now – it's strange living in London, such a big place you think you would never see people you know but I do quite a lot, and now Gormley is one of them! It's great to have public art with a sense of fun as well as something more profound – you don't feel they're intruding in your space. I read before that they were all Gormley, so I maybe relate to them differently – you can get up close and personal to him on Waterloo Bridge [This was one of the four sculptures at ground level, all anatomically correct].

The first woman said 'I couldn't go and join one of them, I might like to but I'm scared of heights'. Her friend took up the conversation again:

Another friend and I, and we hadn't had a drink either, had quite a long conversation with him the other night on the bridge – some of the comments are too inappropriate to repeat! You couldn't do that on your own, chatting to him with that sense of fun. I thought afterwards how extraordinary, my friend is quite introverted and wouldn't normally do that sort of thing – he elicits a real response – he wouldn't say anything back, he's just there. It's quite comforting to think 'they're all around you' – it'll be brilliant if they stay.

Her friend said:

I think people want them to stay because they humanise the city, a lot of buildings can seem too imposing, all concrete and glass, quite dominating and cold, and these figures are saying 'we're on top of it'. A male friend asked me if I felt left out because there were no women. In this era of complex political correctness it's hard to say really. Someone was talking about the Cerne Abbas giant on television – that the word 'man' derives from 'mind' not sexuality.

Her friend said ruefully, 'I've sometimes been called "the chair" and I'd rather be called "man" than "chair" – this isn't the right place to do stuff about equality though I do know there is still a lot to do. Is he exhibitionist?' (JE talks here of the blog comment reported in the newspapers, about the statues being 'just an excuse for him to exhibit his penis'):

> Oh, that's enormously trivialising isn't it . . . I think Gormley represents every person, like in Field, he is focussed on our common humanity – and he is using the body he has to hand. He comes across as someone you can relate to – talented and complicated but not exhibitionist . . . someone I aspire to be.

Nearby a group of two young women and a young man said they were from an art appreciation group. They too embarked on the conversation enthusiastically. The first young woman said:

> They're great, I feel like I'm looking at the ocean – when I was a child I lived by the beach and the harbour and I loved watching the boats coming in and then going again over the horizon, it's a good feeling, about my childhood – and Gormley's also got pieces on a beach.

Her female companion had a more sober view:

> I'm interested in them a lot, and they make me think about being in London at Liverpool Street post the 7/7 disaster – the marksmen were all around on the rooftops and I was in my office. These individual figures are watching and there's a faint air of surveillance about them. But that's when they're high up, you don't get that feeling when they're on the ground like the one at the back of the gallery. Anyway, they do remind me that I'm in a city, which is a contrast to being by the sea.

Their male companion agreed:

> I find them quite mesmerising, I can stop and then feel I'm trying to get a connection with them, there's definitely the sense of being watched by them and also watching them. I can't think of what I might say but I'd want to make some sort of connection – which is interesting when you think you're in a city full of people wanting naturally to have a bit of private space around themselves [JE 'and I'm aware I'm coming into yours'] – it's interesting, you see one lone person and maybe there's a wish to make a connection with, whereas you wouldn't normally want to do that, but why wouldn't you want to have that connection with a person in the street. Of course a person standing naked on top of a building would be different; that makes me think of jumpers, isolated and alone and yet not fragile, at least not these figures, but looking powerful.

The second woman said, 'Yes, they're close to the edge – I think we get a sense of identification and identity, inside and outside ourselves.' Their male companion added 'What would be the relevance of them staying? He's trying to express himself – like on the Beach – these lone anonymous figures staring out, we connect to this, perhaps that's what we all do, we're all looking for something.'

Three extended interviews

A group of two women and a man were very voluble and articulate, and the man began the conversation, even before I had switched on the tape.

Man: 'I think the statues should be on St Paul's and the Gherkin – they say something about the conflict of man and metropolis, and the city dominating human aspirations. These figures rise above the city, and so create some type of humanity, they are spiritually nourishing, yes, they should definitely be on the Gherkin and St Pauls.'

First woman: 'But then they'd be seen as a sort of joke on St Paul's and it might upset people; they'd be sticking two fingers up and they are not there for that. But I do dislike the Gherkin, it's arrogant, so that would be OK, I think, to stick two fingers up to arrogant architects – we don't want buildings that are a pastiche of what's gone before, but a lot of buildings now seem to be about the ego of the architect, look at me! No I don't think they're exhibitionist, he only casts his own body, it's about him.'

Man: 'I agree, they're a celebration of the human form, they say something about a self, they are totally personal, he didn't want to talk about the sexes.'

Second woman: 'I saw in the catalogue he has cast some female figures, but it isn't something that bothers me.'

First woman: 'It's his art, not our art! There are a lot of ways in which feminism got it wrong. Women are not the same as men but they are equal; it went too far.'

Man: 'I think you're lifted up to their level, it's a celebration of the human spirit, they're not looking down on us, I can imagine myself up there but it would be bloody cold!'

Second woman: 'But you'd get such a wonderful view!'

Man: 'I feel there's if you like an unspoken bond between them and me. It's a celebration, touching the transcendental without having to say anything, a bit like being understood without words.'

Second woman: 'I stroked the ones in the gallery, I would probably do that up there, it's a friendly experience [perhaps a parental experience (JE)]. I felt very close to the figures inside when I touched them. I'd touch them but not talk, they don't speak, they're 'completely apart' – there would be a kind of wordless communion.'

Her female friend agreed, but with rather strong reservations:

First woman: 'Yes they are "something apart" – but they don't come across to me as being tender or loving, they are very cold.'

Second woman: 'Not to me, I feel very close to them.'

Man: 'I think they are very private people, I wouldn't intrude in on them unless they made the first moves.' (JE apologises here for her intrusion!)

First woman: 'They are strong and I'd like them to stay.'

Man: 'They add a marvellous presence, and give a spiritual dimension that is totally lacking in the city at the moment which is about Mammon and making money. We need to present another facet and they do that, they add to human experience, the human condition. Yes, I will miss them when they are taken away.'

Another man and a woman sitting nearby were also very interested to have a conversation about their experiences:

Woman: 'It certainly gives us something to look at; makes you feel different about distances, it's not just blocks then, there's more a feeling of being scaled, it's quite odd really, in a way a bit spooky thinking of men walking across roofs, a bit like the exhibition and the white-out space, a sudden appearance like that is a sudden disappearance. It sort of makes you feel you have been put down to scale yourself, you are another little figure in a bigger landscape, makes me feel part of the landscape myself.'

Man: 'It's so interesting, a human form on top of a building, turning it upside down in a way, the buildings usually dominate people, it raises issues about how you display sculpture and where do you put public art; on a plinth? In a gallery? Or places that kind of surprise and shock – I know there was concern about suicide when they first went up, maybe people still think that. But they are on top – I'm not up there with them.'

Woman: 'Yes, in my scale I am definitely down here.'

Man: 'There's the repetition of the figures too, they are not straightforwardly representing or doing anything, their features are smoothed off, they're anyone, Everyman in a way. What is the action they are engaged in? It is surveillance, are we being watched by these brooding figures which is how they can come across sometimes if you catch them at certain angles. They're far from standard although they are all the same. Their location in different places gives different meanings.'

Woman: 'I hadn't seen them as ominous, although having said that you could also say they are slightly spooky, but also playful, and unexpected, a great contrast to blocks of functional architecture – the architecture can have an overwhelming quality and they reduce that feeling, give you more a sense of fun – cocking a snook at architect's seriousness, the blockiness of it, figures on the tops of the building are disarming, you can have a sense like a child of leaping from roof to roof.'

Man: 'They are unexpected, that's so good, it makes you pause, because there's a sort of disjunction, they make you look at the world slightly differently, gives a different sense of scale – the Angel of the North is so vast and then he's also done very small figures in Field, these are human size, not massive or tiny.'

Woman: 'They really open up the space, we don't normally think of the tops of buildings and the sky above them, they make you look up at the sky . . . There are so many figures of women everywhere, why not see a naked man, that's fine.'

Man: 'I think it would have a different meaning because there are different associations to a woman's body – maybe people would say quite different things. As a woman you'd probably feel vulnerable if you saw a naked woman up there. They don't make me feel vulnerable as a man, but it's quite good too to see the male body in a position of vulnerability . . . it doesn't feel abusive in the same way as it might if it were a woman's body. It's tempting to say to them "Jump!" – they look like the suspended figures inside who are falling.'

Woman: 'Oh no, I'd say carry on looking up! I don't think they can see us, for me they are in their own space, in a different plane.'

The man looked very thoughtful, then said slowly:

Man: 'There's something interesting about their posture, reminds me of diving when I was a child, you have your hands straight down and then you lift up on your toes [*he stood up with some energy and did it*] – I think that posture of theirs is almost like that, something to do with high diving – there is that same element of waiting, stillness and concentration.'

Woman: 'Yes they should stay longer but not for ever, because you don't want to lose that element of surprise but maybe then have something else surprising – I love that it comes out of nowhere, it surprises something in all of us.'

Man: 'They could be moved around. You could have a year say not having them, then they could appear in different places. They've got a meaning much beyond most public sculpture.'

Finally I talked to a young woman with two children, while the children were taken off along the embankment by their grandfather:

Young woman: 'They seem like such still figures in this big city landscape to me, I think of them observing time and movement, not threatening; a bit like the tide going in and out. You stop for a second to go where they are in your mind, you hold and let everything else continue round you, be at peace and at one with them, in unmeasured time, not physically but spiritually up there, because they are at one with the concrete environment, being made of industrial materials, they're part of the nature of the city in a way, there are particles that cling to them all, like barnacles. They wouldn't say anything, they just are; you could go alongside them and then embrace that space and time, be as un-intrusive as possible, a bit like the cloud cube, become part of it without interrupting them, join them and then come away again, a sort of fluid connection. You might have a conversation with them emotionally, and see what they see, the people, the buildings, the environment, what's behind you what's in front of you . . . the girls said why are there only men? They find it a bit bizarre, but if there were women too it would perhaps be different, more about sex and sexuality? The artist is a guy, it's his work, they're made of industrial, heavy materials. A woman would be more likely to make something more fluid, softer, echoing her body shape – shadows – these are male, phallic structures. There is industrial concrete all around and because he has used these sort of materials the figures sort of join the furniture – might a female piece in softer materials make it more exhibitionist? I don't know. Should they stay there? Well maybe these things are good to kind of knock you, but then they should just roll away, not to be there as monuments: part of what comes and goes. They kind of work while they're there, for ten days or ten years, but they shouldn't be stuck there for ever, it's good to see them and I guess I might miss them when they're gone because they are very different. I've seen Gormley's work before in different places. I think of them as sort of spiritual mentors: they're not looking at us but up at the sky, and we look up at them and get something from that.'

Discussion

'We're all looking for something', averred one of the young men I interviewed. As I hope these conversations indicate in different ways, this search while diverse, seems also to group around different ideas related, as I suggest, to unconscious processes: wishes, desires and anxieties. The statues, one might hypothesise, inhabit for the beholder what Winnicott (1971) called 'the transitional space'. This was originally conceived of as developing a space between mother and infant during the process of separation and individuation, where the 'transitional object' appears, what he called 'the first non-me object', to aid in the onward journey with the issues to do with separation, loss and mourning (as well too as issues of gain, when the infant turns towards the wider world). This space evolves with maturity into the space where adult play, and creativity, may grow and elaborate into cultural experience:

> I have used the term cultural experience as an extension of the idea of transitional phenomena and of play without being certain that I can define the word 'culture'. The accent indeed is on experience. In using the word culture I am thinking of the inherited tradition. I am thinking of something that is in the common pool of humanity, into which individuals and groups of people may contribute, and from which we may all draw *if we have somewhere to put what we may find* . . . cultural experience begins with creative living first manifested in play.
>
> (Winicott, 1971, p. 116)

While some of those I spoke to saw the figures as benign, benevolent superego figures of an almost advisory kind ('spiritual mentors'), for a few others, specifically two adolescent boys, they had a more threatening mien. It was notable that only one (woman) interviewee felt that the figures were remote and cold: perhaps in identification with critical superegos such as Klein described (Klein, 1975, p. 255).

In terms of the male/female issue, predominantly one could suggest that the male statues were seen as wise (except in the cases of two adolescent boys, who had seen them as threatening) paternal figures. The notion of female figures gave rise to thoughts of women in their sexual rather than maternal role (and the related issue of feminism), although one woman talked of the statues inside the gallery she had stroked 'in wordless communication' which could be seen to be connected to infantile memories of a preverbal communion with mother; what one might term an intimate maternal space. The last interviewee, when she talked of qualities of hardness and softness, seemed perhaps also in touch with this aspect. This was also alluded to, but more tangentially, by those who talked of architecture being 'humanised' by the appearance of the figures: as it were benign parental figures who help the child make sense of the world.

In other ways too there seemed to be a thread of thinking very much in touch with the experience of being a child: running, diving, watching the boats come in to the harbour, and as a grandparent showing grandchildren something of the world around which is exciting and full of potential; a sense of celebration of life and potency, aspiration rather than omnipotence. The joy and re-realisation with which the man described his diving child self seemed a clear link with the theme of potential and exploration. Bachelard (1969, p. 206) quotes the travel writer Diole: 'in deep water the diver loses the ordinary ties of time and space and makes life resemble an obscure, inner poem'. It made me recall in retrospect a patient of mine, a rather depressed boy who defended against feelings by acting out, which behaviour had caused him to be excluded from two schools. When he made (for the first time, successfully) a paper aeroplane, instead of interpreting that he wanted to fly away from his worries, I suggested that he also had a sincere wish to fly in a freer way, to feel less ground down by a history of failure. He looked at me intently and asked 'did it take you a long time to train for your job?' which I took to be his appreciation of the way I could acknowledge both his previous despair and the potential emergence of some hope. Both flying and diving in these contexts refer to hope rather than despair.

The issue of the statues remaining in their places or being taken away provoked different responses, which seemed in some cases to be connected to the idea that they represented 'spiritual mentors' offering a needed containing potential, the desire of the individual to be held in mind: parental figures holding children (or the infantile aspects of the self) by their gaze, which was described by one man as 'mesmerising'. Other people interviewed, while clearly having a sense of their powerful presences, seemed more willing to accept the idea of their being taken away, but perhaps replaced later with something different. Referring back to Freud's conversation with his 'two young friends', the notion of being small and transient in relation to a larger and perhaps unfeeling universe seemed to hover around the edges of some conversations. The thanks I received from many of my interviewees led me to hope that more thoughts might be generated later in their minds.

At the end of her life Melanie Klein wrote a paper 'On the Sense of Loneliness', published posthumously (1963). She talked about the perpetual human wish for 'an understanding without words'. One of my interviewees previously quoted had expressed the same thought. Klein went on to say:

> Full and permanent integration is never possible, for some polarity between the life and death instincts always persists and remains the deepest source of conflict . . . The longing to understand oneself is bound up with the need to be understood by the internalised good object.
>
> (Klein, 1963, p. 302)

It seemed evident to me in the course of these interviews that the real and often deep responses to Gormley's statues over the city is a mark of this longing, present in us all, at an unconscious level: a longing 'surprised' by works of art, or 'the trap' that Gormley himself referred to, that give us, to re-quote Winnicott, 'somewhere to put what we may find'.

Conclusion

In September of that same year, *The Guardian* newspaper published a letter from a reader wondering whether others also felt bereft at the absence of the Event Horizon figures, after they had been taken down. She talked about there being something 'magnificent and comforting' about their presence, and ended, 'they certainly fulfilled a very important function: they persuaded complete strangers to strike up conversations about art'. Perhaps, or so I like to think, she was one of the people who were generous enough to talk to me about the figures and what they might mean to the individual. One lone woman said to me, 'thank you for talking to me, it's nice to be able to think about this.' What was hugely interesting to me in these conversations was the way in which there were revealed so many layers of meaning, some of which I have touched on here. As Gormley himself said recently (2015) this kind of focus on sculpture may elicit 'feelings you didn't know you had' – what takes place in the darkness of the internal world.

Sculpture in the twenty-first century is now very rarely commemorative of 'great figures', and is increasingly recognised as being able to give some sort of identity to public spaces, what might be called a human dimension. The vast and impersonal spaces created by London's city architecture around the South Bank were for a short while given a human dimension by Gormley's figures, and his title 'Event Horizon' resonated with this idea of ourselves as individuals perched on the edge of a vast space, internal as well as external, where different solutions may be posed and meanings sought.

I suggest that these short interviews, while not following the 'accepted' methodological protocol, do attest to the artist's capacity to tap into truths about our nature. The meaning of this particular work lay in a very real sense in the eye of the beholder, with his or her internal preoccupations about flying and falling, seeing and being seen, in the ongoing and fundamental dialectic of the container and the contained.

References

Bachelard, G. (1969) *The Poetics of Space*. New York: Beacon Press.

Bollas, C. (2000) 'Architecture and the Unconscious'. *International Forum of Psychoanalysis*, 9(1/2), 28–43.

Bick, E. (1968) 'The experience of skin in early object relations'. *International Journal of Psychoanalysis*, 49, 484–6.

Bion, W. R. (1959) 'Attacks on linking'. *International Journal of Psycho-Analysis*, 40, 308–15.

Bion, W. R. (1967) *Second Thoughts*. London: Heinemann.

Freud, S. (1915) 'On transience', *S.E. 14*, 303–7. London: Hogarth.

Freud, S. (1939) 'Moses and monotheism'. In J. Strachey (ed.) (1964) Volume XXIII (1937–1939): *Moses and Monotheism, An Outline of Psychoanalysis and Other Works*. London: Hogarth.

Gormley, A. (2007) *Blind Light*. London: Hayward Publishing.

Gormley, A. (2015) 'Being human': Alan Yentob meets the sculptor, BBC 1 Television, November 2015.

Houzel, D. (1995) 'Precipitation anxiety'. *Journal of Child Psychotherapy*, 21(1), 65–78.

Klein, M. (1959) 'Our adult world and its roots in infancy'. In M. Klein (ed.) (1975) *Envy and Gratitude and Other Works 1946–63*. London: Hogarth Press, pp. 247–63.

Klein, M. (1963) 'On the sense of loneliness'. In M. Klein (ed.) (1975) *Envy and Gratitude and Other Works 1946–63*. London: Hogarth Press, pp. 300–14.

Klein, M. (1975) *Envy and Gratitude and Other works 1946–63*. London: Hogarth Press.

Ogden, T. H. (1997) 'Some theoretical comments on personal isolation'. In T. M. Mitrani and J. L. Mitrani (eds), *Encounters with Autistic States*. Northvale, NJ and London: Aronson, pp. 179–93.

Winnicott, D. W. (1965) *The Maturational Processes and the Facilitating Environment*. London: Hogarth Press and Institute of Psychoanalysis; Madison, CT: International Universities Press, 1965; London: Institute of Psychoanalysis and Karnac Books, 1990.

Winnicott, D. W. (1971) 'Transitional objects and transitional phenomena'. In *Playing and Reality*. London: Tavistock Publications (reissued in Penguin Education 1980), pp. 1–30.

Winnicott, D. W. (1989) *Psychoanalytic Explorations*, ed. C. Winnicott, R. Shephard and M. David, Cambridge, MA: Harvard University Press.

CHAPTER 13

THE ELUSIVE PURSUIT OF INSIGHT
Three poems by W. B. Yeats and
the human task

William Butler Yeats died in winter: streams and rivers were frozen, airports were empty, and statues in the city were covered in snow. The thermometer told the world that the day he died 'was a dark cold day'. So said W. H. Auden in his poem 'In Memory of W. B. Yeats' who died in 1939. In his solemn elegy for Yeats, written after the poet's death and published later, the poet W. H. Auden says 'You were silly like us; / Your gift survived it all' (Auden, 1949). What I hope to do in this chapter is to take three poems from Yeats' prolific work and to suggest how like us all he was in his development. This will not then be an attempt to put either a poet or his poetry on the couch per se, except in so far as both partake of the human condition. Poetry survives the individual's death, says Auden, and is modified 'in the guts of the living' – a digestive and assimilative process that one hopes produces growth. I hope to draw forth something from the large and varied output of one of the twentieth-century's greatest English-speaking poets that is representative of differing states of mind experienced within individuals struggling with the task of progressing towards a mature and realistic sense of self. This sense of self will inevitably be prone to instability and will be vulnerable to both internal and external attack, so that, in a sense, this developmental 'line' is actually more of a loop – or even a spiral – much in the way that the Kleinian psychoanalyst Britton (1998, pp. 69–81) describes in the oscillation and either augmentation or diminution that occurs as a normal phenomenon in mental and emotional development in relation to the world inside the individual's mind. Britton talks of the important need to distinguish between these oscillations which result in positive psychic development following periods of turmoil, and more pathological regressions.

As Yeats himself described it in his journals (Foster, 1998) the ordinary man is 'a bundle of accident and incoherence': however, the poet who emerges from the struggle with words and images in a finished work is 'something intended, complete' (at least provisionally, we might add). He talked of a pursuit of 'radiance' being a central task, and I have paraphrased this to encompass something of the human task in the long and often painful journey on the path towards a more realistic sense of identity: what could be called 'seeing the light' about the self.

I want to begin with one of Yeats' best-known poems, 'The Lake Isle of Innisfree'. He wrote it when he was a young man in London, and as he wandered despondently down the street he stopped to stare into a shop window (ibid., p. 79). It was a poem that was to pursue him, often to his irritation, for the rest of his life, as he was asked many times to declaim it (which he did of course with relish) (ibid.):

I will arise and go now, and go to Innisfree,
And a small cabin build there, of clay and wattles made:
Nine bean-rows will I have there, a hive for the honey-bee,
And live alone in the bee-loud glade.
And I shall have some peace there, for peace comes dropping slow,
Dropping from the veils of the morning to where the cricket sings;
There midnight's all a glimmer, and noon a purple glow
And evening full of the linnet's wings.
I will arise and go now, for always night and day
I hear lake water lapping with low sounds by the shore;
While I stand on the roadway, or on the pavements grey,
I hear it in the deep heart's core.

'The deep heart's core' has some affinities, I think, with Wordsworth's 'emotion recollected in tranquillity', and what Yeats is bringing into being for himself and his readers is an image that might also at one level be compared to Wordsworth's daffodils. But I think there are important differences in their internal inspiration. While Wordsworth's daffodils were 'fluttering and dancing', and on show to everyone on the hills of the Lake District, Yeats' Lake Isle is for him alone. He has taken up residence in the small cabin, and his 'nine bean rows' have a proprietorial ring to them – putting his seeds, as it were, on the land he has staked out – as I would like to suggest, some exclusive ownership of the land that may be compared to a very early experience and impulse to be in complete ownership of the mother, to the exclusion of father and siblings. In other words, the staking out of internal territory. The language and the way he deploys it has a sleepy, hypnotic effect, with the repetition of consonants and whole words emphasising a slow contemplative rhythm that one might think could be related to the early infant's experience of the reassuring beat of mother's heart.

There is the idea of a protected space, which of course the small infant does indeed need in order gradually to be introduced to the external and internal stresses of the world via his mother's containment. She takes on his anxieties and fears, ponders on them in her own mind – what Bion (1962) called her 'reverie' – and returns his thoughts to him in a less terrifying form.

Yeats' place of peace seems to describe an escape into the simple life from the complexity and conflict of relationships: his Lake Isle object is suffused with feelings of safety – there is no harsh light. He talks of the 'veils' of the morning (which one could perhaps recast as mother's gentle lidded eyes), the glimmering of night (the dimmed light for the night-time feed), and the hushed feathery image of 'the linnets' wings'; small murmurings at the edges of a soothing world. Again the rhythm is emphasised through alliteration with the low lapping of the lake water, and the whole picture has a soft-focus, almost 'Vaseline on the lens' feel, that could be seen to represent one side of primary experience: what Freud (1927, pp. 66–72) called the 'oceanic bliss' that observers of infants see when a baby is resting close to mother's breast after a satisfying feed, taking in the feed again in phantasy and recollection, with little mouthing movements, while his hands lie close to the breast itself. This vital experience provides the first way in which a baby takes in or introjects a good satisfying experience that then can act as a buffer when he is assailed by the internal monsters of hunger, pain and loneliness.

There follows a good description of this, where after a period of being unsettled a baby finds some temporary peace, and I am grateful to the author for permission to quote this in full:

Mother is stretched out on the settee, and Pierre is lying on top of her, as if he wanted to encompass her whole body. His head is in the hollow of her left elbow, his body on her chest, his feet on her thighs with his left arm dangling, the other tucked behind her back. She offers him her left breast and he takes it instantly. At the beginning he seems to drink eagerly, then he sucks the milk with four or five movements of his lips – a pause – four or five more movements – another pause. Mother looks at him: he has his eyes shut and it seems as if he has fallen asleep, as he has fallen from the nipple. Then he moves his lips several times in the same sucking rhythm as before. He is breathing quite rapidly. His mother leaves him as he has fallen asleep, against her breast. When she moves a little, he moves; his mother dries his lips and he seems to wake up a little, repeating the same suck–pause rhythm, but more slowly now. His hand rests free, grazing the breast in a sort of caress. He is calm but not completely asleep; he begins to make a movement as if to let go of the breast, but takes the nipple again, and his mother helps him.

(Sandri, 1999)

So, then, we have a picture in the Lake Isle of an ideal state, which can possibly be likened, as I have indicated, to the feelings a baby has when digesting a good experience or feed, close to the provider of the feed. These are experiences that need to be repeated for adequate introjection or location within the psyche to form the ego ideal. But there is also the possibility that this good experience can then turn from an ideal to an idealised state that defends against reality: Yeats' island could be seen to represent a turning away from difficulty and an image based on psychic retreat. While Steiner (1993) has powerfully delineated the pathological consequences of retreats based on grievance, there exists within any normal human being the impulse to retreat in the face of difficulty to a state of no suffering, an idealised fusion with a breast/nurturing object that provides refuge from frustration and the delusion that the infant self owns the breast (i.e. mother) exclusively. Britton (1998, p. 112) describes this as a 'wishful psychosis ... a deficit is denied by hallucinating the missing object, or there is the delusion of *being it*' (emphasis in original). He emphasises that this is a particular sort of non-pathological retreat. And we must remember the impulse of the poem, written on a grey, lonely day. 'I will arise and go now' also possesses energy and resolve; a move from despondency. The ideal state is indeed 'gone', and mourned in this poem. Remembering it in 'the deep heart's core' is akin to mourning.

While I have mentioned not wishing to analyse Yeats as a particular individual, it might be worth pointing out that he had a mother who had, according to her husband, 'never shown attention to me or to anyone' (Foster, 1997, p. 8). She was prone to depressive withdrawal, and would often fall asleep while reading to her children. But for Yeats she was 'the most beautiful woman in Sligo' and it is hardly surprising that he projected this idealisation in the face of real difficulty onto the countryside of Sligo in general in his early poetry, and onto the Lake Isle in particular. Grinberg and Grinberg (1999, p. 160) talk of the propensity for migrants to project on to the lost countryside all the human losses they have endured: 'It is the non-human environment, especially the natural surroundings of the individual which have acquired an intense emotional meaning that usually persists unmodified as an object of longing and *a symbol of what is his own*' (my italics).

For the migrant, the loss of country represents one end of a continuum of losses. At the other end lie the ordinary losses originating with what psychoanalysts call 'the absent breast' (O'Shaugnessy, 1964, pp. 36–43), and complicated further in the case of the breast/thinking experience offered by a mother preoccupied by her own distress and so not able to be 'occupied' by the baby's feelings and emotional needs. (It is also important to note that since this 'classical' formulation of the spur to first thought occurring in the space left by the absent breast, there has been more consideration (Alvarez, 1999, pp. 183–96) of the differential qualities of the *present* breast/object as a stimulus to thought.)

So here we have a primary state of mind represented by the Lake Isle, which has necessarily to be modified in order that the individual can move towards a fuller view. There is loss but also gain in this move, and it is essential to keep both in mind when considering any change in a previously maintained psychic equilibrium (Joseph, 1989).

I want to move on to another short poem that sprang from a moment in time and then came to represent for the poet what seems like a pivotal developmental point, where there could be either a move forward or back.

It is no longer summer in 'the bee-loud glade', but winter, on a day full of sunlight and harsh, brilliant contrasts, and the poet is taking a solitary walk:

The Cold Heaven
Suddenly I saw the cold and rook-delighting heaven
That seems as though ice burned and was but the more ice,
And thereupon imagination and heart were driven
So wild that every casual thought of that and this
Vanished, and left but memories, that should be out of season
With the hot blood of youth, of love crossed long ago;
And I took all the blame out of all sense and reason,
Until I cried and trembled and rocked to and fro,
Riddled with light. Ah! When the ghost begins to quicken,
Confusion of the death-bed over, is it sent
Out naked on the roads, as the books say, and stricken
By the injustice of the skies for punishment?

I think it would he hard to conceive of a more radically different tone in this poem from the previous one: gone is the soft, protected and insular world of the Lake Isle. Instead the poet (and the reader) is exposed to a harsh and glittering sky, where opposites unite in a cruel discord, burning and freezing simultaneously. Foster (1997, p. 490) describes this poem in terms of a man looking back on his life and his failed loves, beset with queries about esoteric dilemmas he has puzzled over to do with death, ghosts and dreams.

The soft linnets have been replaced by the wheeling silhouettes of rooks, black against the steely sky. There is a powerful evocation of utter helplessness against the lightning flash of a new realisation. The phrase 'riddled with light' with its possible association to gun bullets and something irrevocably blown apart, holds within itself the paradox of the dark thoughts that accompany this attack of insight.

Heaney (1995, p. 148) describes the poem as a 'spasm of consciousness', where it is the poet's energetic engagement with his technical skills that succeeds in holding together a shattering moment. Heaney demonstrates this by his close textual analysis of the poem from the point of view of poetic technique:

'The Cold Heaven' is a poem which suggests that there is an overall purpose to life; and it does so by the intrinsically poetic action of its rhymes, its rhythms and its exultant intonation. These create an energy and an order which promote the idea that there exists a much greater, circumambient energy and order within which we have our being.

(Heaney, 1995, pp. 147–149)

Heaney's is one reading of the poem and, of course, a perfectly valid one. For my purposes in this chapter I want to focus more on the despair and the painful sense of guilt combined with a feeling of profound alone-ness. This is very different from the wished-for protected 'alone-ness' in 'The Lake Isle'. What I want to suggest is that this represents an oscillating moment on 'the threshold of the depressive position' where there can be either an evasion of the reality of the world as it is rather than as we would like it to be, and a retreat to the Lake Isle frame of mind, or a modifying cast of thought that mediates against the primeval terror of being responsible and thus culpable. In other words, a move from an idealised view of the blameless self to the acceptance of self-divisions, and a concern for the welfare of others in the face of one's more destructive impulses.

Yeats describes the force of the realisation which makes him rock and reel with the pain of it. This would seem to be in the same imaginative terrain as Dante's ninth and last circle of Hell, where those who have betrayed their families, associates and benefactors are buried in varying degrees of ice:

Here the weeping puts an end to weeping,
and the grief that finds no outlet from the eyes
Turns inward to intensify the anguish.

(Musa, 1995, p. 183)

Although Yeats knows already by implication that something has happened that will then become modified by further thinking, at this moment 'I took the blame out of all sense and reason'. This brings thoughts of death, and then of infinite punishment. The unjust skies seem to represent a wrenching away from the gentle protecting maternal influence in the Lake Isle to the Jehovah-like paternal judgement that shows no mercy or ultimate forgiveness. At this moment, far from there being hope of redemption and faith in 'an overall purpose', the poem can be read in the spirit of an individual mind that feels cast out forever, 'naked on the roads', without compass or guide. It is a bitter expulsion from the Garden of Eden that is the Lake Isle.

This seems to me less about the exultation that Heaney suggests than about total despair. This is the agony rather than the ecstasy. The desperate rocking may put one in mind of the rocking rituals of autistic children, as they attempt to block out the pain of separation and loss by fervent self-comforting. This can result in the complete evacuation of the capacity to think; into a black hole where gravity and the space–time continuum collapse. I have talked of this phenomenon in autism elsewhere (Edwards, 1994). I would like here to see the poem rather in the light of more generalised anxieties activated by the bringing together of love and hate in both self and object, with the concomitant realisation of responsibility for destructive impulses and the initial despair that this means as something more negative comes into the idealised picture of the self. There is fear that the attacked object will be lost, just at the moment when the whole picture can include the bad but alongside the undoubted good, which can be really appreciated. To put it at its earliest occurrence: the mother who made the baby wait is undoubtedly also the one that offers him goodness in terms of milk, thoughts and feelings. As I have said, the phrase 'riddled with light' could be construed as representing just such an epiphanic moment, where the realisation itself, the light, forces an acknowledge-ment of hitherto unacknowledged internal darkness – the narcissistic self-image gives way to something that feels initially catastrophic, as Britton (1998, pp. 69–81) puts it, and the self, now feeling infinitely small rather than improbably large, occupying the whole of the island, has a sense of being ejected into the wilderness. What Britton then formulates is a state of affairs that will follow later, 'it is not a state of mind that is realised, but a hope, based on faith, that future developments will bring coherence and meaning'. This hope is what Heaney seems to intuit as being a next step, although actually within the poem itself there seems to be the expression of despair in pure culture. Britton maintains that it is only later that a move forward occurs to something more manageable inside the mind. 'By the time this position (that of the promised land) is arrived at, we are back to the familiar depressive position; the promised land has become Israel and another struggle has begun' (ibid.). In other words, there is a continual 'looping' to-and-fro of states rather than stasis in an idealised 'depressive position'. In 'The Cold Heaven' all responsibility is taken by the self, and the 'burning ice' freezes this moment in time before the oscillation begins; the move towards real reparation of the damage and a more realistic and forgiving view of the self, which brings relief. The crucial point would seem to be, I think, to do with having enough strength to withstand being blinded by the 'bullets' of realisation, 'riddled with light', without resorting to a bullet-proof vest that prevents any realisation entering. Insight marks a pivotal point: there is then a choice about going forward, going back, or remaining in a stuck state, transfixed by 'the light'.

In work with children, in recent years there has been a predominance in our caseloads of deprived and borderline personalities who have not indeed experi-enced in a reliable way the kind of early foundational interactions between caretaker and infant that result in reliable introjections as a buffer against later difficulty. The oscillations between these 'positions' may not be present at all. Months or even years may pass before discernible patterns may emerge, and there may be instant terrified returns to a 'Lake Isle' position at the mere hint of the emergence of a different perspective. Dependence on an object and concern for its welfare could be seen as a kind of luxury to those children for whom defensive denial has actually been the only resort and comfort in situations of deficit and trauma.

For example, a ten-year-old boy I saw who had been severely abused in his family of origin had been a 'late adoption' with his younger sister (See also Chapter 9). Jim was referred to me because of his difficulties making a relation-ship with his adoptive family, particularly his adoptive mother. (I have used this material elsewhere, to illustrate the difficulty such children have with traumatic memories.)

He came to the first assessment meeting with his family, armed, it seemed burdened, by a huge 'Life Story Book'. One of my first thoughts was that at least part of my work would be to help him slowly relegate this to the past in order to free the present and create a less contaminated future. Therapy began, and while he railed against boundary setting (for instance that what he made in the room needed to stay there), he also seemed to appreciate firmness and my capacity to contain and think about his frustration. In the penultimate session of the first term he drew a flower rooted in a pot, which seemed to indicate his sense of being rooted in the therapeutic process. However, at times of breaks, or when Jim felt I thwarted him he would return to a more autonomous 'Lake Isle' state, and he built a castle with huge defences that could only later include a drawbridge that sometimes opened to let me in ... 'My parents look after me; I stay well away from you'. It was clear that by my taking the role in the therapy of the one who had abandoned him, he was able more to appreciate the love of his adoptive parents.

Gradually, through a series of stories about a phoenix and a magic carpet he was able to sort out his defensive use of magic powers from an ordinary, healthy capacity to wish that things had been different. He was amazed when I endorsed his growing view that 'life now' was more important, rather than his obsessive concentration on a chronically difficult life history. This was after nine months of once-weekly meetings:

> After some 'magic' play with characters who flew, I said sometimes he wished he lived in a magic world. 'Yes I do', he said, 'especially at bedtime, but then I have bad dreams. I dream about being Superman flying about, but then people shoot me down. I know it is bad for me to have these thoughts.' I said it was so hard when he wanted to be the boss, but then he feared people like me would get cross and destroy him. But he also wanted people to think he's super too, a boy worth caring about. [He had been badly abused by his original parents.] He smiled, pleased. And I said it was hard to do what grown-ups said, like about bedtime or coming here when *I* said rather than when *he* wanted to. 'Well I sometimes want to come', he said, 'and sometimes I don't.'

Jim needed me to help him overcome difficult experience and to foster growth, and I had to respect his retreats in the service of this, to the 'Lake Island'.

The third poem I want to focus on was one written when Yeats was in his late middle age, and the location has moved from an anonymous sky-filled space where the poet feels adrift in the universe to Coole Park in Ballylee, the beloved home of his friend and patron Lady Gregory. It represented many things to him, culturally and historically, but here I want to concentrate on its emotional significance as the locus for the moving on from implacable insight to something more reflective and philosophical.

The Wild Swans at Coole
The trees are in their autumn beauty,
The woodland paths are dry,
Under the October twilight the water
Mirrors a still sky;
Upon the brimming water among the stones
Are nine and fifty swans.
The nineteenth autumn has come upon me
Since I first made my count;
I saw, before I had well finished,
All suddenly mount
And scatter wheeling in great broken rings
Upon their clamorous wings.
I have looked upon these brilliant creatures.
And now my heart is sore.
All's changed since I, hearing at twilight,
The first time on this shore,
The bell-beat of their wings above my head,
Trod with a lighter tread.
Unwearied still, lover by lover,
They paddle in the cold

Companionable streams or climb the air;
Their hearts have not grown old;
Passion or conquest, wander where they will,
Attend upon them still.
But now they drift on the still water,
Mysterious, beautiful;
Among what rushes will they build,
By what lake's edge or pool
Delight men's eyes when I awake some day
To find they have flown away?

Here the scene is set for late autumnal thoughts; a mature sort of beauty with its own quiet reflections as the water mirrors the sky. There is a dynamic tension in the poem between this stillness and the 'clamorous wings' of the swan couples and in the whole poem with its free-flowing discipline of rhyme and rhythm a temporary acceptance of change, despite the 'sore heart'. This again has some resonances with Wordsworth, both in the idea of the return to a much loved place as Wordsworth returned to Tintern Abbey, and in the inevitable sadness attendant on life – the 'still sad music of humanity', although Yeats' sadness seems more personally located rather projected into humanity as a whole. (Which in a sense can be seen as a more authentic working-through of sorrow: Britton (1998, pp. 129–132) postulates that Wordsworth's rather precocious poetic development gave way later in his life to a retreat to certainty rather than face the inevitable 'loops' of psychological experience.)

We have moved in the bird imagery from the soft linnet and the cawing crows to the swans, with the emphasis on their wildness and their freedom to go where they will, as well as their uxoriousness (swans are known to mate for life). They are seen to 'paddle' in the air: symbolically they represent the union of air and water (Cooper, 1978) and the swan is called 'the bird of the poet'. Here Yeats laments the passing of time 'all's changed' . . . and he seems to feel that his days of passion and conquest, which were causing him such agony of blame in 'The Cold Heaven', are behind him, but embodied in the swans in their upwards passage from the stones by the lake. One could say that at this moment Yeats has projected his own lively engagement with life into these wild birds, and one could debate whether this might be a defensive exclusion of his own energies rather than an 'integrated' perspective. There is the contrast between time passing in a human life and what he sees as the eternal timeless beauty of the birds.

These wild swans could be seen to represent a capacity to leave things in the moment without wishing to constrain them. They are also seen by Yeats as couples, so that the internal image of a parental couple who have their own autonomy has replaced the more primitive and passionate urge to control them. In the last stanza, as the swans drift quietly on the water after their clamorous flight, he wonders where they will go, when he wakes to see they have gone. We could see this as having something to do with an acceptance of his own mortality: that he too must at last 'fly away'; and that he has developed the capacity to accept this and let go, in preparation for his own death. (Symbolically again the swan is seen as 'the bird of death' and its dying song denotes resignation.) This could be seen as at least a temporary integration of opposites and the end of many struggles to come to terms with the finiteness of life. (This kind of integration, hard won, can nevertheless very easily fail under the pressure of fear, hatred of reality, or disbelief, and for Yeats himself there is strong evidence in his very last poems that this could only be achieved through a sort of distanced objectivity – 'Cast a cold eye / On life, on death, / Horseman, pass by!') By talking of himself in the third person in his very last published poem, 'Under Ben Bulben' – 'In Drumcliff churchyard Yeats is laid' – he objectifies himself perhaps as a way of dealing with the inevitability of the death we must all face. By locating energy and passion in the swans at Coole Park rather than himself, one could also think that the acceptance of death at this point means that Yeats may feel he has to be dead to the senses already. Is this mourning or melancholia?

Here there can be seen to be a contrast between what one might call the persecuting guilt of 'The Cold Heaven', where despair and self-reproach all but annihilate the subject, and a more 'depressive' approach, where there is a sense of nostalgia and feelings of responsibility. These feelings are the basis for the wish to repair the objects, to present them with a gift, which links more with Segal's ideas of the creative impulse as being firmly rooted in the depressive position (Segal, 1991). Or to go back to Freud's original work, we could see here the working through of 'normal mourning' as opposed to the more pathological state of mourning where melancholia ensues (Freud, 1917, pp. 237–60).

And yet thinking has moved on since Segal's formulations about the creative impulse being firmly located in the depressive position, and the idea of a perpetual motion between states of mind over the life-span seems not only more akin to the internal lives human beings generally experience, in life as well as on the couch, but also to abandon the notion of morality in creativity, with a 'depressive' cast of mind being a *sine qua non* for 'good' creative work. Ehrenzweig's posthumously published book (1967, pp. 102–9) seems to have links with this notion of the free looping movement that is the hallmark of authentic creativity. An art education lecturer with a solid background knowledge of psychoanalytic principles, he talks of the three phases of the creative act.

Initially the artist (or poet, for the purposes of this chapter) projects what Ehrenzweig calls the schizoid parts of the fragmented self into the internal creative 'womb' (much in the way that the baby, as I have already said, projects his terror and fear into his mother). There then occurs what he calls a 'manic' scanning of these fragments, which begin to come together as the underlying structure of their nature is gradually revealed. I would like to suggest a link between this and the struggle between love, hate and despair in 'The Cold Heaven'. The third phase is when the creator of the work of art re-introjects the hidden substructure into his ego, but at a higher mental level where the integrated work of art can be worked on by the tools and the technique of the creator. In the case of the poet this will be to do with the strength of poetic technique in terms of tone, structure and use of language in a particular way. At which point the poem becomes a 'thing-in-itself' with an independent existence.

Ehrenzweig observes that good art teaching, and creativity itself, is dependent on a great tolerance of anxiety, because of the need to work through the phase of chaos before the pattern emerges, and it requires, as he says, a more than average ego strength. This passage much illuminated for me a remark made by Eliot (1933, p. 140): 'you cannot take heaven by magic, especially if you are, like Mr Yeats, a very sane person.' It is this very management of the different elements in the personality that is the hallmark of the authentic creative act, rather than, I think, the notion of a purely 'depressive position' state as an end-point.

It reminds me of an adolescent girl I saw with her family, where mother was complaining about (among other things) the mess in the kitchen when her daughter made cakes. We could return later in the work of disentangling their mutual negative projections to the metaphor of the cake: there has to be a mess out of which will ensue the finished product. I have talked to several artists and writers who readily identify with the tripartite nature of this process, akin I think also to what is at work in children's play. The process as described by Ehrenzweig has affinities, I think, with the concepts derived from chaos theory. Structure can emerge from chaos, and there ensues a rhythm of chaos, transition and order before a new disequilibrium occurs (Gleick, 1987; Scharff and Scharff, 2000, p. 63) – this also links with Britton's ideas about development beyond the depressive position to a new area of struggle.

I think Ehrenzweig's formulation of the three phases of the creative process has links with the idea of a triangular internal space that develops when the individual leaves 'The Lake Isle' and is able to tolerate separation and to acknowledge his debt to the objects he both loves and hates. This is the space where play is generated, and where later creative life is nourished.

So I would like to suggest that the wild swans can be understood in a number of ways. They represent the tolerance of the autonomy of the parental couple, an acceptance of departure and loss, and also an acceptance that provisional states of mind, hard won, may then be undermined, even necessarily will be so, in order for creativity to remain alive in the self, by the more anxious, angry and destructive parts of the self. As Yeats observes, he will wake one day to find the swans gone, along with his autumnal resignation. He, like the rest of us, will have to take back his projected passion and work with it in order not to become stuck in another form of retreat.

Since first writing this chapter I read Likierman's publication (2001) offering a fresh approach to Klein's work. I think her helpful delineation of two stages of depressive anxiety – what she calls 'the tragic stage' and 'the moral stage' – link with the ideas I have put forward about Yeats' persecuting guilt in 'The Cold Heaven' and his eventual overcoming of it through toleration and an appreciation of reality.

There is, of course, the danger that any theory about the creative act or our understanding of it will become ossified. As Eliot (1933, p. 141) insisted:

> Even when two persons of taste like the same poetry, this poetry will be arranged in their minds in slightly different patterns; our individual taste in poetry bears the indelible traces of our individual lives with all their experience pleasurable and painful. We are apt either to shape a theory to cover the poetry that we find most moving, or – what is less excusable – to choose the poetry which illustrates the theory.

I hope the reader will take the views expressed here as offering just one reading, from a psychoanalytic perspective, of the nature and shape of the creative act and the oscillating states of mind to which we are all prey, as seen in Yeats' three poems. I talked earlier of Yeats identifying 'radiance' as something to which he aspired. I think my own appending of the word 'pursuit', as well as 'insight', conveys something of the chase to pin down, at least in a provisional way, often elusive ideas that do in any case get modified by subsequent thinking. In psychoanalytic culture these are underpinned by a fundamental understanding of the internal world as being prone to primitive mechanisms such as splitting, idealisation and denigration, while the individual struggles towards integration or, rather, one might say management and tolerance of the flux.

I want to end by considering the image of the wild swans linked to a symbol produced by Jim in his therapy, thinking about these 'transformative' images as being related to Bion's ideas about 'O' – a state of mind that might be called 'transcendent' without this necessarily meaning a return to an idealised state.

It is easier to speak of 'O', the 'thing-in-itself', 'the ultimate reality' (Bion, 1970, p. 18) in poetry rather than psychoanalysis, because there hovers over such suggestions the fear of 'wild analysis' and hallucination. Bion himself talks of the need to enter into a near-hallucinatory state without memory or desire. He maintained that verbal, musical and artistic transformations are 'transformations in O': 'I shall use the sign O to denote that which is the ultimate reality represented by terms such as absolute truth . . . the thing-in-itself.' These moments of 'O' could then, he maintained, be translated into 'K' or knowledge, but only when memory and desire have been renounced. These are complex and difficult ideas, not much debated because, I think, of the danger inherent within them for those practising psychoanalysis, but I believe that if the idea is approached through poetry it becomes more graspable.

The relationship between the poem and the reader lies in the space between them, which has links with the space between patient and analyst, containing not only the projections of the poet but the preconceptions of the reader; not only the projections of the patient but of the analyst. Just as no two sessions can be identical, so no two readings of a poem can be identical, because they occur at this interface. The symbols that arise in a poem, and in a session, have a particular meaning in relationship to both poet and reader, analyst and patient. In psychoanalysis, sometimes it may only be necessary to recognise the 'O moment' rather than constrain it with words, even though words are our tools. This chapter is written in the spirit of this understanding: that one's meanings are ultimately one's own, but may also have relevance for others. The swans continue to fly away in each reader's imagination, and by so doing produce their own meanings. As Alvarez (1994, p. 124) puts it, in a chapter about the interpretation of dreams:

> there are as many code-books as there are interpreters . . . the discipline of psychoanalysis is based on the premise that dreams [*and I would add, symbolism in poetry*] are like the glittering fragments of a kaleidoscope, constantly shifting and rearranging themselves when the instrument is passed from hand to hand.

It was a year after work began with Jim that he was able to relax his defensive guard and a series of very moving sessions culminated in his producing a symbol that has, I think, affinities with the wild swans and Bion's formulation of 'O'. He was able to come out from his defensive hiding place and begin to believe that he could rework a difficult internal picture to make room for something new, and to turn to helpful external objects in the process:

> He was drawing the cover for a book he planned to write. It was night-time in the picture, and a rabbit had come out to look around. Then he turned over the page and began again. He drew a tree that had roots but no leaves, and the roots were floating. Then he drew some breast-like hills, with one in the distance, and a straight path to the distant hill. There was a fence on the hill, and I asked about it. He said it was to stop people falling off the hill. The tree's roots were now within the nearer hill, and I talked about his feeling rooted here with a place to think. Perhaps we could think about sad things

and happy things, without his falling off into space. [His growing awareness of being contained by thinking.] He was colouring the hills and then he drew a badger, saying 'It's sunset [the whole sky was red] and he's waking up and coming out'. I simply commented on the badger emerging into the quiet evening, and the beautiful sky. 'Yes', he said, 'and there's a young moon coming up', and he drew it on the right hand side of the page, a thin yellow crescent hanging over the hills.

I think this symbol of the 'young moon' was a reworking of 'Superman': a projected part of himself that could abandon omnipotence and begin a new cycle of growth and renewal. He had needed me to respect his working under cover of darkness for a long while before he could begin to emerge. This was a crucial turning point for Jim: not a flight from despair into idealisation, but a movement towards something new. It is important in our work to recognise the difference (see Alvarez, 1992, p. 179). In this session there was a feeling of awe (on both our parts) that this had been achieved, and after the session he made eye contact with me and said goodbye simultaneously for the first time. In later sessions he was able to appreciate the idea that we made 'stories about my feelings' and said he did his best work in therapy. He still had an enormous amount to work through and resistance was still a feature, but far less so. In a long series of sessions he built a 'tent' in the room, and this could be explored as both a safe internal space for us to work together but also as a space where I had to stay outside with the humiliating wait before being 'adopted' in the sessions by Jim. Within the therapeutic space he could dare more and experiment more in the way Ehrenzweig described with his art students; Jim would describe as an 'art attack' (the name of a children's television programme) the fragments he brought and which we would then attempt to piece together to find out their possible meanings. This vital turning point was reached with the symbol of the young moon, the 'thing-in-itself' an O symbol.

What I hope to have shown in this chapter is something of the ordinary life process that can be traced through three poems, where idealised states that are actually quite rigid under their apparent 'soft-focus', as in 'The Lake Isle of Innisfree', have to give way to notions of flexibility and experimentation that nevertheless depend on an internalised stability in order to unfold. While Yeats was a prolific poet who was important socially and politically, what I have been concentrating on is something that is common to us all. What the human task involves is to find a path between the two poles of Hell and Heaven in the psyche: this may involve occasional epiphanic moments that then need to be slowly built into understanding. Insight on its own is not enough: the uncertainty it brings is an opportunity, a necessity, to move forward and achieve change. While this can be formulated on the page it is extremely hard to live, and involves us all in psychic struggle throughout life, in what Hering (2002, personal communication) has called 'the dialectic between defensiveness and openness'.

Perhaps it is fitting to quote Yeats in his journals again (Foster, 1998) in order to conclude this exploration into what is involved in what I have called the elusive pursuit of insight:

> I suppose that I may learn at last to keep to my own [values and instincts] in every situation in life: to discover and create in myself as I grow old that thing which is to life what style is to letters: moral radiance, a personal quality of universal meaning in act and in thought.

Acknowledgements

Conversations with Al Alvarez, Andrew Baldwin and Christoph Hering have helped me enormously in writing this chapter.

Grateful thanks to *Contrappunto* and to Rosella Sandri for permission to translate and quote her baby observation.

References

Alvarez, A. (1992) *Live Company: Psychoanalytic Psychotherapy with Autistic, Borderline and Deprived Children*. London and New York: Routledge.

Alvarez, A. (1994) *Night: An Exploration of Night Life, Night Language, Sleep and Dreams*. London: Jonathan Cape.

Alvarez, A. (1999) 'Frustration and separateness, delight and connectedness: Reflections of the conditions under which bad and good surprises are conducive to learning'. In A. Alvarez, A. Harrison and E. O'Shaugnessy (eds), *Symposium on Frustration. Journal of Child Psychotherapy*, 25(2), 183–96.

Auden, W. H. (1949) *Selected Poems*. London: Macmillan.

Bion, W. R. (1962) *Learning from Experience*. London: Karnac.

Bion, W. R. (1970) *Attention and Interpretation*. London: Karnac.

Britton, R. (1998) *Belief and Imagination: Explorations in Psychoanalysis*. London: Routledge.

Cooper, J. M. (1978) *An Illustrated Encyclopaedia of Traditional Symbols*. London: Thames & Hudson.

Edwards, J. (1994) 'Towards solid ground: The ongoing psychotherapeutic journey of an adolescent boy with autistic features'. *Journal of Child Psychotherapy*, 21(1), 57–83.

Ehrenzweig, A. (1967) *The Hidden Order of Art*. London: Weidenfeld.

Eliot, T. S. (1933) *The Use of Poetry and the Use of Criticism*. London: Faber & Faber.

Foster, R. F. (1998) *W. B. Yeats: A Life, Volume 1: The Apprentice Mage*. Oxford and New York: Oxford University Press.

Freud, S. (1917) 'Mourning and melancholia'. *S.E., 14*, 237–60. London: Hogarth.

Freud, S. (1927) 'The future of an illusion'. *S.E., 21*, 66–72. London: Hogarth.

Gleick, J. (1987) *Chaos*. London and New York: Viking Penguin.

Grinberg, L. and Grinberg, R. (1999) 'Psychoanalytic perspectives on migration'. In D. Bell (ed.), *Psychoanalysis and Culture*. London: Duckworth, pp. 154–69.

Heaney, S. (1995) *The Redress of Poetry*. Oxford: Oxford University Press.

Joseph, B. (1989) *Psychic Equilibrium and Psychic Change*. London: Routledge.

Likierman, M. (2001) *Melanie Klein: Her Work in Context*. London: Quantum.

Musa, M. (ed. and trans.) (1995) *The Portable Dante*. London: Penguin.

O'Shaugnessy, E. (1964) 'The absent object'. *Journal of Child Psychotherapy*, 1(2): 36–43.

Sandri, R. (1999) 'Il passagio dallo spazio del corpo allo spazio mentale'. *Contrappunto*, 27, 7–25.

Scharff, D. E. and Scharff, J. S. (2000) *Tuning the Therapeutic Instrument*. London and Northvale, NJ: Aronson.

Segal, H. (1991) *Dream, Phantasy and Art*. London: Routledge.

Steiner, J. (1993) *Psychic Retreats*. London: Routledge.

Yeats, W. B., Wikipedia.

INDEX

'A Biographical Sketch of an Infant'
(Darwin) 4
ADHD, and early trauma 71
adhesive identification: as danger to ego
122; described by Darwin 7; as desperate
measure 32–3; with lost object 125
Adult Attachment Interview 51, 63–4
Alvarez, A. 37, 164
anticipatory identification 37
Ariadne 92, 95, 98
arts, and psychoanalysis: in documentary
film 131–9; in film 119–30; in Gormley's
sculpture 140–53; links described
117–118; in memoir 104–16; in Yeats'
poetry 154–65
autism features: as buffer 142; as defence
35; early schooling, therapy for 32;
suspension of mental life 34; see also
Joe (patient)

babies: early defences of 15; enabled in
containment 15; learning from pleasure,
safety 35; observing, observations of
1–2
balance, in observation 14
Bell, C. 6
Bick, E. 3, 14, 18, 32–3, 97
Bion, W. R.: on 'dark matters' 104–5; on
flexibility, new ideas 129; on functions of
models 77–8, 90, 104; on growth,
limitations 94; on knowing, knowing
about 81–2; on moments of 'O' 164
black hole metaphor: defined 31; event
horizon of 141–2; as internal womb 91;
in myth 95; used in therapy 34, 36, 41
Bollas, C. 143
Brian (patient) 54–6

Britton, R. 94, 106–7, 159
buttonhole analogy 52

Cancrini, T. 56
children, late-adopted: art as symbol
110–11; and creative play 98–9; Darren
(patient) 53, 98–100; denial, retreat of
63, 159–60; Gary (patient) 65–72;
mediating factors for 63–4; memory
fragments of 63–4, 109; need for
qualified carers 65; Oedipus as 62; recall
capacity of 64; therapeutic spaces for
164; working with, 61–2
children, of single parents: Brian (patient)
54–6; Darren (patient) 53; described
47–8; Neil (patient) 53; an Oedipal
complexes 49–51; owning narratives 52;
relationships of 51; Thomas (patient)
56–8
chuntering 33, 41
Coetzee, J. M. 52
communication as hallmark of sanity xix
concentric containment 13–14, 28
consulting room, described xvii
Cooper, Andrew 65
counter-transference: author's experience of
34, 98; central role of 29; defined 5; and
emotional state of therapist 15;
examining 105; as instrument of research
128; understanding of 127; used in film
119, 123
creative acts: initiated by paranoid-schizoid
mode 95, 101; as leap to safety, security
95–8; phases of 162–3; preceded by
depressive position 90–1
crying, onset, purposes of 6
cultural experience 151